Microsoft®

# MICROSOFT®
# QUICK C™
# COMPILER

## FOR IBM® PERSONAL COMPUTERS AND COMPATIBLES

# PROGRAMMER'S GUIDE

If you have comments about the software documentation, complete the Documentation Feedback card at the back of this manual and return it to Microsoft Corporation.

If you have comments about the software, complete the Product Assistance Request form at the back of this manual and return it to Microsoft Corporation.

Document No. 410840014-500-R00-0887

# TABLE OF CONTENTS

## Introduction

## Part 1 ◇ Getting Started

# CONTENTS

# Part 2 ◇ The QuickC Programming Environment

# 5   Controlling the Display: the View Menu

# 6   Creating and Saving Programs

# Part 3 ◇ The QuickC Tool Kit

# Appendixes

# Figures

# CONTENTS

# Tables

# INTRODUCTION

Welcome to the Microsoft® QuickC™ Compiler! You have purchased one of the most powerful packages available for working with the C language, an ideal set of tools for beginning programmers and experienced software developers alike.

The Microsoft QuickC Compiler is a full implementation of the C programming language that combines the power, portability, and flexibility of C with a complete development environment. It includes the following features:

■ **Get All the Tools You Need**
   **in an Integrated Programming Environment**

The Microsoft QuickC Compiler provides the program-development tools you need in a single package: an integrated program editor, compiler, and debugger (Chapter 8). Using the Microsoft QuickC Compiler, you can compile, run, debug, edit, and recompile programs without ever leaving the programming environment. The QuickC compiler can create programs for in-memory execution, or it can create stand-alone object files for use in libraries plus executable files for later execution under DOS.

Since most standard C library functions are built into the programming environment, it is not usually necessary to link with an external library. Any standard C library routines that are not built into the environment can be loaded in a user-configurable library known as a Quick library.

■ **Learn Quickly with a WordStar-Compatible Editor**

Learning the QuickC editor is a simple matter. If you are familiar with the MicroPro WordStar® program, you already know most of the QuickC editing commands, since they they are exactly the same as the corresponding WordStar commands. (Section 7.1.1 describes the QuickC editing keys.)

■ **Find Bugs Fast with an Integrated Debugger**

QuickC includes many of the capabilities of professional debuggers, which make it easy to track down errors in program logic. Using the QuickC debugger, you can

- Step through program execution line by line
- Set multiple breakpoints
- Display the values of variables in a separate window during program execution
- Switch between the program and program-output displays
- Search for particular functions in the source program

Sections 8.2–8.2.4 show how to use these debugging facilities. If even this list of features isn't enough, you can debug QuickC programs by using the Microsoft® CodeView® window-oriented debugger provided with the Microsoft C Optimizing Compiler and other Microsoft language products.

## ■   Get Help At Your Fingertips

Do you have a question about the syntax of a C statement? About the types of arguments to a library routine? About the QuickC editor keys? Get answers fast using QuickC's context-sensitive, on-line help facility. Browse through a menu of topics, or simply highlight a function name and press a key. You don't even need to leave the editor; information appears in a separate window at the top of the screen.

## ■   Add Visual Impact to Programs with the Graphics Library

The graphics library provided with the QuickC library gives you the power you need to write sophisticated graphics applications. This library supports the full range of IBM and IBM-compatible display adapters, including the IBM Video Graphics Array (VGA), Monochrome Display Adapter (MDA), Color/Graphics Adapter (CGA), and Enhanced Graphics Adapter (EGA). See Chapter 4 for information about the graphics library.

## ■   Write Programs Fast, Then Optimize
##     with the Microsoft C Optimizing Compiler

Since the Microsoft QuickC Compiler is fully compatible with Version 5.0 of the Microsoft C Optimizing Compiler at the source-file and object-file levels, you are assured of a smooth upgrade path when you need the added flexibility and power that the Microsoft C Optimizing Compiler provides. If you are developing programs with the Microsoft C Optimizing Compiler, you can use the Microsoft QuickC Compiler to speed up the early phases of program development, then use the Microsoft C Optimizing Compiler to fine-tune program performance.

■ **Start Fast with the OS/2-Compatible User Interface**

The user interface for the Microsoft QuickC Compiler is easy to learn. Simply select commands from menus using the keyboard, an optional mouse, or both, or press special keys to carry out commands without opening a menu. The QuickC user interface looks and works very much like the new Microsoft presentation-manager interface to the OS/2 operating system.

■ **Maintain Large Programs Automatically**

Maintaining large programs with large numbers of modules is automatic with the Microsoft QuickC Compiler. As you edit the modules that make up a program, you add them to a "program list." When you rebuild the program, QuickC saves you time by recompiling only the modules that have been changed since the last program build.

The program list is saved in a file that is compatible with the **MAKE** program-maintenance utility; consequently, programs can be updated automatically outside the QuickC programming environment.

■ **Get the Results You Want with These Additional Features**

Microsoft QuickC offers the following additional features:

- A complete tool kit of utility programs to meet almost every programming need. This tool kit includes the **QCL** compiler/linker driver; the Microsoft Overlay Linker, **LINK**; the Microsoft Library Manager, **LIB**; and the Microsoft Program-Maintenance Utility, **MAKE**.

- Simplified memory management using any of four memory models. The **QCL** compiler/linker driver supports the small, medium, compact, and large memory models.

- Outstanding reference documentation. The documentation includes complete reference documentation for the C programming language and standard C library routines, including hundreds of complete program examples.

# System Requirements

The Microsoft QuickC Compiler requires the following minimum configuration:

- An IBM® Personal Computer or strict "compatible" running MS-DOS® or PC-DOS® Version 2.1 or later
- Two floppy-disk drives or one floppy-disk drive and a hard disk
- 448K RAM available memory

# Using This Manual

The Microsoft QuickC Compiler is designed for a wide range of users, from beginners who are new to programming to experienced developers who are fluent in the C language. Different parts of the manual are intended for users with different needs.

The following paragraphs explain how this manual is organized, suggest different paths for different types of users, and describe the other manuals provided in the package.

## How this Manual is Organized

Part 1 of this manual, "Getting Started," explains how to install the Microsoft QuickC Compiler, introduces you to the QuickC programming environment, and describes important features of the C language for users familiar with other languages such as BASIC and Pascal. This part also shows you how to use the graphics library provided with the Microsoft QuickC Compiler.

Part 2, "The QuickC Programming Environment," explains how to edit, compile, and debug programs within the QuickC programming environment.

Part 3 of this manual, "The QuickC Tool Kit," explains how to compile and link programs by using the **QCL** and **LINK** programs; how to build Quick libraries by using **LINK** and build stand-alone libraries by using the **LIB** utility; and how to maintain programs by using the **MAKE** utility.

The appendixes to this manual contain additional information you may find helpful, such as:

- A table of ASCII character codes
- A description of QuickC memory models
- A description of interfaces between Microsoft C and the Microsoft Macro Assembler (MASM)
- A list of error messages

A handy quick reference card included in this manual lists QuickC editing and debugging keys and key sequences.

## What to Read in this Manual

All users should read Chapter 1, "Installing and Starting QuickC," to get instructions for installing the compiler software. If you want introductory hands-on practice with the compiler, you will want to go through the brief sample session described in Section 1.7.4.

Where to go next depends on your particular needs, as described below:

### ■ Users New to Programming and the C Language

If you are learning programming and C at the same time, refer to the list of tutorial texts under "Resources for Learning" in this introduction.

### ■ Programmers Who are New to the C Language

If you have some programming background but have never programmed in C before, refer to Chapter 3, "C Quick Start," for information about particular features of C and the differences between C and other languages such as BASIC and Pascal.

### ■ Users Who Want to Program with QuickC Graphics

Read Chapter 4, "Graphics Quick Start," for instructions on writing programs with the graphics functions provided with the Microsoft QuickC Compiler.

■ **Users Who are New
to Integrated Programming Environments**

Read Chapter 2, "Introducing the QuickC Programming Environment,"
for an introduction to the components of the QuickC programming
environment. Then read Part 2, "The QuickC Programming Environment," to learn how to use the editor, compiler, and debugger built into
the QuickC environment.

■ **Users Who Are Interested
in Other Tools Provided with QuickC**

Read Part 3, "The QuickC Tool Kit," for descriptions of the **QCL**
compiler/linker driver, the **LINK** linker, the **LIB** library manager, and
the **MAKE** program-maintenance utility.

## Other Manuals You Get with QuickC

Two additional manuals are provided in the Microsoft QuickC Compiler
package:

- The *Microsoft C Language Reference* decribes Microsoft's ANSI-
  compatible implementation of the C language.
- The *Microsoft C Run-Time Library Reference* describes the more
  than 350 library routines and 34 include files provided with the
  Microsoft QuickC Compiler.

## Notational Conventions

This manual uses the following notation:

| Example of Convention | Description of Convention |
|---|---|
| `Example` | The typeface shown in the left column is used to simulate the appearance of information that would be printed on the screen or by the printer. |
| *placeholders* | Words in italics are placeholders in command-line and option specifications for types of information that you must supply. Italics are also occasionally used in the text for emphasis. |

**DOS NAMES,**
**FILE NAMES,** and
**MACROS**

Bold capital letters are used for the names of executable files and files provided with the product, for environment variables, for manifest constants, for macros, and for registers. These commands include built-in DOS commands such as **SET**, as well as the names of programs provided with the QuickC package.

**Reserved words**

Bold type indicates text that must be typed as shown. Text that is normally shown in bold type includes operators, keywords, library functions, commands, options, and preprocessor directives. Examples include the C keyword **int** and the function name **fopen**.

*⟦optional items⟧*

Double brackets enclose optional fields in command-line and option specifications.

*{ choice1|choice2}*

Braces and a vertical bar indicate that you have a choice between two or more items. Braces enclose the choices, and vertical bars separate the choices.

"Defined term"

Quotation marks set off terms defined in the text. For example, the term "far" appears in quotation marks the first time it is defined. Quotation marks also set off command-line prompts in text.

Some C constructs require quotation marks. Quotation marks required by the language have the form " " rather than " ".

Repeating
elements...

Three dots (also known as "ellipsis dots") following an item indicate that more items having the same form may be entered.

A column of dots in syntax lines and program examples shows that a portion of the program has been omitted.

KEY NAMES

Small capital letters are used for the names of keys you must press. Key sequences are indicated by small capitals separated by a plus sign (+). Examples include ENTER and CTRL+C.

The names of the keys in this manual correspond to the names printed on IBM Personal Computer key tops. If you are using a different machine, these keys may have slightly different names.

The group of cursor-movement (sometimes called "arrow") keys located on the numeric keypad to the right of the main keypad are called the DIRECTION keys. Each individual DIRECTION key is referred to either by the direction of the arrow on the key top (LEFT, RIGHT, UP, DOWN), or by the name on the key top (PGUP, PGDN).

The carriage-return key is referred to as ENTER.

## Resources for Learning

You may want to explore C further with one or more of the books listed below. They are listed in ascending order of difficulty, from beginning to advanced.

Hancock, Les, and Morris Krieger. *The C Primer, 2d ed.* New York: McGraw-Hill, 1985. (A beginner's guide to programming in the C language.)

Schildt, Herbert. *C Made Easy.* Berkeley, CA: Osborne/McGraw-Hill, 1985. (A good introduction to C for the reader who already knows BASIC.)

Waite, Mitchell, Stephine Prata, and Donald Martin. *C Primer Plus.* Indianapolis, IN: Howard W. Sams, Inc., 1984. (The best-selling introduction to the C language.)

Plum, Thomas. *Learning to Program in C.* Cardiff, New Jersey: Plum Hall, Inc., 1983. (A widely used introductory college text on computer programming using the C language.)

Kochan, Stephen. *Programming in C.* Hasbrouck Heights, NJ: Hayden Book Company, Inc., 1983. (A comprehensive introduction to C with some emphasis on the UNIX® environment.)

Harbison, Samuel P. and Guy L. Steele, Jr. *C: A Reference Manual, 2d ed.* Englewood Cliffs, NJ: Prentice-Hall, Inc., 1987. (An outstanding reference to the C language. The second edition incorporates the ANSI standard.)

Kernighan, Brian W., and Dennis M. Ritchie. *The C Programming Language.* Englewood Cliffs, NJ: Prentice-Hall, Inc., 1978. (The original, classic C book. Known to insiders as "K & R" or as "the white book." Useful after you have learned C.)

Tondo, Clovis L., and Scott E. Gimple. *The C Answer Book.* Englewood Cliffs, NJ: Prentice-Hall, Inc., 1985. (A collection of answers to the exercises in K & R. A companion volume to K & R.)

Jaeschke, Rex. *Solutions in C.* Reading, Massachusetts: Addison-Wesley, 1986. (A useful collection of C programming tips.)

Ward, Robert. *Debugging C.* Indianapolis, Indiana: Que Corporation, 1986. (A guide to the techniques of debugging C programs.)

Schustack, Steve. *Variations in C.* Redmond, Washington: Microsoft Press, 1985. (A guide to programming business applications in C.)[*]

Hansen, Augie. *Proficient C.* Redmond, Washington: Microsoft Press, 1987. (A guide to advanced C programming in the MS-DOS environment.)[*]

## Getting Help from Microsoft

If you feel you have discovered a problem in the software, please report the problem using the Product Assistance Request at the back of this manual.

If you have comments or suggestions regarding any of the manuals accompanying this product, please use the Documentation Feedback Card, also at the back of this manual.

---

[*]Microsoft Press books are available wherever books and software are sold. To order by phone, call 1-800-638-3030; in Maryland, call collect 824-7300. For a complete catalog of Microsoft Press books, write to: Microsoft Press, 16011 NE 36th Way, Box 97017, Redmond, WA 98073-9717.

# PART 1

# GETTING STARTED

# CHAPTERS

# PART 1

# ◇ GETTING STARTED

This part of the manual will get you started programming with the Microsoft QuickC Compiler.

Chapter 1 explains how to install the compiler by using the **SETUP** program and how to start and exit from the QuickC programming environment; it also describes a sample session in which you can load, compile, and run a program by using the QuickC compiler.

Chapter 2 describes the QuickC programming environment and common operations within it. This chapter is designed for users who want to experiment with QuickC before reading about menus and commands in detail.

Chapter 3 introduces the C programming language to users who are familiar with other languages such as Pascal or BASIC.

Chapter 4 shows how to write graphics programs by using the graphics-library routines.

# CHAPTER 1

# INSTALLING AND STARTING QUICKC

# CHAPTER

This chapter tells you how to install and start the Microsoft QuickC Compiler. Before you begin using the compiler, be sure to

1.  Back up your product disks (see Section 1.1).

2.  Check the contents of your disks (see Section 1.2).

3.  Read the **READMEDOC** file on your working copy of the Product distribution disk to learn about changes and additions made to the software after this manual was printed.

4.  Run the **SETUP** program to install the software (see Sections 1.3.1.1–1.3.1.2 and 1.3.2.1–1.3.2.2).

5.  Set up your DOS environment so that QuickC can find the files that it needs (see Section 1.4).

Several DOS procedures are mentioned in this chapter. In particular, the DOS **SET** and **PATH** commands are used to give values to DOS environment variables. If you are unfamiliar with any of the DOS procedures mentioned, consult your DOS user's guide for instructions.

---

*Note*

In this manual, the term "DOS" is used to refer to both MS-DOS and PC-DOS.

---

## 1.1   Backing Up Your Disks

After you have unwrapped the disks in your package, the first thing you should do is to make working copies, using the DOS **COPY** command or the **DISKCOPY** utility. Save the original disks for making future working copies.

## 1.2   Checking Disk Contents

When you open your compiler package for the first time, you may want to verify that you have a complete set of software. The Product distribution disk included in your compiler package contains a file that is named **PACKING.LST**; this file lists and describes the files and manuals that make up the Microsoft QuickC package.

To accommodate new features that may be added to the Microsoft QuickC Compiler, certain files or programs can be moved to disks other than the disks described in this manual. If you cannot find a file or program that you need, see the **PACKING.LST** file to find out which distribution disk contains that file or program.

# 1.3   Installing QuickC

Use the **SETUP** program provided on your working copy of the Libraries #1 distribution disk to install your QuickC software. The sections that follow give information about

1.  Exactly what **SETUP** does when it installs compiler software
2.  How to run **SETUP** to install the compiler software on a hard-disk or floppy-disk system
3.  How to set up the DOS environment so that QuickC can find the files that it needs

---

*Note*

If you also have Version 5.0 of the Microsoft C Optimizing Compiler, skip the installation procedure described here and run the version of **SETUP** provided with the Microsoft C Optimizing Compiler. The Version 5.0 **SETUP** installs both the Microsoft C Optimizing Compiler and the Microsoft QuickC Compiler. See Chapter 2 of the *Microsoft C Optimizing Compiler User's Guide* for instructions.

---

## 1.3.1   Installing on a Hard-Disk System

Sections 1.3.1.1–1.3.1.6 give instructions for installing the Microsoft QuickC Compiler on a hard-disk system.

### 1.3.1.1   What SETUP Does on a Hard-Disk System

When you install QuickC on a hard-disk system, the **SETUP** program does the following:

- Copies all necessary files to the directories or disks you specify.

- Builds a stand-alone library for each memory-model/math-package combination you specify on the **SETUP** command line. Many standard C library routines are built into the QuickC programming environment; however, in some cases, the QuickC compiler searches the libraries that **SETUP** builds to find routines that cannot be found otherwise. Also use these libraries if you create programs outside of the QuickC programming environment.

- Creates a batch file named **NEW-VARS.BAT** that sets the values of DOS environment variables so that QuickC can find the files it needs.

- Creates a file named **NEW-CONF.SYS** containing the appropriate settings for the **files** and **buffers** parameters in your **CONFIG.SYS** file.

### 1.3.1.2   Running SETUP on a Hard-Disk System

When you are ready to run **SETUP**, insert your working copy of the Libraries #1 distribution disk in drive A. Then enter a command line of the following form:

**SETUP H C:\ ** *dest* **{ S|M|C|L }** ... **{ EM|87 }** ... ⟦**GR**⟧ ⟦\ *bin*⟧ ⟦\ *incl*⟧ ⟦\ *lib*⟧

---

*Warning*

Several of the arguments that you give **SETUP** are directory names. If the directory you specify does not exist, **SETUP** creates the directory automatically.

**SETUP** overwrites the existing files as it installs new files with the same names. Do not give **SETUP** the name of an existing directory, unless you don't mind overwriting the files in that directory or you know that no files in that directory have the same names as the compiler files.

---

Each item (or "argument") on the **SETUP** command line shown above gives **SETUP** information about how you want to install the QuickC compiler. Optional arguments are shown in double brackets (⟦ ⟧). If you leave out an optional argument, **SETUP** uses the appropriate default. Some optional arguments allow you to type a question mark (**?**) to choose the default.

These are the arguments you can type on the **SETUP** command line; for a brief on-line explanation of these arguments, type **SETUP** with no arguments while the Program distribution disk is in drive A.

| Argument | Meaning |
| --- | --- |
| H | Type **H** to tell **SETUP** that you are installing on a hard-disk system. |
| C:\ *dest* | Type **C:** to tell **SETUP** that you are installing on drive C, immediately followed by the name of the "destination" directory for the installation. **SETUP** considers all other names that you give on the command line to be subdirectories of this directory. |
| S, M, C, L | Type one or more of these letters, separated by spaces, to tell **SETUP** which memory models you will use. Type **M**, since the medium memory model is the default for the QuickC programming environment. If you will be developing programs outside of the QuickC programming environment (using the **QCL** command discussed in Chapter 9, "Compiling and Linking Programs"), type **S**, since the small memory model is the default for the **QCL** command. Also, if you will be using them, type **C** (compact memory model), or **L** (large memory model). |
| | **SETUP** uses the memory-model arguments and the floating-point-math arguments (see below) that you give to determine which libraries to build. Combined libraries speed up the process of creating programs; however, because the combined libraries are large, you should specify only those memory models that you know you will use. (If you use more than one memory model, you may also want to use the uncombined libraries instead of taking up disk space for combined libraries; see Section 1.4 for more information.) |
| EM, 87 | Type either or both of these arguments to tell **SETUP** how you want to handle floating-point math operations in your programs. |
| | Ordinarily, type **EM** for this option to tell QuickC that you will be using a floating-point emulator rather than an 8087 or 80287 coprocessor. (See Section 9.3.5 if you need more information about handling floating-point math in programs.) |

Type **87** if you develop programs that perform scientific, mathematical, or financial calculations with real numbers and that will always run on systems with coprocessors. Typing **87** builds an additional library, which requires substantial disk space, but creating programs with this library makes them smaller and faster.

**GR**　　Type **GR** if you want to build the QuickC graphics functions (described in Chapter 4 of this manual and in the *Microsoft C Run-Time Library Reference*) into the library that **SETUP** builds. This option makes the library approximately 50K larger. If you do not give this option, graphics functions are not included. The QuickC compiler must be able to find the library that is named **GRAPHICS.LIB** if your program uses QuickC graphics functions. See Section 1.5 for more information.

\\*bin*　　Type the subdirectory of *dest* in which you want to install the compiler executable files, including the compiler, linker, and utilities. If you leave out this argument or type a question mark (**?**) for it, **SETUP** uses the \\**BIN** subdirectory by default.

\\*incl*　　Type the subdirectory of *dest* in which you want to install include files. If you leave out this argument or type a question mark (**?**) for it, **SETUP** uses the \\**INCLUDE** subdirectory by default.

\\*lib*　　Type the subdirectory of *dest* in which you want to install library files. If you leave out this argument or type a question mark (**?**) for it, **SETUP** uses the \\**LIB** subdirectory by default.

**SETUP** automatically creates the following subdirectories:

- A subdirectory named \\**TMP** that the compiler uses for temporary files during compilation
- A subdirectory of the executable-file directory named \\**SAMPLE**, in which **SETUP** installs demonstration programs

■　**Examples**

```
SETUP H C:\ M EM ? ? ?
```

The command line above tells **SETUP** to install the compiler software in the default subdirectories of the root directory (\\) on hard-disk drive C.

11

The default subdirectories are **\BIN** for compiler and utility executable files, **\INCLUDE** for include files, and **\LIB** for library files. **SETUP** builds the appropriate library for the medium memory model and the emulator floating-point math package and names this library **MLIBCE.LIB**.

```
SETUP H C:\QC S M C L EM GR 87 \BINDIR \INC \LIBS
```

The command line above tells **SETUP** to install the compiler software in the given subdirectories of the \QC directory on hard-disk drive C. Executable files are installed in \QC\BINDIR; include files are installed in \QC\INC; library files are installed in \QC\LIBS; and demonstration files are installed in \QC\BINDIR\SAMPLE. Library files are built for all available memory models and floating-point math packages (eight libraries total). Each library includes the Microsoft C graphics functions.

### 1.3.1.3  Building Libraries on a Hard-Disk System

After you press ENTER, **SETUP** begins to build and install libraries. **SETUP** prompts you when to swap disks in drive A.

**SETUP** reads each memory-model argument (**S**, **M**, **C**, or **L**) and floating-point-math argument (**EM** and **87**) that you have given on the command line and builds one library for each possible combination of the two. **SETUP** displays the names of the libraries it is building as it builds them.

**SETUP** also names the libraries it builds based on the memory model(s) and floating-point-math package(s) you choose. Each default library name has the following form:

**{ S | M | C | L } LIBC { E | 7 } .LIB**

The first character of the library name is the same as the memory-model argument: **S** for the small (default) memory model, **M** for the medium memory model, **C** for the compact memory model, or **L** for the large memory model. The last character of the base name (the part of the name before the .LIB extension) is determined by the floating-point-math argument: **E** if the **EM** argument was given, or **7** if the **87** argument was given.

For example, the library named **MLIBCE.LIB** supports the medium memory model and the emulator floating-point-math package, the defaults for the QuickC programming environment. The library named **SLIBC7.LIB** supports the small memory model and the 8087/80287 floating-point-math package, which can be used only for programs run on machines with a math coprocessor.

*Note*

For ease of discussion, the remainder of this manual uses the default names to identify libraries that support particular combinations of memory models and math packages.

### 1.3.1.4 Deleting Library Components

**SETUP** displays the following additional prompt:

```
Setup no longer needs the library sub-components and you do not
normally need them to compile and link your C program. Do you want
to delete them? [y/n]
```

If you use combinations of memory models and floating-point-math packages other than those you gave on the **SETUP** command line, you may want to keep the uncombined libraries. However, if you will only be using the models and math packages supported by your combined libraries, you can delete the uncombined libraries. Enter **Y** or **y** to delete the uncombined libraries, or enter **N** or **n** if you want to keep them.

### 1.3.1.5 Completing Installation

**SETUP** performs several additional steps, including creating the **NEW-VARS.BAT** and **NEW-CONF.SYS** files.

### 1.3.1.6 Setting Up the DOS Environment on a Hard-Disk System

The final step of installation is to set up the DOS environment so that the QuickC compiler can find the files that it needs.

**SETUP** automatically creates a batch file named **NEW-VARS.BAT**. Use **NEW-VARS.BAT** to set up your DOS environment variables so that the compiler and linker can find the files they need.

If you wish, you can add the **SET** commands in the **NEW-VARS.BAT** file to your **AUTOEXEC.BAT** file so that the DOS environment is set up correctly each time you boot your system.

In addition to **NEW-VARS.BAT**, **SETUP** creates a file named **NEW-CONF.SYS.** This file sets the **files** and **buffers** parameters to appropriate values for the Microsoft QuickC Compiler. You can either replace your existing **CONFIG.SYS** file with **NEW-CONF.SYS** or copy the **buffers** and **files** settings from **NEW-CONF.SYS** to your existing **CONFIG.SYS** file.

**SETUP** installs **NEW-VARS.BAT** and **NEW-CONF.SYS** in the subdirectory of *dest* where you installed the QuickC executable files (by default, in *dest*\**BIN\SAMPLE**).

## 1.3.2 Installing on a Floppy-Disk System

Sections 1.3.2.1–1.3.2.4 give instructions for installing the Microsoft QuickC Compiler on a floppy-disk system. Note that these instructions assume that you will be running **SETUP** from drive A; if you prefer to run **SETUP** from drive B, simply substitute "drive B" for "drive A" and "drive A" for "drive B" in the following instructions.

### 1.3.2.1 What SETUP Does on a Floppy-Disk System

When you install QuickC on a floppy-disk system, the **SETUP** program builds a stand-alone library for each memory-model/math-package combination you specify on the **SETUP** command line. Many standard C library routines are built into the QuickC programming environment; however, in some cases, the QuickC compiler searches the libraries that **SETUP** builds to find routines that cannot be found otherwise. Also use these libraries if you create programs outside of the QuickC programming environment.

## 1.3.2.2 Running SETUP on a Floppy-Disk System

Before you run **SETUP** on a floppy-disk system, determine how many blank, formatted floppy disks you will need to hold the libraries that **SETUP** builds. You need one blank, formatted disk for each memory model you will be using, plus one "scratch" disk; if you will be using only the default memory model for the QuickC programming environment (medium model), two disks are all you need. **SETUP** places each library that it builds on a separate floppy disk.

After you format the required number of disks, insert your working copy of the Libraries #1 distribution disk in drive A. Then enter a command line of the following form:

**SETUP F B: { S|M|C|L} ... {EM|87} ⟦GR⟧**

Each item (or "argument") on the **SETUP** command line gives **SETUP** information about how you want to install the QuickC compiler. Optional arguments are shown in double brackets (⟦ ⟧). If you leave out an optional argument, **SETUP** uses the appropriate default. Some optional arguments allow you to type a question mark (**?**) to choose the default.

These are the arguments you can type on the **SETUP** command line; for a brief on-line explanation of these arguments, type **SETUP** with no arguments while the Program distribution disk is in drive A.

| Argument | Meaning |
|---|---|
| F | Tells **SETUP** that you are installing on a floppy-disk system. |
| B: | Type **B:** to tell **SETUP** that you are creating libraries on the disks in drive B. |
| S, M, C, L | Tells **SETUP** which memory model(s) you will use. Type one or more letters, separated by spaces. Type **M**, since the medium memory model is the default for the QuickC programming environment. If you will be developing programs outside of the QuickC programming environment (using the **QCL** command discussed in Chapter 9, "Compiling and Linking Programs"), type **S**, since the small memory model is the default for the **QCL** command. Also, if you will be using them, type **C** (compact memory model), or **L** (large memory model). |

**SETUP** uses the memory-model arguments and the floating-point-math argument (see below) that you give to determine which libraries to build. Combined libraries speed up the process of creating programs; however, because you need a separate library disk for each library that you create, type letters only for the memory models that you know you will use. (If you use more than one memory model, you may also want to use the uncombined libraries instead of taking up disk space for combined libraries; see Section 1.4 for more information.)

**EM, 87**    Type either **EM** or **87** to tell **SETUP** how your programs will handle floating-point-math operations: using software that emulates an 8087 or 80287 coprocessor (**EM**) or using an actual coprocessor (**87**).

Generally, type **EM** for this argument, since programs created within the QuickC environment use the emulator.

If you develop programs that perform scientific, mathematical, or financial calculations with real numbers and that will always run on systems with coprocessors, rerun **SETUP** and type **87** for this argument. Typing **87** builds an additional library, which requires substantial disk space, but creating programs with this library makes them smaller and faster.

**GR**    Type **GR** if you want to include the QuickC graphics functions (described in Chapter 4 of this manual and in the *Microsoft C Run-Time Library Reference*) in the library that **SETUP** builds. This option makes the library approximately 50K larger. If you do not give this option, graphics functions are not included. The QuickC compiler must be able to find the **GRAPHICS.LIB** library if your program uses QuickC graphics functions. See Section 1.5 for more information.

■ **Example**

SETUP F B: M EM

The command line above tells **SETUP** to build the appropriate library for the medium memory model and for the floating-point emulator, **MLIBCE.LIB**, on floppy-disk drive B.

### 1.3.2.3 Building Libraries on a Floppy-Disk System

After you press ENTER, **SETUP** begins to build and install libraries. **SETUP** installs one library per disk; it prompts you when to swap, in drives A and B, the required Libraries distribution disks, the disks on which you are installing new libraries, and your scratch disk.

**SETUP** reads each memory-model argument (**S**, **M**, **C**, or **L**) and the floating-point-math argument (**EM** or **87**) that you have given on the command line and builds one library for each possible combination of the two. **SETUP** displays the names of the libraries it is building as it builds them.

**SETUP** also names the libraries it builds based on the memory model(s) and floating-point-math package(s) you choose. Each default library name has the following form:

{ S | M | C | L } LIBC { E | 7 } .LIB

The first character of the library name is the same as the memory-model argument: **S** for the small (default) memory model, **M** for the medium memory model, **C** for the compact memory model, or **L** for the large memory model. The last character of the base name (the part of the name before the **.LIB** extension) is determined by the floating-point-math argument: **E** if the **EM** argument was given or **7** if the **87** argument was given.

For example, the library named **MLIBCE.LIB** supports the medium memory model and the emulator floating-point-math package, the defaults for the QuickC programming environment. The library named **SLIBC7.LIB** supports the small memory model and the 8087/80287 floating-point-math package, which can be used only for programs run on machines with a math coprocessor.

*Note*

For ease of discussion, the remainder of this manual uses the default names to identify libraries that support particular combinations of memory models and math packages.

### 1.3.2.4 Setting Up the DOS Environment on a Floppy-Disk System

The final step of installation is to set up the DOS environment so that QuickC can find the files that it needs. Type the following DOS commands:

```
SET PATH=A:;
SET LIB=A:;
SET INCLUDE=A:\INCLUDE;
```

These commands tell QuickC to look for executable files and library files in the root directory of the disk on drive A and for the include files in the **\INCLUDE** directory of the disk in drive A. These settings hold until you next reboot your system. You may want to add these commands to your **AUTOEXEC.BAT** file so that they are carried out automatically when you reboot.

Before you run QuickC, enter the following values in your **CONFIG.SYS** file, then reboot your system:

```
files=15
buffers=10
```

# 1.4   Using Uncombined Libraries

The **SETUP** program builds combined libraries because creating programs with uncombined libraries takes more time. If you use many different combinations of memory models and floating-point-math packages, you may not want to use up the disk space required for all of the combined libraries you need. Instead, you may use the individual library components. Note that using uncombined libraries has the following disadvantages:

- You must generally type longer command lines to compile and link programs.

- You must tell the linker not to use the libraries it would normally use and explicitly give it the names of the appropriate uncombined libraries.

- Linking with uncombined libraries takes longer than linking with combined libraries.

The following uncombined libraries are provided with the Microsoft QuickC Compiler (where *m* indicates the appropriate memory model):

| Library | Purpose |
| --- | --- |
| *m*LIBC.LIB | Standard run-time library; contains all of the routines included in the Microsoft C run-time library except math routines that require floating-point support. |
| *m*LIBFP.LIB | Floating-point math library; required whenever your program uses EM.LIB or 87.LIB. |
| EM.LIB | Model-independent floating-point emulator; used to perform floating-point operations. |
| LIBH.LIB | Model-independent "compiler helper" functions; used to handle complex operations such as 32-bit multiplication and division. |
| 87.LIB | Model-independent 8087/80287 floating-point library; provides minimal floating-point support and can only be used when an 8087 or 80287 coprocessor is present. |

The following list shows each combined library built by **SETUP** and the corresponding uncombined libraries:

| Combined Library | Uncombined Libraries |
| --- | --- |
| *m*LIBCE.LIB | *m*LIBC.LIB, *m*LIBFP.LIB, LIBH.LIB, and EM.LIB |
| *m*LIBC7.LIB | *m*LIBC.LIB, *m*LIBFP.LIB, LIBH.LIB, and 87.LIB |

If you choose to use uncombined libraries, copy the uncombined libraries you need from your working copies of the Libraries #1, Libraries #2, and Libraries #3 distribution disks to the subdirectory you created for libraries on your hard disk (by default, *dest*\LIB). If you are running on a floppy-disk system, use your working copies of these distribution disks. The following list shows where to find each type of library:

| Libraries | Distribution Disk |
| --- | --- |
| Model independent | Libraries #1 |

| Medium and small model | Libraries #2 |
| Compact and large model | Libraries #3 |

See Section 9.4.2.3 for more information about specifying uncombined libraries.

## 1.5   Using the Microsoft C Graphics Library

If you decided not to include graphics in the combined libraries built by **SETUP**, but you still want to use Microsoft C graphics routines in your programs, QuickC must be able to find the **GRAPHICS.LIB** library, which contains the graphics routines. This library is included on the Libraries #1 distribution disk in your package. If you installed QuickC on a hard-disk system, copy this library to the subdirectory where you told **SETUP** to install libraries.

If you create a graphics program within the QuickC environment, set up a program list for that program as described in Section 6.2.6. Then add **GRAPHICS.LIB** to the program list as described in Section 6.2.7.

If you create a graphics program outside the QuickC environment, you must link with **GRAPHICS.LIB** explicitly. You have the following choices:

- Specify **GRAPHICS.LIB** on the **QCL** or **LINK** command line as described in Section 9.4.2.3.
- Specify **GRAPHICS.LIB** in the **CL** environment variable, as described in Section 9.3, or in the **LINK** environment variable, as described in Section 9.5. Specifying **GRAPHICS.LIB** in the DOS environment links your program with **GRAPHICS.LIB** automatically.

## 1.6   If You Have a Mouse

You can use QuickC with or without a mouse. Where appropriate, this manual describes procedures with the keyboard and with the mouse, so you can use either or both.

*Note*

> Microsoft QuickC is designed for use with the Microsoft Mouse. Many manufacturers advertise their pointing devices as being compatible with the Microsoft Mouse. QuickC may work with some of these devices if they are fully compatible, especially if they emulate the function calls of the Microsoft Mouse. For details, check with your mouse manufacturer.

The following mouse-specific terms are used in this manual:

| Term | Definition |
| --- | --- |
| Point | Move the mouse until the pointer rests on what you want to point to. |
| Press | Hold down the mouse button. |
| Click | Quickly press and release the mouse button. Click refers to the left button unless otherwise indicated. |
| Drag | Hold down the left mouse button while moving the mouse across a flat surface, such as a desk top. |
| Double click | Click the left mouse button twice in rapid succession. |

## 1.7  Running the QuickC Compiler

The following sections explain how to start and exit the Microsoft QuickC Compiler, gives steps for a sample compilation, and explains options that you can give on the **QC** command line to change its behavior on start-up.

### 1.7.1  Starting the QuickC Compiler

After you have installed the compiler software and set up your DOS environment variables, you are ready to start QuickC. Which of the following methods is used depends on whether you are using a hard-disk or a floppy-disk system:

- On a hard-disk system, you can start the QuickC compiler from any directory, provided that you used **NEW-VARS.BAT** to set up the environment. Otherwise, execute the DOS **CD** command to move to the directory where you installed the **QC.EXE** file. Then simply type

  QC

- On a floppy-disk system, make drive B the current drive. Place your working copy of the Product distribution disk in drive A and the disk you will use for your programs in drive B. Start QuickC using the following command:

  A:QC

  When the QuickC screen appears, swap your working copy of the Work distribution disk in drive A.

To load a C source file automatically when you start QuickC, type the file name after **QC** on the command line. The QuickC compiler also allows you to give a number of arguments and options on the command line; the following section describes these arguments.

## 1.7.2  The QC Command

With the **QC** command, you can control the operation of QuickC by using command-line options. These options can be given in any order, as long as the name of the source file you are loading is given last on the command line. Here is the full syntax:

QC [ [/b] [/g] [/h] [/l *quicklib*] [*sourcefile*] ]

The following list describes the available **QC** options:

| Option | Effect |
| --- | --- |
| /b | Starts the Microsoft QuickC Compiler in black-and-white mode. Use this option if you are using a composite monitor on your system. |
| /g | Try this option if you are using a color graphics adapter (CGA). QuickC automatically adjusts the way it updates the screen to accommodate your hardware. On some machines it is possible to update the screen faster than the QuickC default. The /g option causes QuickC to update the screen as fast as possible. If you see "snow" (dots flickering on the screen) when you update large areas of the screen (for example, with PGUP), then your |

hardware cannot handle the speed and you should restart QuickC without the **/g** option. This option has no effect on machines with enhanced graphics (EGA) or monochrome adapter (MA) cards.

**/h**  Starts QuickC using as many lines as possible for the display adapter in use. For example, the IBM Enhanced Graphics Adapter (EGA) can display 43 lines when attached to an IBM Enhanced Color Display.

**/l** *quicklib*  Type the name of a Quick library, if you want to load one. If your programs use C library routines that are not built into the QuickC programming environment, you can compile them faster by loading a Quick library containing these routines. (See Table 6.1 for a list of built-in C library routines and Section 10.1 for information about creating and using Quick libraries.)

*sourcefile*  Type the name of a C source file if you want to load that file for editing or compiling when you start QuickC.

## 1.7.3  Leaving QuickC

To leave QuickC and return to the operating system, follow these steps:

1.  Type ALT+F to display the File menu.
2.  Type X to execute the Exit command.

Other ways to leave QuickC are described in Chapter 6, "Creating and Saving Programs."

If you leave QuickC without writing your program to disk, a prompt asks if you want to save the program. Type the name you want to give the file, then press ENTER.

## 1.7.4  Sample Compilation

This sample compiling session will give you hands-on practice with QuickC. During this session, you will compile the demonstration program **CFLOW.C**, which outlines the function calls and dependencies in any C source file.

The steps below will take you through the compilation process:

1. If you have a hard-disk system, the **CFLOW.C** program is in the directory that **SETUP** created for sample programs (by default, *dest*\\**BIN**\\**SAMPLE**).

   If you have a floppy-disk system, place your working copy of the Product distribution disk in drive A and your working copy of the Libraries #2 distribution disk in drive B.

2. If you are running on a hard-disk system, type

   ```
   qc cflow.c
   ```

   and press ENTER to start QuickC and load **CFLOW.C**. If you are running on a floppy-disk system, type

   ```
   a:qc cflow.c
   ```

   and press ENTER.

3. Press ALT+R to open the Run menu.

4. Press C to execute the Compile command.

5. A box (known as a "dialog box") for the Compile... command appears. For now, just press ENTER. When QuickC has finished compiling your program, the Compile dialog box disappears from the screen.

6. Press ALT+R to open the Run menu again.

7. Press ALT+O to execute the Set Runtime Options command.

8. A dialog box for the Set Runtime Options command appears. Type `cflow.c` in the Command Line text box and press ENTER.

9. Press ALT+R to open the Run menu again.

10. Press S to run your program. If it runs without errors, QuickC displays the following message:

    ```
    Program returned (0). Press any key
    ```

11. Press any key to return to the QuickC view window.

12. Press the ALT+F keys to open the File menu again.

13. Press X to exit QuickC and return to DOS.

## 1.8 Saving Options: the QC.INI Initialization File

**QC.INI** is the initialization file that QuickC uses to save settings for the Options... command on the View menu and the Compile... command on the Run menu. The Options... settings determine the colors used to display different types of text, tab-stop indenting, and the presence of scroll bars in the windows. The Compile... settings control various aspects of the compilation process.

If you have changed any of the Options... or Compile... settings when you exit from QuickC, these changes are written to a file named **QC.INI**. **QC.INI** is not supplied on any of the distribution disks. It is created only when changes are made to the View menu Options... settings. If you use only the default settings, **QC.INI** is never created.

When QuickC starts, it looks for **QC.INI** first in the current directory, then in the directories given by the **PATH** environment variable. If QuickC does not find **QC.INI**, it uses the default View menu Options... settings. If you change the Options... settings, QuickC writes the new **QC.INI** file to the directory where it was originally found.

Note that you can have multiple **QC.INI** files in separate directories; QuickC uses the version in the directory from which you start QuickC.

# CHAPTER 2

## INTRODUCING THE QUICKC PROGRAMMING ENVIRONMENT

This chapter introduces the QuickC programming environment. It describes the parts of the environment and shows how to perform common operations within the environment, including: opening menus and dialog boxes; choosing commands and options; and selecting and scrolling text.

This chapter provides essential information if you want to experiment with the programming environment before learning in detail about the individual menus and commands in Part 2 of this manual.

## 2.1   The QuickC Screen

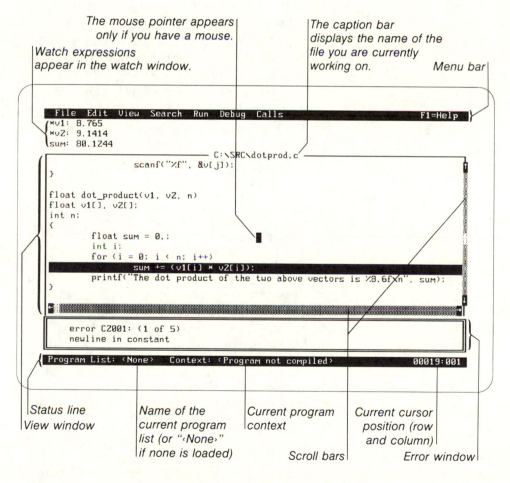

Figure 2.1  The QuickC Screen

Figure 2.1 illustrates the components of the QuickC screen. The list below describes these components:

| Element | Description |
| --- | --- |
| Cursor | A flashing underscore or block that shows where text you enter will appear on the screen. If QuickC is in insert mode, the cursor is a flashing underscore; if it is in overtype mode, the cursor is a flashing block. (See Section 7.1.2 for information about overtype mode.) |
| Mouse pointer | A small rectangular block that appears in the center of the screen if you have a mouse installed. |
| View window | The area of the screen where you enter and edit the text of your program and trace through your program during debugging. |
| Menu bar | The bar at the top of the screen that contains the names of the QuickC command menus. |
| Title bar | The bar below the menu bar that displays the name of the file being edited in the view window. If no file is loaded, or if you are working on a new program, `untitled.c` appears in the title bar. |
| Scroll bars | Bars along the right and bottom margins of the screen that show your relative position in the file. If you have a mouse, scroll bars also give you a convenient way to move text up and down or right and left within the view window. Scroll bars can be toggled on and off through the View Options... dialog box. |
| Status line | The last line on the screen showing current program list and the program context. If you have loaded a program list, `Program List:` is followed by the name of the program list. Otherwise, `Program List:` is followed by `<none>`. (See Chapter 6, "Creating and Saving Programs," for a description of program lists.) If the program has not yet been compiled, `Context:` is followed by `Program not compiled`. If the program has been compiled but is not being executed, `Context:` is followed by `Program not running`. If you are running or stepping through |

the program, the name of the current source file, followed by the the name of the function that is currently being executed, appears after Context:. On the far right, the current cursor position is displayed as a combination of line and column numbers. Just to the left of this cursor-position display, the letter C appears when the CAPS LOCK key is toggled on, and N appears when the NUM LOCK key is toggled on.

Watch window                    A window that appears on the screen only when you are using the Add Watch... command. See Section 8.2.3.1 for more information about the watch window and the Add Watch... command.

Error window                    Appears on the screen only when your program causes compilation or run-time errors. See Section 5.5 for more information about the error window.

## 2.2   Using QuickC Menus

QuickC commands are organized in "menus" on the menu bar. A sample menu, File, is shown in Figure 2.2.

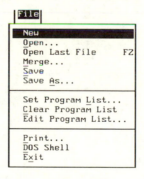

**Figure 2.2  Sample Menu**

Commands followed by dots ( . . .) prompt you for additional information when you select them. Commands without dots are executed as soon as you select them.

## 2.2.1  Contents of QuickC Menus

The following list describes the QuickC menus and the commands they contain:

| Menu | Actions of Commands |
| --- | --- |
| File | Create, load, merge, print, or save source files. Other commands on this menu set up or edit the list of source files in a program, temporarily exit to DOS, and end the QuickC session. |
| Edit | Delete, add, or copy source-file text. |
| View | Customize the appearance of the QuickC programming environment and specify what QuickC displays. |
| Search | Find or replace text in source files, find functions during debugging, or display source-file lines that cause compilation errors. |
| Run | Compile and run programs and set compile-time and run-time options for programs. |
| Debug | Control the use of debugging features such as watch expressions, breakpoints, and screen swapping. |
| Calls | Does not contain commands. Instead, it shows the hierarchy of functions that have been called by other functions and allows you to move the cursor to the point where any of the displayed functions are called. |
| Help | Control the display of help information. The Help menu is described in Section 2.6 of this manual, "Getting Help: the Help Menu." |

## 2.2.2  Choosing Commands from Menus

In the QuickC environment you have several ways to display menus and select commands. Use the method you find most convenient.

■ **Keyboard**

To select a command with the keyboard, perform the following steps:

1. Press the ALT key plus the key with the first letter of the menu name. This opens the menu.

2. Press the key corresponding to the highlighted or underlined letter in the command name. If a command is already highlighted, press ENTER to select it.

A second way to select commands is the following:

1. Press ALT.
2. Move the highlight from command to command using the DIREC-TION keys.
3. Press ENTER to carry out the highlighted command.

To cancel any command before you carry it out, press ESC.

Note that the ALT key is "sticky": when pressed, it highlights the first entry in the menu bar, File. It is also a "toggle": if you press the key again, its state is reversed. Therefore, if you press ALT+R, the Run menu opens. If you immediately press ALT again, the Run menu disappears, and the Run selection in the menu bar is highlighted. If you press ALT once more, the highlight disappears completely.

If more than one command on a menu has the same first letter, one of those commands has a letter other than the first letter highlighted (indicated here in boldface). For example, on the File menu both the **O**pen... and the Open **L**ast File commands begin with "O." Press O to execute the **O**pen... command, or press L to execute the Open Last File command. Pressing ESC turns off a menu display completely, whereas pressing ALT closes it but leaves the menu name selected. To open a menu and then open other menus on the menu bar, open a menu and then use the LEFT or RIGHT key to open either adjacent menu.

■ **Mouse**

To choose a command with the mouse, click the menu name with the left mouse button. Then click the command with the left mouse button.

To cancel a command with the mouse, click anything except a menu with the left mouse button.

### 2.2.3  Shortcut Keys for Commands

A key name appears to the right of some menu commands, as shown in
Figure 2.3.

Figure 2.3  Shortcut Keys

These are "shortcut keys." Use the shortcut keys to carry out a command
without first opening the menu and selecting the command. For example,
simply press F2 to load the most recently edited file without having to
open a menu. Table 2.1 lists the QuickC shortcut keys.

Table 2.1

QuickC Shortcut Keys

| Menu | Command | Key(s) |
|------|---------|--------|
| File | Open Last File | F2 |
| Edit | Undo | ALT+BACKSPACE |
| | Cut | SHIFT+DEL |
| | Copy | CTRL+INS |
| | Paste | SHIFT+INS |
| | Clear | DEL |
| View | Output Screen | F4 |
| Search | Selected Text | CTRL+\ |
| | Repeat Last Find | F3 |
| | Next Error | SHIFT+F3 |
| | Previous Error | SHIFT+F4 |
| Run | Continue | F5 |
| Debug | Delete Last Watch | SHIFT+F2 |
| | Toggle Breakpoint | F9 |

## 2.3   Using Dialog Boxes

QuickC displays a "dialog box" when it needs additional information or when it needs you to confirm an action you have chosen. The dialog box contains areas where you enter information, select options to commands, or activate controls to execute or cancel a command. While QuickC displays a dialog box, any input you type at the keyboard affects the item in the dialog box that has the "input focus." The flashing underscore appears in the item that has the input focus.

Many items in dialog boxes are options that you can turn on or off. To turn the option with the input focus on or off, press SPACEBAR. To move the input focus to an option and turn it on or off in a single step, press ALT and type the highlighted letter in the option name.

Clicking an item with the mouse affects it, regardless of the input focus.

In this section, the Compile... and Open... dialog boxes shown in Figure 2.4 are used as examples to illustrate the parts of a dialog box.

*Select only one from each group of circular buttons.*     *Select any number of check boxes.*

```
Program List: |Lexer
Current File: |C:\SRC\lexer.c

Warning Levels     Output Options          Miscellaneous
  ( · ) Level 0    ( ) Obj                 [ ] Debug
  ( ) Level 1      ( · ) Memory            [ ] Pointer Check
  ( ) Level 2      ( ) Exe                 [ ] Stack Check
  ( ) Level 3      ( ) Syntax Check Only   [X] Language Extensions
                                           [ ] Optimizations


Include:  [                                            ]

Define:   [                                            ]


  [ Build Program ]   [ Compile File ]   [ Rebuild All ]   [ Cancel ]
```

*Press ENTER from anywhere in the dialog box to choose the command button with the input focus (double outline).*     *To choose a command button, move the input focus to that button and press SPACEBAR.*

*Type the text in a text box.*

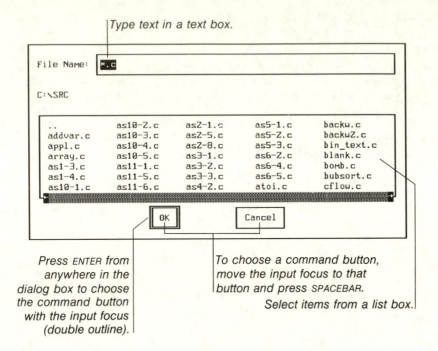

*Type text in a text box.*

```
File Name: *.c

C:\SRC

..          as10-2.c    as2-1.c    as5-1.c    backw.c
addvar.c    as10-3.c    as2-5.c    as5-2.c    backw2.c
appl.c      as10-4.c    as2-8.c    as5-3.c    bin_text.c
array.c     as10-5.c    as3-1.c    as6-2.c    blank.c
as1-3.c     as11-1.c    as3-2.c    as6-4.c    bomb.c
as1-4.c     as11-5.c    as3-3.c    as6-5.c    bubsort.c
as10-1.c    as11-6.c    as4-2.c    atoi.c     cflow.c

              OK              Cancel
```

*Press ENTER from anywhere in the dialog box to choose the command button with the input focus (double outline).*

*To choose a command button, move the input focus to that button and press SPACEBAR.*

*Select items from a list box.*

**Figure 2.4  Sample Dialog Boxes**

Dialog boxes contain some or all of the following elements:

| Element | Description |
| --- | --- |
| Text box | A space in which to enter information for commands, such as a file name or text you are searching for. |
| | A text box has the input focus when a flashing underscore appears in the box. This indicates that you can enter or edit the text in the box. If you type more text than a text box can hold, the text box scrolls to the left to allow you more room to enter text. |
| | To correct typing errors in a text box, press BACKSPACE or use the QuickC editing keys described in Section 7.1.1. To move the input focus from the text box to the next or previous item in the dialog box, press TAB or SHIFT+TAB, respectively. To move the input focus to *any* item in the dialog box, press ALT and type the highlighted letter in the item name. |

List box

A box that lists the files matching the specification in a text box. List boxes give you an alternative way to select a file for a command: instead of typing the file name in the text box, you can select it from the file names listed in the list box.

The file name with the input focus appears in reverse video. This file name is the currently selected file name. The currently selected file name also appears in the text box. To move the input focus to a different file name, press the DIRECTION keys or type the first character of the file name. To carry out the command by using the selected file name, press ENTER.

Check boxes

Options preceded by opening and closing brackets ([ ]), which let you select one or more options from a group of options.

To move the input focus forward and backward between check boxes, press the TAB and SHIFT+TAB keys.

To turn the check box with the input focus on or off, press SPACEBAR. When a check box is turned on (that is, selected), an X appears in the box.

To turn *any* check box on or off, press ALT and type the highlighted letter in the option name.

Command button

A square box with a label that indicates what choosing the button will do.

When a command button has the input focus, it has a double outline. The command button with the input focus indicates the action carried out when you press ENTER or SPACEBAR. To move the input focus forward and backward between command buttons, press TAB and SHIFT+TAB, or press ALT and type the letter that is highlighted in the command box.

To execute the command with the options you have chosen from the dialog box, press SPACEBAR or ENTER. After the command is executed, the dialog box disappears.

| | |
|---|---|
| Circular buttons | Options preceded by opening and closing parentheses ( () ), which indicate that you may select only one option from the group. |
| | To move the input focus forward and backward between circular buttons, press UP and DOWN. |
| | To turn the circular button with the input focus on or off, press SPACEBAR. When a circular button is turned on (selected), a highlight appears inside of it. |
| | To turn *any* circular button on, press ALT and type the highlighted letter in the option name. |
| | After you have selected a circular button from a group of circular buttons, press TAB or SHIFT+TAB to move on. |

Often, a dialog box opens with options already chosen. These usually are the options that were chosen the last time the command was selected. For example, the Options... dialog box might open with the options set from the last time you changed them this session.

To select a check box, circular button, or command button with the mouse, use these two steps:

1. Point to the option.
2. Click it with the left mouse button.

## 2.4   Selecting Text

When you work with the QuickC environment, you need to "select" the text that the next command or action will affect.

■   **Keyboard**

To select text, either in a work area (for instance, a list window) or in a text box, hold down the SHIFT key while you press DIRECTION keys to move the cursor over the text you want to select. You can use different key combinations to select more than one character of text at a time. These key combinations are listed in Table 7.1.

■ **Mouse**

To select text, point to the left of the text you want to select and drag the mouse pointer over the text.

# 2.5 Scrolling

Often, a program or procedure is too big to fit in the visible portion of a view window. To view information that won't fit in the window, you can move the text up, down, right, or left. This is called "scrolling."

■ **Keyboard**

To scroll with the keyboard, once you have reached the last character on the screen, press the DIRECTION key for the direction you want to scroll. For example, to scroll right, go to the rightmost character on the screen and keep pressing the RIGHT key. To scroll more than one character at a time, refer to Table 2.2.

**Table 2.2**

**Scrolling with the Keyboard**

| To Scroll: | Press: |
| --- | --- |
| Down one screen | PGDN |
| Up one screen | PGUP |
| Left one screen | CTRL+PGUP |
| Right one screen | CTRL+PGDN |

■ **Mouse**

If you have a mouse installed, you can use the scroll bars at the bottom and right margins of the active window to scroll text up, down, left, or right.

To scroll with the mouse, point to the "scroll box" (the dark box on a scroll bar) and drag it to a position on the bar that corresponds to the general location you want. To scroll a page at a time, place the mouse pointer in the scroll bar between the scroll box and the top or bottom of the scroll bar, and click the left button. To scroll one line or one character at a time, click the arrows at either end of the scroll bars.

## 2.6  Getting Help: the Help Menu

If you need information about QuickC editing keys or menus, C language features, or C library functions, QuickC makes it fast and easy to get help. You can tell QuickC to display help information about any C keyword or function name in the view window while you are editing your source file. Or, if you prefer, you can browse through a list of help topics to find the information you need.

To see QuickC help information while no other help information is being displayed, press F1. The first panel of QuickC help information, a list of commonly used QuickC editing keys, appears over the view window.

Use the commands on the Help menu to view information about the QuickC keyboard commands or about C statement and function syntax. Figure 2.5 shows the Help menu.

---

06 The Help Menu

---

**Figure 2.5  The Help Menu**

The commands in the Help menu are described below:

| Command | Action |
|---|---|
| General... | Displays information about using Help, and about the QuickC menu and keyboard commands. There are several panels of general information. Press N (next) and P (previous) to move between panels. |
| Topic | Displays information about a C keyword or function. |
| Close Help | Removes the help information from your screen. |

It is faster to use the shortcut keys described in Table 2.3 instead of the menu to display help information.

**Table 2.3**

**Help Shortcut Keys**

| Menu Command | Shortcut Key |
|---|---|
| General | F1 |
| Topic | SHIFT+F1 |
| Close Help | ESC |

For example, to display information about a C keyword or function, do the following:

1. Place the cursor anywhere on the word (including the space after the last letter).

2. Press SHIFT+F1 to display information about that keyword.

If you press SHIFT+F1 while the cursor is not on a C keyword or function, a dialog box appears listing topics (in uppercase letters). To display information from this list of topics, do the following:

1. Use the DIRECTION keys to select a topic.

2. Press ENTER. A list of the functions related to that topic appears; proceed to step 3.

3. Use the DIRECTION and ENTER keys as described in steps 1 and 2 to display information about any function listed under that topic.

To return to your program, press ESC.

# CHAPTER 3

## C QUICK START

This chapter introduces the basics of the C programming language using a brief, outline format. It is designed to get you "up and running" with C as quickly as possible.

It is assumed you are familiar with programming in Pascal or BASIC. If you are completely new to programming, you can use this chapter and one of the books listed below to learn computer programming and the C language.

To speed your learning, each topic occupies only two pages. The topics are presented in order of increasing complexity and in the approximate order of their appearance in C programs. For example, the discussion of variable declarations precedes the discussion of conditional statements.

Each section first defines and describes a topic (such as formatted I/O), then goes on to outline its operation. Each section ends with a C program or program segment that highlights the topic.

## ■ Further C Resources

You may want to explore C further with one or more of the books listed below:

Hancock, Les, and Morris Krieger. *The C Primer, 2d ed.* New York: McGraw-Hill, 1985. (A beginner's guide to programming in the C language.)

Kochan, Stephen. *Programming in C.* Hasbrouck Heights, NJ: Hayden Book Company, Inc., 1983. (A more comprehensive introduction to C with some emphasis on the UNIX environment.)

Plum, Thomas. *Learning to Program in C.* Cardiff, New Jersey: Plum Hall, Inc., 1983. (A widely used introductory college text on computer programming using the C language.)

Schildt, Herbert. *C Made Easy.* Berkeley, CA: Osborne/McGraw-Hill, 1985. (A good introduction to C for the reader who already knows BASIC.)

Waite, Mitchell, Stephen Prata, and Donald Martin. *C Primer Plus.* Indianapolis, IN: Howard W. Sams. Inc., 1984. (The best-selling introduction to the C language.)

# 3.1   The Structure of C Programs

All C programs contain preprocessor directives, declarations, definitions, expressions, statements, and functions.

■ **Preprocessor directive**

A preprocessor directive is a command to the C preprocessor (which is automatically invoked as the first step in compiling a program). The two most common preprocessor directives are the #**define** directive, which substitutes text for the specified identifier, and the #**include** directive, which includes the text of an external file into a program.

■ **Declaration**

A declaration establishes the names and attributes of variables, functions, and types used in the program. Global variables are declared outside functions and are visible from the end of the declaration to the end of the file. A local variable is declared inside a function and is visible from the end of the declaration to the end of the function.

■ **Definition**

A definition establishes the contents of a variable or function. A definition also allocates the storage needed for variables and functions.

■ **Expression**

An expression is a combination of operators and operands that yields a single value.

■ **Statement**

Statements control the flow or order of program execution in a C program.

■ **Function**

A function is a collection of declarations, definitions, expressions, and statements that performs a specific task. Braces enclose the body of a function. Functions may not be nested in C.

■   **main function**

All C programs must contain a function named **main** where program execution begins. The braces that enclose the **main** function define the beginning and ending point of the program.

■   **Example: General C program structure**

```
                          /* preprocessor directives */
#include <stdio.h>        /* include standard C header file */

#define PI 3.14           /* define symbolic constant */

float area;               /* global declaration */

int square (int);         /* function prototype */

main()

{                         /* beginning of main function
                             and program */

    int radius_squared;   /* local declaration */

    int radius = 3;       /* declaration and initialization */

    radius_squared = square (radius); /* pass a value
                             to a function */

    area = PI * radius_squared;        /* assignment statement */

    printf ("area: %6.2f\n", area);

}           /* end of main function & program */

square (r)      /* function head */
{
    int r_squared;      /* declarations here are known only  */
                        /* to square                         */
    r_squared = r * r;

    return (r_squared); /* return a value to calling statement */

}
```

## 3.2   Declarations

Declarations establish the names and types of variables, and the types of functions defined elsewhere.

■   **Standard data types**

The C language defines a standard set of data types, including character (**char**), integral (**int**), and floating point (**float**).

■   **Declaring variables and functions**

Declare variables before using them in a C program. Variables do not have to be initialized, but you can give them initial values in definition statements.

Functions can be declared explicitly in a function declaration before the definition of their contents. Functions with a return type other than **int** must be declared before using them. Without an explicit declaration, the first reference to a function will assume an **int** return.

■   **Creating new type names**

Use the **typedef** declaration to create new type names for existing data types. The use of **typedef** declarations can make programs more portable and reliable.

A defined type can serve as a reminder of the type of operations allowed with the variable (such as logical operations). Use the **typedef** keyword to shield programs against portability problems. Use a **typedef** declaration for data types that are machine dependent; only the **typedef** declaration will need to be changed when the program is moved. Finally, use the **typedef** keyword to provide better documentation for a program. A type called "employee" is easier to understand than one declared as a complex structure. A few typical **typedef** names and their associated meanings are shown below:

| typedef Name | Meaning |
| --- | --- |
| ulong | Unsigned long integer |
| bool | Integer (tested for zero/non-zero conditions) |
| string | Pointer to character |

### ■ Example: C declarations and defined types

```
#include <stdio.h>
typedef unsigned long ulong;      /* programmer-defined types */
typedef unsigned short ushort;
typedef int bool;
typedef char *string;
/* typical function declaration:
   function name -- get_avg
   return value  -- float
   expected parameters -- two integers
*/
float get_avg (int, int);   /* function prototype */
main()
{
   int matrix [3] [3];  /* 2-dimensional matrix declaration */

   struct date {          /* structure declaration */
        int month;
        int day;
        int year;
   };

   /* once created, the typedef names can be used */
   bool true = 1;
   string example_string;
   example_string = "text";
   printf ("string: %s\n",example_string);
   printf ("bool: %d\n",true);
}
```

# 3.3 Preprocessor Directives and Include Files

External text files can be incorporated into a C program with the preprocessor #include directive. The preprocessor is automatically invoked as the first step of compilation. It interprets the preprocessor directives and then sends the modified C source file to the compiler.

An #include directive instructs the preprocessor to substitute the contents of the external file for the line containing the directive.

## ■  C header files

C header files are typically created to contain common variable and function declarations. Such files can then be "included" into any source program that uses the variables or functions contained within it. External files that are to be used in #include directives are also known as "header" files and by convention have the DOS file-name extension .h.

The #include directive is a command to the preprocessor. The # must be the first non-white-space character on the line. The line does not end with a semicolon. Generally, the #include directive usually appears at the beginning of the program file before the main function.

Use a header file to store commonly used definitions and declarations or machine-specific constants in one place. This file simplifies the task of maintaining a set of declarations and definitions used by several source programs. The C run-time library functions use external files for their definition and declaration. Before using a library function, the appropriate external file should be included in the C program.

## ■  Controlling the include-file search path

The format used for the header file specification in the #include directive determines the search path.

Three possible formats are allowed:

- Angle brackets specify that the current working directory is not initially searched. The search begins in the directories specified in the compiler command line and then continues in the standard directories specified in the include environment variable. Use angle brackets to specify header files supplied by the compiler.

- Double quotation marks specify that the file search begins in the directory in which the source file is found, then the directories specified on the compiler command line, and finally the standard directories. Use quotation marks to specify files supplied by the programmer.

- An unambiguous path name given in either form (within quotation marks or brackets) specifies that only that path name will be searched.

■   **Example:  Including external files**

```
#include <stdio.h>      /* standard C I/O header file --
                           look in standard directory */

#include <math.h>       /* math functions header */

#include <graph.h>       /* graphics header file */

#include "local.h"      /* local header file --
                           look in directory where
                           source code resides  */

#include "c:\test\math87.h" /* look for specified file only
                           on disk drive C and only in
                           subdirectory "test" */

main()

{
   .
   . /*  body of C program  */
   .
}
```

# 3.4  Variable Declarations

Declare all variables before using them. Variables in C do not have to be initialized before use. Uninitialized variables contain values that are unpredictable.

- **Data types**

A declaration consists of a type specifier that is followed by a list of variables having that type. Variables in a declaration list are separated by commas.

- **Scope**

The location of a variable's declaration determines the scope (or visibility) of the variable.

Global variables are declared outside of any function. A global variable can be accessed anywhere inside the source file in which it is declared. It is also accessible from other source modules. Global variables are generally declared at the beginning of the program text before the **main** function and after any #**include** directives.

Local variables are declared within a function and are known only in the function where they are declared. Local variables are generally declared at the beginning of the function before any executable statements.

- **Storage requirements**

The storage requirements for the basic data types are shown below:

| Type | Storage[1] (bytes) | Range of Values[1] |
|------|-------------------|--------------------|
| char | 1 byte | –128 to 127 |
| int | —— | —— |
| short | 2 bytes | –32,768 to 32,767 |
| long | 4 bytes | –2,147,482,648 to 2,147,482,647 |
| unsigned char | 1 byte | 0 to 255 |
| unsigned | —— | —— |
| unsigned short | 2 bytes | 0 to 65,535 |
| unsigned long | 4 bytes | 0 to 4,294,967,295 |
| float | 4 bytes | $\pm$ 3.4E–38 to 3.4E+38 |
| double | 8 bytes | $\pm$ 1.7E–308 to 1.7E+308 |

[1]Where storage or range of values are unspecified, they are implementation dependent.

The types **int** and **unsigned** are implementation dependent. For the 8086 and 80286 family of machines, **int** is equivalent to **short** and **unsigned** is equivalent to **unsigned short**.

■ **Register variables**

A register variable is an integer or pointer variable stored in a machine register. This storage speeds up programs by increasing the speed of variable access. If no machine registers are available, the declaration will be made but a register will not be used for storage.

■ **Example: Variable Declarations**

```
#include <stdio.h>   /* standard C header file */

float pi=3.14159;    /* global declaration & initialization */

typedef unsigned short ushort;      /* ushort is now a synonym
                                       for unsigned short */

main()
{
     int i = 0;        /* local integer declaration
                          and initialization */

     ushort limit;     /* variable limit is of type ushort,
                          equivalent to unsigned short */
     register int j;   /* store variable j in machine register */
     .
     . /* body of the main function follows declarations */
     .
}

function1()
{
     int x=47;    /* Integer declaration and initialization.
                     x is "known" locally only in function1 */
     .
     . ... body of function1 follows declarations
     .
}
```

# 3.5 Statements, Expressions, and Operators

A C statement consists of program-control keywords (such as **for** or **while**), expressions, or function calls. An "expression" is a combination of operands and operators that yields a single value when evaluated. An "operator" specifies how its operands are to be manipulated. An "operand" is a constant or variable value manipulated in an expression.

■ **Statement format**

All statements end with a semicolon. Two or more statements can appear on one line, separated by semicolons. A null statement consists of a single semicolon.

■ **Compound statements**

Compound statements are collections of other statements enclosed by braces ({ }). A compound statement can appear anywhere a simple C statement appears. No semicolon occurs after the closing brace. A compound statement is also known as a "block."

■ **Expressions**

An expression consists of an operator and its operands. An expression can occur wherever a value is allowed. Any expression terminated with a semicolon is a statement. In C, assignments are considered to be expressions.

■ **Assignment operation**

An assignment operation specifies that the value of the right-hand operand is to be placed in the storage location specified by the left-hand operand.

■ **Operators**

C contains more than 40 operators covering the range from the basic arithmetic operations to logical and bitwise operations. C operators produce a result that can be nested inside a larger expression. Operators can also be combined with the assignment operator (=) to form a compound assignment operator of the following form:

```
x += y;
```

■ **Type conversions**

Explicit type conversions can be made with a "cast" or "coercion" operation that consists of a type enclosed in parentheses. The example below coerces the variable i (previously declared to be **int**) to be of type **float**:

```
(float) i
```

■ **Increment and decrement operators**

Use the increment operator (++) and the decrement operator (− −) to increment and decrement variables, respectively. Use these operators in either the prefixed or postfixed position. In the prefix form, the operand is incremented or decremented and its new value is the result of the expression. In the postfix form, the immediate result of the expression is the value of the operand *before* it is incremented or decremented. In use, these operate as shown below:

```
if (i-- > 0)    /* compare i to zero then decrement i */
    printf ("compared then decremented");
if (--i > 0)    /* decrement i and then compare to zero */
    printf ("decremented then compared");
```

■ **Examples: Annotated C expressions**

```
while ((c = getchar ()) != EOF)
```

The example above, a nested expression, calls the **getchar** function, which returns an integer. It then stores the result in the variable c, then compares c to the constant EOF, which gives either a true or false value. This value determines whether the body of the **while** loop will be executed.

```
a = b = 7;
```

The multiple assignment statement above stores the value 7 in b, then stores the contents of b (which is 7) in a.

```
x += 7;
a <<= b;
```

The first compound statement above increments x by 7. The second compound statement shifts a left by b bits.

# 3.6   Function Declaration and Definition

A function declaration establishes the attributes (such as name, arguments expected, and return type) of a function. A function definition specifies the actual content of a function.

## ■   Function declaration

A function declaration consists of a return type, the function name, and optionally an argument-type list. It declares the characteristics of the function but does not define its contents. Functions can be declared implicitly or with a forward declaration. An implicit declaration occurs whenever a function is called without a prior declaration or definition of the function. An explicit function declaration ("forward declaration") consists of the function declaration and it makes known the characteristics of a function before it is defined or used.

## ■   Function definition

A function definition contains a function header and a function body. A function header consists of the type of data returned by the function, followed by the function name and a list of the function's formal parameters. The function body consists of local declarations and a compound statement (or "block") that specifies what the function does.

## ■   Return types

The return type specifies what type of data the function returns. The return type is any fundamental, structure, or union type except an array or a function; the **void** type specifies that a function does not return any value. The default function-return type is **int**. You should not write functions that have structure or union return types. The large size of these objects will result in poor program performance.

## ■   Argument-type list and function prototypes

A function declaration's argument-type list specifies the types of arguments to the function. The use of argument-type lists is also known as "function prototyping." The argument-type list contains one or more type names that specify the types expected for each argument. Use the type name **void** to specify that a function does not accept arguments.

■ **Formal parameters**

The formal parameters of a function declaration are variables that receive the values of arguments passed to the function.

■ **Passing arguments to functions**

All arguments (except arrays) are passed by value. That is, a copy of the argument (not its address) is passed to the function. As a result, a C function does not alter the contents of a variable passed to it. The only variation to the pass-by-value rule occurs when the argument passed to the function is an address. Here, the pointer indirectly allows the function to alter the contents of a variable with the given address.

■ **Example: Function declaration and definition**

```
#include <stdio.h>        /* standard function declarations */
#include <stdlib.h>       /* contains atof prototype declaration */
typedef char *string;
main()
{
    string ascii_number;
    float float_number;
    ascii_number = "-6.02E-23";
    printf ("string: %s\n", ascii_number);
    /* the next line generates a compiler warning message */
    float_number = atof();        /* too few arguments */
    float_number = atof (ascii_number);/* correct call */
    printf ("number: %e\n", float_number);
}
```

The C program above shows how the use of function prototypes can warn you of incorrect function calls.

The function **atof** converts a character string to a floating-point number. The function prototype contained in the file **stdlib.h** specifies that the function expects one argument.

# 3.7   Looping Statements

The **for** and **while** statements provide looping capabilities in C so that you can repeatedly execute statements.

■   **The for statement**

Use the **for** statement to repeat a statement or compound statement a specified number of times. It consists of three parts:

1.   A loop-initialization expression (*init-expr*)

2.   A test expression (*cond-expr*) evaluated before each iteration

3.   A loop expression (*loop-expr*) executed at the end of each iteration of the loop

Its format is shown below:

**for** ([*init-expr*]; [*cond-expr*]; [*loop-expr*])
　　*statement*

First, *init-expr* is evaluated. Then, while *cond-expr* evaluates to a nonzero value, *statement* is executed. At the end of the loop, *loop-expr* is evaluated. When *cond-expr* becomes 0, control passes to the statement following the body of the **for** loop.

Each expression in the **for** loop can be any valid C expression. Any or all of the three expressions can be omitted. If omitted, the semicolons must remain. Multiple expressions can be put within the parts of the **for** statement by separating the multiple statements from one another with commas. A typical use of multiple statements would be the initialization of several values in the *init-expr* portion of the **for** loop, as shown below:

```
for (i=1, j=1; i<= 100; i++)    /* initialize i and j */
```

■   **The while statement**

The **while** loop consists of a test expression (*test-expr*) that is evaluated before the body of the loop is executed. If *test-expr* is false, the loop is never executed. The format of the **while** statement is:

**while** ([*test-expr*])
　　*statement*

The body of a **while** loop consists of a statement or a compound statement. If the test expression is true, the body of the loop is executed until the expression becomes false.

## ■ Ending the for or while statement

The **for** and **while** statements normally end when the test expression in the loop becomes false. Use the **break**, **goto**, or **return** statement whenever it is necessary to exit a loop early.

Use the **continue** statement to terminate an iteration without exiting the loop. The **continue** statement passes control to the next iteration of the **for** or **while** statement.

## ■ Example: Using for and while loops

```c
#include <stdio.h>
main()
{
    int i, done;
    printf ("table of squares (every sixth number)\n");
    printf ("\nfor loop\n");
    printf ("number\t\tsquare\n");
    for (i=0; i<= 20; i+=6)
        printf ("%d\t\t%d\n",i, i*i);
    printf ("\nwhile loop\n");
    printf ("number\t\tsquare\n");
    i = 0;
    while (i <= 20) {
        printf ("%d\t\t%d\n",i, i*i);
        i += 6;
    }
    printf ("\nwhile (nonzero test expression version)\n");
    printf ("number\t\tsquare\n");
    i = 0;
    done = 0;
    while (!done) {      /* will execute until done = 1 */
        printf ("%d\t\t%d\n",i, i*i);
        i += 6;
        if (i > 20)
            done = 1;
    }
}
```

The program above uses **for** and **while** loops to calculate a table of squares for every sixth number between 0 and 20.

# 3.8   Conditional and Branching Statements

The **if** and **switch** statements provide conditional and branching capabilities in C.

■   **The if statement**

If the test expression in an **if** statement is true, the body of the **if** statement executes. Otherwise, the program continues with the next statement. An **if** statement can have an **else** clause. However, because C does not offer an "else if" clause, use nested **if** statements to accomplish the same effect. Without explicit direction, C pairs each **else** with the most recent **if** that lacks an **else**. Group statements between braces to make your intention clear to the compiler. Typical **if** statements are shown below:

```
if (x < 0)
    printf ("Square root operation invalid\n");
if (x >= 0)
    {
    answer = sqrt (x);
    printf ("square root is: %6.2f\n", answer);
    }
```

■   **The switch statement**

The **switch** statement takes the place of a large number of nested **if** and **else** clauses. The **switch** statement transfers control to a statement within its body. The statement receiving control is the statement whose **case** constant expression (an integer or character constant, or a constant expression) matches the value of the **switch** test expression. Execution begins at the selected statement and continues through the end of the body or until a statement transfers control out of the **switch** body. Use the **break** statement to end processing of a particular case within the **switch** statement. Without the **break**, the program falls through to the next case.

A **default** statement executes if there is no matching **case** constant expression for the **switch** test expression. If the **default** statement is omitted and no matching **case** is found, none of the statements in the **switch** body is executed. No two **case** constants within the same **switch** statement can have the same value. A sample **switch** statement is shown below:

```
switch (i) {
   case 1:
           printf ("number 1\n");
           break; /* continues after closing brace */
   case 2:
   case 4:
           printf ("even\n"); /* executes if i==2 or i==4 */
           break; /* continues after closing brace */
   default:
           /* prints if i not equal to 1, 2 or 4 */
           printf ("number not in our test list\n");
   }
```

## ■ Example: Using if and switch statements

```
#include <stdio.h>
#include <ctype.h>   /* necessary with conversion function
                         toupper */
main ()
{
   char response [10];
   char test_char;
   printf ("Please enter your response (yes/no/quit): ");
   scanf ("%s", response);   /* formatted input into a string */
   if (toupper(response[0]) == 'Q') {    /* test for q */
     printf ("program exit\n");   /* execute if equal to q */
     exit(1);
   }
   switch (response[0]) { /* switch based on first character */
      case 'y':             /* multiple case labels */
      case 'n':
         printf ("lowercase y or n as first letter\n");
         break;
      default:
         printf ("not a lowercase y or n as first letter\n");
         break;
   }
   test_char = toupper(response[0]);   /* convert to uppercase */
   switch (test_char) {
      case 'Y':
         printf ("Response is yes\n");
         break;
      case 'N':
         printf ("Response is no\n");
         break;
      default:
         printf ("Please enter a yes or no\n");
   }
}
```

# 3.9  Arrays and Strings

An "array" is a collection of data elements of a single type. A "string" is an array of characters that is terminated with the null character ('\0').

- **Array types**

The base type of the elements of an array determines the array's type. The base type of an array can be any valid C type, including so-called "aggregate" or constructed types such as structures.

- **Array storage**

The elements of an array are stored in contiguous memory locations and with increasing memory address from first element to last. Arrays are stored by row. (That is, all of the columns of the first row are stored, then the columns of the second row, and so on.) An array name without brackets is a pointer to the first element of the array. The initial element of an array has a subscript of 0.

- **Strings**

A string in C is an array of characters that terminates with the null character ('\0'). Arrays representing strings must allow space for the storage of the final null character.

- **Passing arrays to functions**

When an array is passed to a function, only the address of the initial element of the array is passed to the function. Omit dimensions when declaring arrays as parameters being passed into a function since the function needs to know only the starting address of the array. Since an address is passed to the function, the function can alter the contents of the array.

## ■ Example: Using arrays

```c
#include <stdio.h>        /* standard header file */
typedef char * string;    /* rename a 'char' type to string */

int strlen (string);      /* function prototype */

/* declare & initialize test character array (string) */

char test_string [] = "This is a C string";

main()
{
    int x;
    x = strlen1 (test_string);
    printf ("length (array method): %d\n",x);
}

/* array & subscript version of strlen */

strlen1 (s)
char s[];
{
    int i = 0;
    while (s[i] != '\0')
        i++;
    return (i);
}
```

The program above finds the length of a string by counting the characters in the string until it finds the terminating null character.

## 3.10  Introducing Pointers

A pointer is a variable that contains the machine address of a variable, rather than the data itself. Use pointers to create and manipulate data structures, to allocate memory dynamically, and to provide pass-by-reference function calls.

### ■  Creating pointers

A pointer can point to an object of any type, including aggregate types such as structures, or even to a function. Declare a pointer by preceding the name of the object with the indirection operator (*), which means "pointer-to." A pointer always points to an object of a particular type (that is, it contains the address of a value of a particular type). Initialize pointers before you use them because values contained in uninitialized pointers are unpredictable and likely to cause program problems. Some examples of pointer declarations appear below:

```
int * intptr;           /* pointer to int */     .
char * name;            /* pointer to char */
```

### ■  Pointer storage requirements

The amount of storage required for a pointer is the number of bytes required to specify a machine address. On the 8086 family of machines a near pointer requires 16 bits and a far pointer requires 32 bits of storage.

### ■  Pointer operators

The asterisk symbol (*) is the indirection operator and denotes "the data being pointed to."

The ampersand symbol (&) is the address-of operator. When an object is preceded by the address-of operator, the expression evaluates to the address at which the object is stored.

### ■  Pointers and functions

Pointers provide pass-by-reference function arguments. When arrays are passed to functions, only the address of the initial element is passed.

■   **Pointer manipulations**

Only certain operations are valid with pointers: adding a pointer and an integer (incrementing a pointer); subtracting an integer from a pointer (decrementing a pointer); subtracting two pointers (calculating the number of elements between them); and comparing two pointers.

Whenever a pointer is incremented or decremented by an **int**-type unit, C scales the value of the **int** by the size of the object pointed to. This ensures that an increment of one, for example, will always point to the next data item regardless of the size of the item.

■   **Examples: String-length functions using pointers**

```
/* pointer-incrementing version of strlen */
strlen1 (s)
char *s;
{
    int i;
    for (i=0; *s != '\0'; s++)   /* increment pointer variable s */
        i++;
    return (i);
}

/* pointer-subtraction version of strlen */
strlen2 (s)
char *s;
{
    char *p = s; /* set p to point to first character of s */
    while (*p != '\0')
        p++;                 /* advance to next character */
    return (p-s);
}
```

The two functions above can be substituted for the string-length function found in Section 3.9, "Arrays and Strings." Instead of an array, these two functions use pointer manipulations to determine the length of a string passed to the function.

# 3.11   Pointers to Functions

A pointer variable can be declared to point to any complex object, including a structure or a function. Use pointers to functions to create "generic" functions that manipulate data of any type.

## ■   Creating pointers to functions

Declare a pointer to a function as shown below:

```
int (*number_compare) ();
```

The type of the variable number_compare is "pointer to a function that returns an integer." The parentheses around *number_compare are required. Without them, the C language would use its precedence rules to interpret the line as a declaration of a function that returns a pointer to an **int** item—not the same thing at all.

## ■   Using pointers to functions

The most common use of pointers to functions is passing them as arguments to other functions. The C library function **qsort**, for example, performs a "quick sort" on an array of data elements. This function takes as one of its arguments a pointer to a function that performs the actual comparison of the elements of the array. The comparison function can contain a comparison operation on any type. As a result, **qsort** can be used to sort an array of any type. The actual comparison is made by the user-supplied function and not by **qsort**.

Use only the assignment, comparison, and indirection operators with function pointers; all other operations are undefined.

## ■   Example: Creating a generic function using pointers

The example program below uses a pointer to a function to build a generic comparison function. The function compare is passed a parameter that is a pointer to the appropriate comparison function (string or numeric). Once this information is passed into compare, the appropriate comparison is made and the result printed out.

```
#include <stdio.h>
#include <ctype.h>
main ()
{
    int number_compare ();
    int string_compare ();
    char s1[80], s2[80];
    printf ("generic test for equality\n");
    printf ("enter first item:\n");
    gets (s1);
    printf ("enter second item:\n");
    gets (s2);
    if (isalpha (*s1))
        compare (s1, s2, string_compare); /* pass address */
    else
        compare (s1, s2, number_compare); /* pass address */
}

compare (a, b, compare_function)
char *a, *b;
/* pointer to function that returns an int value*/
int (*compare_function) ();
{
    /* use indirection operator
        to invoke correct compare function */
    if ((*compare_function) (a,b))
        printf ("equal\n");
    else
        printf ("not equal\n");
}
number_compare (a,b)
char *a, *b;
{
    if (atoi (a) == atoi (b))
        return (1);
    else
        return (0);
}
string_compare (a,b)
char *a, *b;
{
if (strcmp (a,b))
    return (0);
else
    return (1);
}
```

# 3.12   Structures

A "structure" is a collection of data elements of different types that are logically related.

## ■   Creating structures

When you define a structure data type, the definition specifies the elements and data types of the structure and creates a structure data type. The individual variables within the structure are called "members," and the name of the structure is called the structure "tag." A structure data type is defined by a declaration of the form:

**struct**   *structure-name* {
        *member-declarations*
};

A date structure type, for example, is created with the following definition:

```
struct date
    {
       int month;
       int day;
       int year;
    };
```

After a structure data type has been defined, you can declare a variable to be of the defined type. The structure tag must be preceded by the keyword **struct**. The declaration below defines a variable  todays_date to be of type struct date:

```
struct date todays_date;
```

## ■   Variables within structures

A variable that is an element of a structure type can be used just like any other variable. The member-of operator (.) specifies the name of the structure member and the structure of which it is a member. The variable month within the structure variable  todays_date is given the value 12 by the assignment shown below:

```
todays_date.month = 12;
```

■   **Structures and pointers**

Pointers to structures can be declared, as can pointers to any other data type. C uses a special symbol $(->)$ to refer to the member of a structure pointed to by a pointer.

■   **Operations with structures**

Only three operations are allowed with a structure variable: you may take its address with the address-of operator (&); you may access one of its members; and you may assign one structure to another with the assignment operator.

■   **Example: Using structures**

```
#include <stdio.h>
#include <time.h>
main ()
{
    struct tm *current_time;
    time_t long_time;      /* time value */
    time (&long_time);     /* get number of seconds into long_time */
    /* convert to time structure */
    current_time = localtime(&long_time);
    /* use member-selection operator to access
        individual element of structure */
    printf ("hour: %d\n", current_time->tm_hour);
}
```

The program above uses the member-selection operator to access individual elements of the structure  tm, which contains time information. It then prints the current value of the hour.

The function **localtime** is not contained in the core of QuickC library routines. As a result, you will need to use the program list feature of the QuickC environment to compile this program. See Section 6.1 for details on using program lists.

# 3.13   Using C Input/Output Functions

The standard C run-time library provides a complete set of input and output (I/O) functions for the C programmer.

■   **Single-character I/O—getchar and putchar**

The **getchar** function "gets" the next character from the keyboard and returns it as the function's value. The **putchar** function "puts" a character to the screen.

■   **Formatted output—printf**

The **printf** function prints formatted output on the screen. The arguments to **printf** comprise a format string enclosed within double quotation marks, followed by a list of variable names, if any, that are to be printed. Literal text within the format string is printed as it appears in the string. Escape sequences within the format string insert special characters into the output. The more commonly used escape sequences are listed below:

| Escape Sequence | Character |
|---|---|
| \n | New line |
| \t | Tab |
| \' | Single quotation mark |
| \" | Double quotation mark |
| \\ | Backslash |

■   **Formatted input—scanf**

The **scanf** function reads formatted input from the keyboard. The arguments to **scanf** comprise a format string enclosed within double quotation marks, followed by a list of variable names to be read. The arguments used in the **scanf** function must be pointers to variables and not the variables themselves. This is required so that the **scanf** function can alter the variable's contents.

■ **Format string specifications**

Conversion specifications mark the place within a control string where variable contents are to be printed or read. The first variable corresponds with the location of the first percent-sign symbol (%) and so on through the list of conversion characters. The following list shows the most common conversion specifications:

| Conversion Specification | Meaning |
|---|---|
| %d | Decimal notation |
| %u | Unsigned decimal notation |
| %o | Unsigned octal notation |
| %x | Unsigned hexadecimal notation |
| %e | Exponential notation |
| %f | Floating-point notation |
| %c | Single character |
| %s | String |

■ **Example: Using the C I/O functions**

```
#include <stdio.h>
typedef char * string;
main()
{
    char c, j;
    int i;
    string item1[10], item2[10];
    float x;
    printf ("please enter a single character:\n");
    c = getchar();
    printf ("\tthe character just input was -- %c\n",c);
    printf ("\nenter a digit, a string, a float, and a string: ");
    scanf ("%d %s %f %s", &i, item1, &x, item2);
    printf ("\n\ayou entered\n");
    printf ("%d\n%s\n%f\n%s", i, item1, x, item2);
    printf ("\n\nexample of conversion specifications:\n");
    printf ("decimal\toctal\thex\tcharacter\n");
    for (j = 65; j<=70; j++)
        printf ("%d\t%o\t%x\t%c\n", j,j,j,j);
}
```

# 3.14   Using File I/O Functions

The standard C run-time library provides a complete set of file input and output functions for the C programmer.

## ■   The FILE structure

The standard I/O header file **stdio.h** contains the definition of a structure called **FILE** that determines the internal character of a file.

## ■   Opening and closing files

Before a file can be used, it must be opened by the standard library function **fopen**. After use, it should be closed by the library function **fclose**.

The function **fopen** takes an external DOS file name and returns a file pointer used in later calls to file I/O functions. The file pointer is a pointer to a structure of type **FILE**. An **fopen** function call also specifies the mode of the file — read, write, or append.

If you attempt to open, for writing or appending, a file that does not exist, it is created, if possible. If an error occurs when opening a file, **fopen** returns the null pointer value **NULL**.

Use the function **fclose** to close a file safely before you exit the program.

## ■   Single character file I/O—fputchar and fgetchar

The **fputchar** function puts a character into the specified file. The **fgetchar** function gets a character from the specified file. A return value of **EOF** indicates that an attempt was made to read past the end-of-file.

## ■   Formatted file I/O—fprintf and fscanf

The **fprintf** function prints formatted output to the specified file. Its formatting is controlled by a format string that operates like the format string for the **printf** function.

The **fscanf** function reads formatted input from the specified file with the same format string features that are used with the **scanf** function. A return value of **EOF** indicates that an attempt was made to read past the end-of-file.

## ■ Example: Using C file I/O

```
#include <stdio.h>
#include <ctype.h>
main()
{
    FILE *fopen(), *fp_in, *fp_out;
    char fn_in[12], fn_out[12];  /* allow room for filename.ext */

    printf ("enter name of input file: ");
    scanf ("%s", fn_in);
    printf ("enter name of output file: ");
    scanf ("%s", fn_out);
    fp_out = fopen (fn_out, "w");
    fp_in = fopen (fn_in,"r");
    /* check for nonexistent input file; exit if fopen failed */
    if (fp_in == NULL) {
        printf ("No input file %s\n",fn_in);
        exit (1);
    }

    /* if fopen is OK then execute the rest of the program */
    convert_file(fp_in,fp_out);
    printf ("\nFile %s cleaned up\n",fn_in);
    printf ("Output in file: %s\n",fn_out);
    fclose (fp_in);
    fclose (fp_out);
    return (0);
}
convert_file (input,output)
FILE *input, *output;
{
    int c;
    /* get characters until EOF */
    while ((c = getc (input)) != EOF){
        if (isupper(c))    /* convert case */
            c = tolower (c);
        else
            c = toupper (c);
    fputc(c,output);  /* print it to the output file */
    }
}
```

The program above changes the case of all the characters within a file.

## 3.15  Accessing Command-Line Arguments in C

Command-line arguments in C provide a way of passing arguments to a program when it begins execution.

■ **Basics of command-line arguments**

In the DOS environment, any information listed after the program's name is known as a command-line argument. The C language provides a mechanism for accessing these arguments. The **main** function accesses the command-line arguments with two parameters. The arguments are listed below with a brief description of their contents:

| Argument | Description |
|----------|-------------|
| *argc* | The "argument count" is the number of command-line arguments. The final argument is given by `argv[argc-1]` since C arrays start with a zero subscript. |
| *argv* | The "argument vector" is a pointer to an array of character strings that contain the command-line arguments, one per string. |

■ **Using command-line arguments**

The easiest way to learn about command-line arguments is to see a simple program using this feature. The program below prints out the number of arguments and the contents of the argument vector:

```
#include <stdio.h>
main(argc,argv)       /*main function
                        using command-line arguments*/
char *argv[];         /* argument vector */
int argc;             /* argument count */
{
   int i;
   printf ("argc: %d\n", argc);   /* print no. of arguments */
   for (i = 0; i < argc; i++)     /* print argument contents */
      printf ("argv [%d]: %s\n", i, argv[i]);
}
```

Remember to specify a few command-line arguments with the Set Runtime Options item from the Run menu when you create and run this program. Also note that in DOS versions prior to 3.0, the value of *argv*[**0**] contains the string "C," not the name of the program.

■  **Using DOS wild-card characters**

Normal compilation produces a program that does not recognize the DOS
file-name wild-card characters (* and ?). Link your program's object file
with the appropriate *m***SETARGV.OBJ** file (the *m* refers to the memory
model) to use DOS file-name wild cards.

When the wild-card file name is expanded, all files that match the name
are passed into the program. If no matches are found, the argument is
passed literally.

■  **Example: Command-line processing**

```
#include <stdio.h>
#include <ctype.h>
main(argc,argv)
char *argv[];
int argc;
{
    FILE *fopen(), *fp_in, *fp_out;
    /* check for correct number of arguments */
    if (argc != 3) {
        printf ("correct usage is:\n");
        printf ("convcase input-file output-file\n");
        exit(0);
    }
    fp_out = fopen (argv[2], "w");
    fp_in = fopen (argv[1],"r");
    /* check for nonexistent input file; exit if fopen failed */
    if (fp_in == NULL) {
        printf ("input file error : %s\n",argv[1]);
        exit (1);
    }
    /* if fopen is OK then execute the rest of the program */
    convert_file(fp_in,fp_out);
    printf ("\nFile %s converted\n",argv[1]);
    printf ("Output in file: %s\n",argv[2]);
    fclose (fp_in);
    fclose (fp_out);
    return (1);
}
convert_file (input,output)
{
/*
    The contents of the convert_file function
    are the same as in Section 3.14
*/
}
```

The program above is a modification of the example program in Section
3.14, "Using File I/O Functions." It accepts the names of the files as
command-line arguments, with the input file name preceding the output
file name.

# CHAPTER 4

# GRAPHICS QUICK START

This chapter briefly outlines the fundamentals of graphics programming. It is designed to quickly give you the basic foundation for any graphics project you can design.

To speed your learning, each topic occupies only two pages. The topics are presented in order of increasing complexity and in the approximate order of their appearance in graphics programs.

Each section first defines and describes a topic (such as video mode), then goes on to outline its operation. Each section ends with a graphics program or program segment that highlights the topic.

---

*Important*

To run the graphics examples shown in this chapter, your computer must have graphics capability. This may be either built in or in the form of a graphics adapter card and a video display (either monochrome or color) that supports pixel-based graphics.

You must include the graphics library in your program list to make an executable C program. The details of this process are in Section 6.1.

---

■　**Further Graphics Resources**

You may want to explore microcomputer graphics further with one or more of the references listed below:

Artwick, Bruce. *Microcomputer Displays, Graphics, and Animation.* Englewood Cliffs, NJ: Prentice-Hall, Inc., 1985. (Discussion of microcomputer graphics and animation from the creator of *Flight Simulator.*)

Cockerham, John T. "The EGA Standard." *PC Tech Journal* 4:10 (October 1986): 48-79. (Discussion of the EGA.)

Hummel, Robert L. "Get the Full EGA Color Spectrum." *PC Magazine* (June 23, 1987): 311-328. (Discussion of EGA color palettes.)

International Business Machines. *Enhanced Graphics Adapter* (manual part # 6280131). (The official technical reference to the EGA; available from IBM, 1-800-426-7282.)

Norton, Peter. *The Peter Norton Programmer's Guide to the IBM PC.* Redmond, WA: Microsoft Press, 1985. (The standard guide to the "inside" of the IBM PC family of computers. Several chapters devoted to video modes, with the exception of the EGA and VGA modes.)

# 4.1  Structure of a Graphics Program

All graphics programs follow these five basic steps:

1. Include the graphics library.
2. Set the video mode.
3. Determine the video-configuration parameters.
4. Create and manipulate graphic figures.
5. Restore the initial configuration before exiting the program.

■  **Include the graphics library**

The include file **graph.h** defines the variables, function prototypes, and manifest constants used in graphics programming. Include this file in all programs that use the graphics routines.

■  **Set the video mode**

The first step in a graphics program is to set a video mode that allows graphics operations. Ten graphics modes are supported in the C graphics library. These are listed in Section 4.2.

The process of setting the video mode is shown below:

1. Set the highest-level video mode needed for the program. Check the return value for failure.

2. If you are unable to set the initial video mode, continue the attempt with less demanding modes until a mode can be set or until there is no mode of sufficient resolution for the program. If no valid video mode is found, return from the function and print an error message.

■  **Determine the video configuration**

Call the **_getvideoconfig** function to determine the characteristics of the video mode. This information includes such things as the number of x and y pixels in each dimension, and the number of colors allowed.

■    **Restore the initial configuration**

Restore the system to its initial video mode by calling the function _set-
videomode with the _DEFAULTMODE manifest constant. Failure to
do this may cause the machine to "lock up" when another program is run.


■    **Example: Skeleton graphics program**

```
#include <stdio.h>
#include <graph.h>        /* graphics include file */
int set_mode (void);      /* prototype */
struct videoconfig vc; /* configuration data */
char error_message [] = "This video mode is not supported";

main ()
{
/* program requires 640 x 200 resolution */
    if (!set_mode()){                        /* if set_mode fails */
        printf ("%s\n", error_message);      /* print message    */
        exit (0);                            /* and exit         */
    }
    _getvideoconfig (&vc); /* video configuration data in vc */
            .
            .  /* do graphics operations here */
            .
    /* restore video mode */
    _setvideomode (_DEFAULTMODE);
}

    /* function to set mode;
        assume program requires 640 x 200 resolution */
int set_mode ()
{
    if (_setvideomode(_HRES16COLOR))     /* VGA or EGA */
        return (_HRES16COLOR);
    if (_setvideomode(_HRESBW))          /* VGA, EGA or CGA */
        return (_HRESBW);
    else
        return (0);
}
```

The program above shows an outline of a graphics program.

## 4.2  Setting the Video Mode

All graphics programs operate in a graphics screen mode, which determines the screen size (in pixels) and the number of colors allowed. The mode set by the program must be compatible with the hardware configuration.

■ **Available modes**

The constants listed below are used to set the video mode. The dimensions are given in terms of pixels for graphics mode and in terms of rows and columns for text modes.

| Constant | Video Mode | Mode Type |
| --- | --- | --- |
| _DEFAULTMODE | Restores screen to original mode | Both |
| _TEXTBW40 | 40 x 25 text, 16 gray | Text |
| _TEXTC40 | 40 x 25 text, 16/8 color | Text |
| _TEXTBW80 | 80 x 25 text, 16 gray | Text |
| _TEXTC80 | 80 x 25 text, 16/8 color | Text |
| _MRES4COLOR | 320 x 200 pixels, 4 color | Graphics |
| _MRESNOCOLOR | 320 x 200 pixels, 4 gray | Graphics |
| _HRESBW | 640 x 200 pixels, BW | Graphics |
| _TEXTMONO | 80 x 25 text, BW | Text |
| _MRES16COLOR | 320 x 200 pixels, 16 color | Graphics |
| _HRES16COLOR | 640 x 200 pixels, 16 color | Graphics |
| _ERESNOCOLOR | 640 x 350 pixels, BW | Graphics |
| _ERESCOLOR | 640 x 350 pixels, 4/16 color | Graphics |
| _VRES2COLOR | 640 x 480 pixels, 2 color | Graphics |
| _VRES16COLOR | 640 x 480 pixels, 16 color | Graphics |
| _MRES256COLOR | 320 x 200 pixels, 256 color | Graphics |

■ **Selecting the video mode**

Select a video mode with the required resolution for the project at hand. You will need to make trade-offs between increased resolution versus increased availability of colors. Call the _setvideomode function with one of the constants listed above to set the video mode.

A return value of 0 indicates that the hardware does not support the selected mode. Take appropriate exit action if the hardware configuration does not support the required graphics mode.

After the video mode has been set, call the _**getvideoconfig** function to determine the parameters of the mode selected (such as the dimensions of the screen). Put the video-configuration information into the video-configuration structure for use by other graphics functions. Use the video-configuration structure rather than absolute numbers to specify video screen characteristics. This ensures portability to other screen configurations (CGA, EGA, or VGA).

■   **Resetting the video mode**

Always reset the video mode to the default mode that was present on entry into the program by calling _**setvideomode** with the _**DEFAULTMODE** parameter. Failure to restore the video environment after a graphics program may cause the machine to "lock up" when another program is run.

■   **Example: Setting the video mode**

```
#include <stdio.h>
#include <graph.h>
int set_mode (void);
struct videoconfig vc;
char error_message [] = "This video mode is not supported";
main()
{
    if (!set_mode()) {
        printf ("%s\n", error_message);
        exit(0);
    }
    _getvideoconfig (&vc);   /* put configuration data into vc */
        .
        .    /* the body of the program goes here */
        .
    _setvideomode (_DEFAULTMODE);   /* restore video mode */
}
int set_mode()
{
/* assume that the program requires 640 x 200 resolution */
if (_setvideomode(_HRES16COLOR))
    return (_HRES16COLOR);
if (_setvideomode(_HRESBW))
    return (_HRESBW);
else
    return (0);
}
```

## 4.3 Getting the Video Configuration

All graphics configuration information is contained in a structure of type **videoconfig**. The template for this structure is defined in **graph.h**. Once the video mode has been set, the video-configuration information must be determined.

■ **The videoconfig structure variable**

Declare a variable to be of type **videoconfig** to receive the video configuration information. This structure variable will be used in the call to **_getvideoconfig** in the following format:

```
struct videoconfig vc;     /* structure variable declaration */
    .
    .
    .
_getvideoconfig (&vc);     /* structure variable use */
```

■ **Contents of the videoconfig structure**

The **videoconfig** structure is defined in the graphics header file **graph.h**, and it contains the following items:

```
struct videoconfig {
    short numxpixels;     /* number of pixels on x axis */
    short numypixels;     /* number of pixels on y axis */
    short numtextcols;    /* number of text columns available */
    short numtextrows;    /* number of text rows available */
    short numcolors;      /* number of actual colors */
    short bitsperpixel;   /* number of bits per pixel */
    short numvideopages;  /* number of available video pages */
};
```

■ **Using the video configuration information**

Use the video configuration information to determine the dimensions of the screen. In *any* graphics mode, the center of the screen is given by the following coordinates:

```
xcenter = vc.numxpixels/2 - 1;  /* x coordinate of center */
ycenter = vc.numypixels/2 - 1;  /* y coordinate of center */
```

The variable `vc.vcnumxpixels` is the number of x pixels and `vc.vcnumypixels` is the number of y pixels in the current video mode.

■   **Example: Accessing the video-configuration structure**

```
#include <stdio.h>
#include <ctype.h>
#include <graph.h>

struct videoconfig vc;   /* variable vc of type videoconfig */

/* define an array of video modes and mode names
   since the numbers are not continuous */

int modes[12] = {_TEXTBW40, _TEXTC40, _TEXTBW80, _TEXTC80,
   _MRES4COLOR, _MRESNOCOLOR, _HRESBW, _TEXTMONO,
   _MRES16COLOR, _HRES16COLOR, _ERESNOCOLOR, _ERESCOLOR};

char *modenames[] = {"TEXTBW40", "TEXTC40", "TEXTBW80",
                     "TEXTC80", "MRES4COLOR", "MRESNOCOLOR",
                     "HRESBW", "TEXTMONO", "MRES16COLOR",
                     "HRES16COLOR", "ERESNOCOLOR", "ERESCOLOR"};
main()
{
    int i;
    /* test all video modes */
    for (i=0; i<= 11; i++) {
        _setvideomode (modes[i]);
        _getvideoconfig (&vc);
        printf ("\n video mode:\t%s\n",modenames[i]);
        printf (" x pixels:\t%d\n",vc.numxpixels);
        printf (" y pixels:\t%d\n",vc.numypixels);
        printf (" text columns:\t%d\n",vc.numtextcols);
        printf (" text rows:\t%d\n",vc.numtextrows);
        printf (" # of colors:\t%d\n",vc.numcolors);
        printf (" bits/pixel:\t%d\n",vc.bitsperpixel);
        printf (" video pages:\t%d\n",vc.numvideopages);
        printf (" Hit return for next video mode");
        _setcolor (2);
        _rectangle (_GBORDER,0,0,vc.numxpixels-5,
        vc.numypixels-5);
        getchar();
        _clearscreen (_GCLEARSCREEN);
    }
    _setvideomode (_DEFAULTMODE);
}
```

The program above calls each possible video mode and prints the video-configuration information about it. The program also draws a rectangle around the edges of the screen.

## 4.4   Using the Color Text Modes

Two color text modes, _TEXTC40 and _TEXTC80, can be used with
the CGA, EGA, and VGA displays. These modes display any of 16 foreground colors with any one of 8 background colors.

■   **Basics of text color selection**

In a text mode, each displayed character requires two bytes of video
memory. The first byte contains the ASCII code representing the character, and the second byte contains the display attribute. In the CGA color
text modes, the attribute byte determines the color and whether it will
blink. Sixteen colors are available: the CGA pixel values, and the default
EGA and VGA pixel values. Since the EGA and VGA palette can be
remapped, these values can be made to correspond to any set of 16 colors
with the appropriate palette mapping. (See Sections 4.6 and 4.7 for information on remapping EGA and VGA pixel values, respectively.)

■   **Using text colors**

Use the _gettextcolor function to find the pixel value of the current text
color.

The pixel values in the range 0–15 are interpreted as normal color. Pixel
values in the range 16–31 are the same colors as those in the range 0–15,
but with blinking text.

Set the color in text modes with the _settextcolor function. This function uses a single argument which specifies the pixel value to be used for
text operations. A pixel value of 0 produces no visible output, since it
always represents the current background color. The text color does not
affect normal C output. The _outtext function should be used to output
colored text.

The pixel values for color text modes are defined below:

| No. | Color | No. | Color | No. | Color | No. | Color |
|-----|-------|-----|-------|-----|-------|-----|-------|
| 0 | Black | 4 | Red | 8 | Dark gray | 12 | Light red |
| 1 | Blue | 5 | Magenta | 9 | Light blue | 13 | Lt. magenta |
| 2 | Green | 6 | Brown | 10 | Light green | 14 | Yellow |
| 3 | Cyan | 7 | White | 11 | Light cyan | 15 | Bright white |

■    **Example: Viewing text colors**

```c
#include <stdio.h>
#include <graph.h>
char buffer [255];
main ()
{
    int i,j;
    long int delay;
    _setvideomode (_TEXTC80);
    for (j=0; j<= 7; j++) {
        _setbkcolor (j);                /* background colors */
        _settextposition (1,1);
        printf ("bkcolor: %d\n", j);
        for (i=0; i<= 15; i++) {
            _settextcolor (i);          /* text colors */
            _settextposition (5+i,1);
            sprintf (buffer, "Color: %d\n", i);
            _outtext (buffer);
        }
            /* pause */
            for (delay = 0; delay <= 200000; delay++);
                        ;
    }
    _clearscreen (_GCLEARSCREEN);
    _setvideomode (_DEFAULTMODE);
}
```

The program above cycles through all background color and text color combinations.

## 4.5  Using the CGA Color Graphics Modes

The CGA color graphics modes (that is, _MRES4COLOR and
_MRESNOCOLOR) display four colors (or shades of gray) selected
from one of several predefined palettes of colors. They display these foreground colors against a background color selected from a set of 16 possible
colors.

■  **CGA color graphics**

In a graphics mode, a pixel can be represented as a one-, two-, or four-bit
value depending upon the mode selected. This representation is known as
the "pixel value." In addition to the pixel value there is an ordinal color
representation. Each color that can be displayed in a particular video
mode is represented by a unique ordinal value. The mapping of pixel
values onto the actual display colors produces a "palette" of colors that
can be displayed.

The CGA color graphics modes provide four palettes of four colors. A
palette defines a subset of all possible colors, and it consists of the background color (pixel value 0) and three set foreground colors. A palette
defines the characteristics of the entire display.

The background color may be any one of the 16 available colors. With the
CGA hardware, the palette of foreground colors is predefined and cannot
be changed. The palette number is an integer value that selects one of the
predefined palettes.

■  **Using palettes**

Four palettes are available in the _MRES4COLOR video mode. Use the
_selectpalette function to select one of these palettes. The table below
shows the correspondence between the pixel values and colors for each
palette. The background color may be set to any of the 16 possible colors.

| Palette Number | Pixel Value | | |
|---|---|---|---|
| | 1 | 2 | 3 |
| 0 | Green | Red | Brown |
| 1 | Cyan | Magenta | Light gray |
| 2 | Light green | Light red | Yellow |
| 3 | Light cyan | Light magenta | White |

Use the _**MRESNOCOLOR** video mode with black-and-white displays to produce palettes consisting of various shades of gray. The _**MRESNOCOLOR** mode will also produce colors when used with a color display. However, only two palettes are available with a color display. Use the _**selectpalette** function to select one of these predefined palettes. The table below shows the correspondence between the pixel values and colors for each palette.

| Palette Number | Pixel Value | | |
|---|---|---|---|
| | 1 | 2 | 3 |
| 0 | Blue | Red | Light gray |
| 1 | Light blue | Light red | White |

You may use the _**selectpalette** function only in conjunction with the _**MRES4COLOR** and _**MRESNOCOLOR** video modes.

■   **Example: Viewing palette colors**

```
#include <stdio.h>
#include <graph.h>
long bkcolor[8] = {_BLACK, _BLUE, _GREEN, _CYAN,
                   _RED, _MAGENTA, _BROWN, _WHITE};
char *bkcolor_name [] = {"_BLACK", "_BLUE", "_GREEN",
    "_CYAN", "_RED", "_MAGENTA", "_BROWN", "_WHITE"};
main()
{
 int i, j, k, delay;
 _setvideomode (_MRES4COLOR);   /* uses CGA color mode */
 for (k=0; k <= 7; k++) {
   _setbkcolor (bkcolor[k]);
   for (i=0; i<= 3; i++) {
     _selectpalette (i);
     for (j=0; j<=3; j++) {
       _settextposition (1,1);
       _setcolor (j);
       printf ("background color: %8s\n", bkcolor_name[k]);
       printf ("palette: %d\ncolor: %d\n",i,j);
       _rectangle (_GFILLINTERIOR,160,100,320,200);
       for (delay=0; delay <= 20000; delay++)
           ;
     }
   }
 }
 _setvideomode (_DEFAULTMODE);
}
```

This program sets the video mode to _**MRES4COLOR** and then cycles through background colors and palette combinations.

# 4.6   Using the EGA Color Graphics Modes

Use the _MRES16COLOR, _HRES16COLOR, or _ERESCOLOR
video modes to display the best color graphics with an EGA adapter. The
CGA modes will also display on the EGA but with the lower CGA resolution and decreased color options.

- **EGA color graphics modes**

In a graphics mode, a pixel can be represented as a one-, two-, or four-bit
value depending upon the mode selected. This representation is known as
the "pixel value." In addition to the pixel value there is an ordinal color
representation. Each color that can be displayed in a particular video
mode is represented by a unique ordinal value. The mapping of pixel
values onto the actual display colors produces a "palette" of colors that
can be displayed.

A palette of colors is available whenever one of the EGA graphics modes is
used. The EGA palettes may be remapped and redefined by the program.
The default palette for the EGA modes is the same as the palette for the
color text modes.

- **Remapping individual colors**

Use the _remappalette function to remap one pixel value to a specified
color, which must be a color supported by the current video mode. For
example, the function below remaps the pixel value 1 to the value _RED.
After this statement, whatever was displayed as blue will now appear as
red:

```
_remappalette (1, _RED);   /* reassign blue to red */
```

- **Remapping a set of colors**

Use the _remapallpalette function to remap all of the pixel values simultaneously. The function's argument points to an array of color numbers
reflecting the remapping. The first color number in the list will become the
new color associated with the pixel value of 0.

The number in a function call to set the color (such as _setcolor) is an
index into the palette of colors available. In the default text palette, an
index of 1 refers to blue. When a palette is remapped, the order of colors
in the palette is changed. As a result, the color produced by a given pixel
value also changes. The number of colors mapped depends on the number
of colors supported by the current video mode.

The **_remappalette** and **_remapallpalette** functions work in all modes but only with the EGA or VGA hardware. The **_remappalette** and **_remapallpalette** functions fail and return a value of –1 when you attempt to remap a palette without the EGA or VGA hardware.

■    **Sample: Remapping color palettes**

```
#include <stdio.h>
#include <graph.h>

main()
{
    _setvideomode (_ERESCOLOR);
    _settextposition (1,1);   /* normal palette */
    printf ("Normal palette");
    _setcolor (4);    /* red in default palette */
    _rectangle (_GFILLINTERIOR, 50,50,200,200);
    getchar();       /* wait for Enter key */
    _remappalette (4, _BLUE);     /* make red into blue */
    _settextposition (1,1);
    printf ("Remapped palette");
    _setcolor (4);    /* blue */
    _rectangle (_GFILLINTERIOR, 50,50,200,200);
    getchar();    /* wait for Enter key */
    _remappalette (4, _RED);    /* restore */
    _settextposition (1,1);
    printf ("Restored palette");
    _setcolor (4);    /* red */
    _rectangle (_GFILLINTERIOR,50,50,200,200);
    getchar();    /* wait for Enter key */
    _clearscreen (_GCLEARSCREEN);
    _setvideomode (_DEFAULTMODE);
}
```

This program draws a rectangle with a red interior. In the default EGA palette, the pixel value 4 maps to the color red. This pixel value is remapped to **_BLUE** in this program and the rectangle is redrawn. Finally, the pixel value is remapped back to the original color.

## 4.7   Using the VGA Color Graphics Modes

Use the video modes _ VRES2COLOR, _ VRES16COLOR, and
_ MRES256COLOR with the VGA display. EGA and CGA modes can
also be used with the VGA hardware, but with either lower resolution or
decreased color choices.

- **VGA color graphics modes**

In a graphics mode, a pixel can be represented as a one-, two-, or four-bit
value depending upon the mode selected. This representation is known as
the "pixel value." In addition to the pixel value there is an ordinal color
representation. Each color that can be displayed in a particular video
mode is represented by a unique ordinal value. The mapping of pixel
values onto the actual display colors produces a "palette" of colors that
can be displayed.

The VGA color graphics modes operate with a range of 262,144 (equivalent to 256K) colors. The _ VRES2COLOR graphics mode displays two
colors, the _ VRES16COLOR graphics mode displays 16 colors, and the
_ MRES256COLOR graphics mode displays 256 colors from the available VGA colors.

The large number of possible colors in the VGA is made possible by the
use of three bytes of information to represent the intensities of red, green,
and blue for each screen pixel. In each byte, the two high-order bits must
be 0. The remaining six bits represent the intensity of blue, green, and red
(reading from high-order byte to low-order byte). Three colors, each with
six bits of intensity, yield $64^3$ or 262,144 colors.

For example, equal values of red, green, and blue are used to make low-
intensity white so that the three-byte color number would be

```
blue            green            red
00011111     00011111       00011111
high ----------------> low order
```

Because of the splitting of color numbers between bytes, the color numbers
are not continuous (as is the case with CGA or EGA modes).

The 16 colors of the default palette for the _ VRES16COLOR mode and
the first 16 colors of the default palette in the _ MRES256COLOR mode
are the same as that for the color text modes.

- ### Remapping individual colors

Use the _remappalette function to remap one pixel value to a specified color number. The function below remaps the pixel value 1 to the color value given by the manifest constant _RED (which represents red). After this statement is executed, whatever was displayed as blue will now appear as red.

```
_remappalette (1, _RED);   /* reassign blue to VGA red */
```

- ### Remapping a set of colors

Use the _remapallpalette function to remap all of the available pixel values simultaneously. The function's argument points to an array of color numbers reflecting the remapping. The first color number in the list will become the new color associated with the pixel value of 0.

The number in a function call to set the color (such as _setcolor) is an index into the palette of colors available. In the default text palette, an index of 1 refers to blue. When a palette is remapped, the order of colors in the palette is changed. As a result, the color produced by a given pixel value also changes. The number of colors mapped depends on the number of colors supported by the current video mode.

The _remappalette and _remapallpalette functions work in all modes but only with the EGA or VGA hardware. The _remappalette and _remapallpalette functions fail and return a value of −1 when you attempt to remap a palette without the EGA or VGA hardware.

Manifest constants for the default color numbers are supplied so that the remapping of VGA colors is compatible with EGA practice. The names of these constants are self-explanatory. For example, the color numbers for black, red, and light yellow are represented by the manifest constants _BLACK, _RED, and _LIGHTYELLOW.

All of the VGA display modes operate with any VGA video monitor. Colors are displayed as shades of gray when the monochrome analog display is connected.

- ### Example: Remapping VGA color palettes

```
long colors1 [16] = {_BLACK, _BLUE, _GREEN, _RED, _RED, _MAGENTA,
      _BROWN, _WHITE, _GRAY, _LIGHTBLUE, _LIGHTGREEN, _LIGHTRED,
      _LIGHTRED, _LIGHTMAGENTA, _LIGHTYELLOW, _BRIGHTWHITE};
```

The array of color numbers above remaps the default VGA palette so that the cyan and light cyan colors are displayed as red and light red.

# 4.8   Understanding Coordinate Systems

A "coordinate system" is used to identify a pixel location relative to a horizontal and vertical axis. In a graphics mode, each pixel on the screen can be located by means of a unique pair of coordinates. The graphics library of functions supports two coordinate systems: a physical system and a logical system.

■   **Physical coordinates**

The "physical-coordinate system" places the origin (or the coordinate pair 0,0) at the upper-left corner of the screen. Increasing positive values of the x coordinate extend from left to right. Increasing positive values of the y coordinate extend from top to bottom. Thus, the bottom-right corner of the screen has an x coordinate equal to the number of x pixels available in the particular graphics video mode. Likewise, the bottom-right corner of the screen has an y coordinate equal to the number of y pixels available in the particular graphics video mode.

The physical-coordinate system contains only positive values with the x coordinate ranging from 0 (upper-left corner) to the number of x pixels (right margin) and the y coordinate ranging from 0 (upper-left corner) to the number of y pixels (bottom margin)

The physical-coordinate system is dependent on the hardware and display configuration, and cannot be changed.

■   **Logical coordinates**

A "logical-coordinate system" is created by moving the origin to a more "logical" position relative to the absolute physical coordinates. It is defined with the **_setlogorg** function, which sets a new logical origin. Initially, the default logical-coordinate system is identical to the physical-coordinate system.

After the origin is moved, the x and y coordinates maintain their orientation. As x increases, the pixel position moves from left to right on the screen. As y increases, the pixel position moves from top to bottom on the screen.

## ■ Repositioning the origin

The program segment below repositions the origin to the center of the screen:

```
_getvideoconfig (&vc);
_setlogorg (vc.numxpixels/2-1, vc.numypixels/2-1);
```

The call to the function **_getvideoconfig** returns the configuration information in the structure variable vc. The configuration structure contains the data on screen size. This is used (after an appropriate division) to reposition the origin to the center of the screen.

## ■ Resetting to physical coordinates

Reset the logical origin to the physical origin (which is the upper-left pixel of the screen) with the function **_setlogorg**. An example of resetting the logical origin is shown below:

```
_setlogorg(0,0);
```

## ■ Converting between coordinate systems

Use the **_getlogcoord** function to translate the physical coordinates to logical coordinates. The logical coordinates are returned in an **xycoord** structure. Use the **_getphyscoord** function to translate the logical coordinates of a specified pixel to physical coordinates. The physical coordinates are returned in an **xycoord** structure. The form of these two functions is shown below:

**_getlogcoord** $(x,y)$;
**_getphyscoord** $(x,y)$;

## ■ Example: Finding the screen centerpoint

```
_getvideoconfig (&vc);      /* get videoconfig information */
x = vc.numxpixels/2 - 1;    /* determine x and y midpoints */
y = vc.numypixels/2 -1;
_setlogorg (x, y);          /* reposition origin */
```

This program segment finds the screen center point for any video mode and sets the logical origin there.

# 4.9   Plotting Points

The simplest graphics functions operate at the single-pixel level. Any individual pixel can be accessed, examined, and set.

### ■   Moving to a particular screen point

Change the current graphics position with the **_moveto** function. This function moves the current position (where the next graphics operation takes place) to the specified logical coordinate. Its format is

```
_moveto (10,10); /* 10 pixels from left & 10 pixels
                    down from the logical origin */
```

### ■   Setting and clearing pixels

Use the **_setpixel** function to set a pixel located at the indicated logical coordinate to the current color. Its format is

```
_setpixel (10,10);   /* sets pixel at 10,10 to current color */
```

Reset a pixel by setting it to the background color (which is always pixel value 0). Shown below is the sequence of commands necessary to clear the specified pixel:

```
_setcolor (0);         /* set color to background color */
_setpixel (x, y);      /* effectively clear pixel */
```

### ■   Example: Setting pixels

The `hyppix.c` program below draws a hypocycloid, a figure created by rolling one circle inside another. The math-function library **math.h** is included because of the calls to the cosine and sine functions. The video mode used is CGA compatible. The curve is drawn during a **while** loop, which can be terminated by a keystroke. For interesting patterns, make the circle ratio larger than the pen position and do not use purely integer values. A particularly interesting pattern arises if the circle ratio is 3.2 and the pen position is 1.6. (More information on hypocycloids and other cycloids can be found in the "Mathematical Recreations" column of the May, 1987, issue of *Byte* magazine.)

```c
/* hyppix.c -- hypocycloid plotter (pixel version ) */
#include <stdio.h>
#include <graph.h>
#include <math.h>
#include <conio.h>
struct videoconfig vc;
char error_message [] = "This video mode is not supported";
main()
{
    if (_setvideomode(_MRES4COLOR) == 0) {
        printf ("%s\n", error_message);
        exit(0);
    }
    _getvideoconfig (&vc);
    hypcycle();          /* call drawing function */
    _clearscreen(_GCLEARSCREEN);
    _setvideomode (_DEFAULTMODE); /* restore video mode */
}
hypcycle()
{
    float pi=3.14159;                      /* declare and initialize */
    float a,h,b,r,x0,y0,x,y, ang;
    int i;
    x0 = vc.numxpixels/2 -1;
    y0 = vc.numypixels/2 -1;
    printf ("circle ratio (>=1): ");
    scanf ("%f", &r);
    printf ("\npen position (>1): ");
    scanf ("%f",&h);
    _clearscreen(_GCLEARSCREEN);
    _setcolor (1);
    _moveto (x0,0);                        /* draw axes */
    _lineto (x0,vc.numypixels);
    _moveto (0,y0);
    _lineto (vc.numxpixels,y0);
     a = 0.5*r*vc.numypixels/(r+h-1);
    b = a/r;
    h = h*b;
    _setcolor (2);
    ang = 0;
    while (!kbhit()) {                      /* draw hypocycloid */
        for (i=1; i<= 20; i++) {
            ang = ang + 2*pi/100;
            x = x0+(a-b)*cos(ang)+h*cos(ang*(a-b)/b);
            y = y0-(a-b)*sin(ang)+h*sin(ang*(a-b)/b);
            _setpixel (x,y);
        }
    }
}
```

## 4.10   Drawing Lines

Use the _ **moveto** and _ **lineto** functions to draw lines between any two points. The line may be drawn with either a solid or patterned line style.

■   **Moving to a specified location**

Use the _ **moveto** function to move to the logical-coordinate position given by the pair of points specified in the function. The form of the _ **moveto** statement is as follows:

```
_moveto (25, 25); /* move to logical coordinate 25,25 */
```

■   **Drawing lines**

Use the _ **lineto** function to draw a line from the present cursor position to the pair of endpoints specified in the function. Once the line has been drawn successfully, the current position is set to the coordinates specified in the _ **lineto** function. The color used is the current color. After executing the _ **moveto** function above, the _ **lineto** call below would draw a line from the point (25,25) to the point (100,100) and set the new current position to (100,100):

```
_lineto (100,100);   /* draw line from current position
                     /* to 100,100 */
```

■   **Drawing dashed or patterned lines**

The line-style mask controls the appearance of a line. The mask is a 16-bit template used for line drawing. Each bit in the mask represents a pixel in the line. If a bit's value is 1, the corresponding pixel is set to the current color. If a pixel is 0, the pixel is set to the background color. The default mask is a solid line (0xFFFF).

The _ **setlinestyle** function affects the line used in the _ **lineto** and _ **rectangle** functions.

The following is an example that changes the line style to a dashed line:

```
_setlinestyle (0xAAAA);   /* line style 1010101010101010 */
```

■ **Example: Line drawing**

```c
#include <stdio.h>
#include <graph.h>
#include <conio.h>
struct videoconfig vc;
char error_message [] = "This video mode is not supported";
main()
{
    if (_setvideomode(_MRES4COLOR) == 0) {
        printf ("%s\n", error_message);
        exit(0);
    }
    _getvideoconfig (&vc);
    _setlinestyle (0x0001);
    _moveto (0,0);                      /* draw figure */
    _lineto (0,150);
    _setlinestyle (0x0bb0);
    _lineto (150,150);
    _setlinestyle (0x0ff0);
    _lineto (150,0);
    _setlinestyle (0xffff);
    _lineto (0,0);
    getchar();                          /* wait for return */
    _clearscreen(_GCLEARSCREEN);        /* clear entire screen */
    _setvideomode (_DEFAULTMODE);       /* restore video mode */
}
```

The program above draws a rectangle with four different line styles for each side.

# 4.11   Describing Graphics Objects

This section defines the fundamental concepts used to describe graphic objects.

■   **Bounding rectangle**

A bounding rectangle defines the space in which a circular figure is drawn. For a circular figure, the center of the bounding rectangle defines the center of the circular figure. In a sense, the bounding rectangle is the "square hole" into which the round object fits. A bounding rectangle is defined by the coordinates of the upper-left corner and the lower-right corner of the rectangle. The other two corners are implied in the call.

■   **Border**

The border of circular objects is drawn in the current color and with a solid line style. The border of a rectangular object is drawn in the current color and with any line style specified by the **_setlinestyle** function. If no value has been specified for the border, the default solid line style (0xFFFF) is used.

■   **Fill flag**

Use the fill flag to specify whether a figure is to be filled using the current fill mask or if the figure is to remain empty. The **_GFILLINTERIOR** constant specifies the object should be filled, and **_GBORDER** specifies that only the border is to be drawn.

■   **Start and end vector**

The arc or pie wedge starts at the point where the bounding rectangle intersects the start vector and ends where it intersects the end vector.

■   **The aspect ratio**

The aspect ratio is the number of pixels in the vertical line divided by the number of pixels in the horizontal line. To draw squares (or circles), you have to scale their dimensions with the aspect ratio.

The aspect ratio depends on two factors:

1. A horizontal row has more pixels than a vertical column of the exact same physical length in all screen resolutions, because of the spacing of pixels and their elongated horizontal shape.

2. A video-display screen is wider than it is high, typically by a ratio of 4:3.

## ■ Calculating the aspect ratio

The formula for computing the aspect ratio for a given video mode is

$$\text{aspect ratio} = (\textit{screenwidth}/\textit{screenheight}) * (\textit{ypixels}/\textit{xpixels})$$

where *screenwidth* and *screenheight* refer to the physical dimensions of the display screen, and where *xpixels* and *ypixels* refer to the current screen resolution (as measured in pixels).

## ■ Example: Drawing correctly proportioned figures

```
#include <stdi.h>
#include <math.h>
#include <graph.h>
struct videoconfig vc;
char error_message [] = "This video mode is not supported";
main ()
{
    float ar, x, y;
    if (_setvideomode (_MRES4COLOR == 0) {
        printf ("%s\n", error_message);
        exit (0);
    }
    _getvideoconfig (&vc);
    /* screen dimensions 10 x 6.5 inches */
    ar = (float) (10 * vc.numypixels) / (6.5 * vc.numxpixels);
    y = 100*ar;
    x = 100;
    _setlogorg (vc.numxpixels/2 - 1, vc.numypixels/2 - 1);
    _setcolor (1);
    _rectangle (_GFILLINTERIOR, -x, -y, x, y);
    _setcolor (3);
    _ellipse (_GFILLINTERIOR, -x, -y, x, y);
    getchar ();
    _clearscreen (_GCLEARSCREEN);
    _setvideomode (_DEFAULTMODE); /* restore video mode */
}
```

This program uses the aspect ratio to correctly draw a square and a circle. The circular figure highlights the concept of a bounding rectangle.

# 4.12 Drawing Basic Shapes

The basic shapes available with the C graphics library are the rectangle, the ellipse, the arc, and the pie-shaped wedge.

## ■ Drawing rectangles

Use the _ **rectangle** function to draw a rectangle. The arguments to the function specify the coordinates of the opposite corners. The other corners are implied. Use the fill-flag parameter to specify whether the rectangle is to be drawn with the border only or it is to be filled with the current color. The two commands below draw a rectangle in the upper-left quadrant of the screen. The opposite corners are at the coordinates (0,0) and (25,25).

```
_rectangle (_GBORDER,0,0,25,25);          /* draw border only */
_rectangle (_GFILLINTERIOR,25,25,0,0);   /* fill interior */
```

## ■ Drawing circles and ellipses

Use the _ **ellipse** function to draw an ellipse. The parameters to the function specify the opposite corners of a bounding rectangle. The center of the ellipse is the center of the bounding rectangle. If the bounding rectangle is a square, the ellipse is a circle. The command below draws two ellipses in the upper left quadrant of the screen:

```
_ellipse (_GBORDER,0,0,25,25);           /* draw border only */
_ellipse (_GFILLINTERIOR,25,25,0,0);    /* fill interior */
```

If the concept of a bounding rectangle is a little confusing, you can call the _ **ellipse** function using only the center point $(x, y)$ and the radius $(r)$, as shown below:

```
_ellipse (_GBORDER, x-r, y-r, x+r, y+r); /* draw border only */
```

## ■ Drawing arcs and pies

An arc is a segment of an ellipse; in other words, a short, curved line. A pie is a pie-shaped wedge consisting of an elliptical arc whose center and two endpoints are joined by lines. The pie-shaped area is filled with the current color.

An arc or pie is drawn by specifying the opposite corners of a bounding rectangle and by specifying the endpoints of the vectors that determine the endpoints of the pie or arc. The center of an arc or pie is the center of the bounding rectangle. The arc or pie starts at the point where the vector defined by the center of the bounding rectangle and the third pair of points intersects the bounding rectangle. The arc or wedge ends at the point where the vector defined by the last pair of points and the center of the bounding rectangle intersects the bounding rectangle. The arc or pie is drawn using the current color, moving in a counterclockwise direction. An arc is not a closed figure; therefore, it is not filled. The pie-shaped area, however, is filled with the current color. The examples below show the use of these calls:

```
/* bounding rectangle determined by coordinates: (0,0) and (50,50)
   beginning vector (center of bounding rectangle) & (0,100)
   ending vector (center of bounding rectangle) & (100,100) */
_arc (0, 0, 50, 50, 0, 100, 100, 100);
_pie (_GFILLINTERIOR, 0, 0, 50, 50, 0, 100, 100, 100);
```

## ■  Example: Figure drawing

```
#include <stdio.h>
#include <graph.h>
#include <math.h>
struct videoconfig vc;
char error_message [] = "This video mode is not supported";
main()
{
    int x = 50;
    int y = 40;
    if (_setvideomode(_MRES4COLOR) == 0) {
        printf ("%s\n", error_message);
        exit(0);
    }
    _getvideoconfig (&vc);
    _setlogorg (vc.numxpixels/2 - 1, vc.numypixels/2 - 1);
    _setcolor (1);
    _setlogorg (vc.numxpixels/2 - 1, vc.numypixels/2 - 1);
    _setlinestyle (0x5555);
    _rectangle (_GBORDER, -x, -y, x, y);
    _setcolor (2);
    _ellipse (_GFILLINTERIOR, -x, -y, x, y);
    _setcolor (3);
    _pie (_GFILLINTERIOR,-x, -y, x, y, -x-10, y+10, x+10, y-10);
    getchar();
    _clearscreen (_GCLEARSCREEN);
    _setvideomode (_DEFAULTMODE); /* restore video mode */
}
```

# 4.13  Filling Figures with Patterns

Use the _ **floodfill** function to fill any enclosed figure with a pattern of pixels. An enclosed figure is a figure with no gaps in the line defining its border.

- **Filling shapes with patterns**

Use the _ **floodfill** function to fill any enclosed figure with a pattern specified by the *fillmask* parameter. The fill mask is an 8-by-8-bit template array with each bit representing a pixel in the overall template pattern. If the bit is 0, the pixel is left alone. If a bit is set to 1, the pixel is assigned the current color value. The fill-mask pattern is repeated over the entire area to be filled. The default fill mask is for a solid fill pattern.

The fill mask operates in a transparent, overlay mode. If a bit in the mask is 0, the pixel on the screen is left alone. A 1 in the mask causes the pixel to be set to the current color. Differently colored fill patterns can be created by setting the color between calls to the _ **floodfill** function.

A nonsolid border (line style not equal to 0xFFFF) can lead to unpredictable filling when used with _ **floodfill** and to possible overflow of the graphics area.

Use the _ **getfillmask** function to return the current fill mask. Use the _ **setfillmask** to set the current fill mask to a specified value. Shown below is the format of the fill-mask functions:

_ **getfillmask** (*fillmask*);
_ **setfillmask** (*fillmask*);

Use a **NULL** fill mask to reset the fill mask to a solid fill pattern as shown below:

```
_setfillmask (NULL);   /* reset fill mask to solid fill */
```

- **Creating a fill mask**

The fill mask is an 8-by-8-bit array that is generally defined in terms of a character array. Create a fill mask as shown below:

1. Draw the pattern for a tile in a grid with eight columns and eight rows. Place a one (1) in any box to represent an "on" pixel.

2. Convert the 8-bit binary numbers in each row to decimal integers.

3. Create an array of these eight digits as shown below:

```
/* fill mask for X pattern
        binary              decimal
    representation          equivalent
        10000001                129
        01000010                66
        00100100                36
        00011000                24
        00011000                24
        00100100                36
        01000010                66
        10000001                129 */
    char fill_mask [] = {129, 66, 36, 24, 24, 36, 66, 129};
```

4. Draw a figure and paint its interior, using the newly created fill mask.

```
_setfillmask(fill_mask);
_rectangle (_GFILLINTERIOR,50,50,25,100);
```

■ **Example: Filling regions with patterns**

```
#include <stdio.h>
#include <graph.h>
char mask1 [] = {0,66,36,24,24,36,66,0};    /* 2 fill patterns */
char mask2 [] = {0,24,0,102,102,0,24,0};
char error_message [] = "This video mode is not supported";
main()
{
    if (_setvideomode(_MRES4COLOR) == 0) {
        printf ("%s\n", error_message);
        exit(0);
    }
    _setfillmask (mask1);
    _setcolor (1);                      /* use multiple colors */
    _rectangle (_GBORDER,0,0,150,150);
    _setcolor (2);
    _floodfill (100,100,1);         /* stop at border of color 1 */
    _setcolor (3);
    _setfillmask (mask2);
    _floodfill (100,100,1);
    getchar();                          /* wait for carriage return */
    _clearscreen(_GCLEARSCREEN);
    _setvideomode (_DEFAULTMODE); /* restore video mode */
}
```

# 4.14   Drawing and Storing Figures

Complex figures can be drawn and stored in memory for later use in animations. The ▁getimage function stores an image in memory, and the ▁putimage function draws a stored image on the screen.

- ### Saving images to memory

The dimensions of the screen image saved are determined by a bounding rectangle. Use the ▁getimage function, as in the example below, to copy the entire area defined by the bounding rectangle to a buffer in memory:

```
_getimage (0, 0, 10, 10, buffer);
```

The bounding rectangle is in the upper-left corner of the screen bounded by the coordinates (0,0) and (10,10). The variable `buffer` is a pointer to the storage buffer for the screen image.

- ### Determining storage requirements for ▁getimage

The buffer must be large enough to hold the image. Use the function ▁getimagesize to determine the size needed to store the image before attempting to store the image. The example at the end of this section also shows how the **malloc** function is used to allocate the buffer storage required.

- ### Displaying images from memory

Use the ▁putimage function to copy the rectangular image stored in the buffer back to the screen, with its upper-left corner at the specified point. The function call below takes the image from the buffer in memory and copies it to the position on the screen with the upper left-corner coordinate of (50,50). The final parameter is the "action-verb" argument which determines how the memory image interacts with the current screen image.

```
_putimage (50,50,buffer,_GPSET);
```

■ **The _putimage action-verb argument**

The action-verb argument controls how the stored image interacts with what is already on the screen. The action-verb manifest constants cause the following display operations:

| Constant | Action |
|----------|--------|
| _GPSET | Direct transfer |
| _GPRESET | Direct transfer, color inverted |
| _GAND | Logical AND of transfer and screen image |
| _GOR | Superimposition of an image onto an existing image |
| _GXOR | Screen inversion where a point exists in buffer |

■ **Example: Drawing and storing a figure**

```
draw_and_store_figure ()
{
    _setbkcolor (0);
    _setcolor (1);
    _rectangle (_GBORDER,0,0,10,10);
    _setcolor (2);
    _rectangle (_GFILLINTERIOR,1,1,9,9);
    _setcolor (3);
    _moveto (1,1);
    _lineto (9,9);
    _moveto (1,9);
    _lineto (9,1);
    buffer=(char far *)malloc((unsigned int)
            _imagesize(0,0,10,10));
    _getimage (0,0,10,10, buffer);
}
```

This function draws a figure, determines the size required to store the image in memory, and then places the figure into a memory buffer for later use in an animation application. (This function will reappear in Section 4.15, "Using Animation," in a complete C animation program.)

# 4.15   Using Animation

Simple animation can be done by drawing figures, erasing them, and then moving to a new location and redrawing them. For faster, more effective animation of complex figures, use the _getimage and _putimage functions.

■   **Creating animation**

Create an image using output from other graphics functions, and then take a "snapshot" of that image with _getimage, copying it to memory. With _putimage, you then reproduce anywhere on the screen the image stored with _getimage.

The two action verbs best suited for animation are _GXOR and _GPSET. Animation done using _GPSET is faster, but erases the screen background. In contrast, _GXOR is slower, but preserves the screen background.

■   **Using _GXOR in animation**

Animation with _GXOR is done with the following four steps:

1.   Put the object on the screen with _GXOR.

2.   Calculate the new position of the object.

3.   Put the object on the screen a second time at the old location, using _GXOR again—this time to remove the old image.

4.   Go to step 1, but this time put the object at the new location.

Movement done with these four steps leaves the background unchanged after step 3. Flicker can be cut down by minimizing the time between steps 4 and 1, and by making sure that there is enough time delay between steps 1 and 3. If more than one object is being animated, every object should be processed at once, one step at a time.

■   **Using _GPSET in animation**

If it is not important to preserve the background, animation can be performed using the _GPSET option. If the border of the bounding rectangle around the image is as large as or larger than the maximum distance the object will move, then each time the image is put in a new location, the border will erase all traces of the image in the old location.

## ■ Example: Animation using memory storage of images

```
     .
     .        previous includes from hyppix.c
     .
#include <malloc.h>      /* needed for buffer use */
     .
     .        declarations from hyppix.c
     .
char far *buffer;  /* used with _getimage & _putimage */
main()
{    .
     .        body of program from hyppix.c
     .
}
hypcycle()
{    .
     .        declarations and initialization from hyppix.c
     .
     draw_and_store_figure();   /* place figure in buffer */
     _clearscreen (_GCLEARSCREEN);
     .
     .        drawing of axes as in hyppix.c
     .
     /* plot points and put image from buffer to screen */
     while (!kbhit()) {
          for (i=1; i<= 20; i++) {
               ang = ang + 2*pi/100;
               x = x0+(a-b)*cos(ang)+h*cos(ang*(a-b)/b);
               y = y0-(a-b)*sin(ang)+h*sin(ang*(a-b)/b);
               _putimage (x,y,buffer,GXOR);
               for (j=1; j<=6000; j++)
                    ;
               _putimage (x,y,buffer,GXOR);
          }
     }
}
draw_and_store_figure()
{    .
     .        function contents from previous section
     .
}
```

The hypocycloid program from Section 4.9 has been modified to draw the curve using the stored pattern and to draw this curve over a background on the screen. The `draw_and_store_figure` function is from Section 4.14, and it uses the **_getimage** function to store a complex graphics figure in a buffer area. The skeleton of the program is shown above with notations of the changes.

# PART 2

# THE QUICKC PROGRAMMING ENVIRONMENT

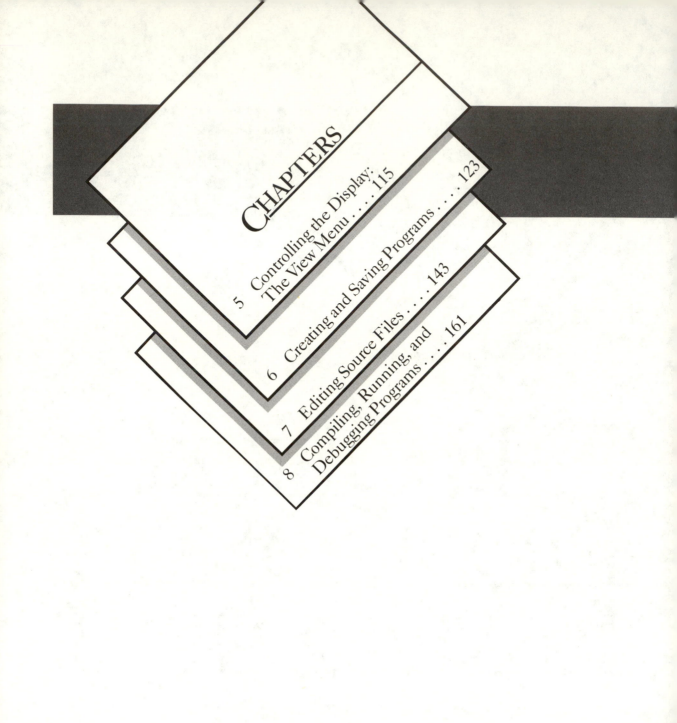

# CHAPTERS

# PART 2

◇ THE QUICKC
PROGRAMMING ENVIRONMENT

This part of the manual describes how you can use the QuickC programming environment to create, compile, debug, and run programs. This section shows you how to use the QuickC menu commands to

- Customize the QuickC display by using the commands in the View menu (Chapter 5)
- Create a new source file containing QuickC source code, or load an existing source file, using the commands in the File menu (Chapter 6)
- Enter the source file using the editing commands, the Edit menu, and the Search menu (Chapter 7)
- Compile, debug, and run the program using the Run menu (Chapter 8)

# CHAPTER 5

# CONTROLLING THE DISPLAY: THE VIEW MENU

Use the commands from the View menu to

- Open windows
- Display program output
- Customize your screen's appearance

The View menu is shown in Figure 5.1.

**Figure 5.1  The View Menu**

The commands on the View menu perform the following actions:

| Command | Action |
| --- | --- |
| Source... | Displays the current program list. |
| Include | Displays a given include file. |
| Options... | Customizes the display by changing background and foreground colors, setting tab stops, and controlling the display of scroll bars. |
| Output Screen | Shows you the output screen. The shortcut key for this command is F4. |
| Errors | Opens or closes the error window at the bottom of the QuickC screen. |

The following sections describe how to use the commands on the View menu.

## 5.1   Viewing the Program List: the Source... Command

Use the Source... command to look at any module in the current program list. This command is active only if you have loaded a program list with the Set Program List... command in the File menu. (See Section 6.2.6, "Creating and Loading Program Lists: the Set Program List... Command," for information on using this command.) This command provides a fast way to move between modules without having to use the Open command. Using Source... is easier than using Open... because

- The Source... command lists only files that are part of the program list; the Open... command may list many more files.

- The Source... command lists files in the program list that reside in other directories; the Open... command lists only files in the current directory.

When you choose the Source... command, the dialog box shown in Figure 5.2 appears:

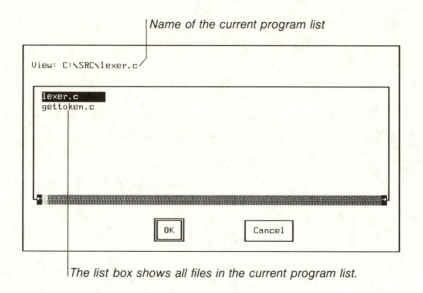

Figure 5.2  The Source... Dialog Box

All modules in the list are displayed, regardless of the drive or directory where they reside. Use the DIRECTION keys to select the module you want to view. Then press ENTER to display the module.

## 5.2 Viewing Include Files: the Include Command

Use the Include command to display include files. You can display include files in one of two ways:

1. Use the DIRECTION keys to move the cursor until it is resting on the same line as an **#include** directive; then choose the Include command to display that include file.

2. Choose the Include command and press ENTER. A dialog box appears. The default file specification in the File text box is *.h. Choose the include file from the list box and choose the OK command button.

After viewing an include file, press F2 to return to the file you were editing.

## 5.3 Customizing the Display: the Options... Command

The Options... command lets you change the appearance of the QuickC screen. With the Options... command you can change the foreground and background screen colors, alter the way program lines are displayed, remove the scroll bars, or change the tab spacing.

When you select Options... from the File menu, the dialog box shown in Figure 5.4 opens.

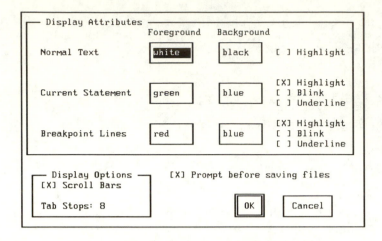

**Figure 5.3  The Options... Dialog Box**

The following options in the Display Attributes box determine the screen's colors:

| Option | Use |
|---|---|
| Normal Text | Specifies colors used to display program statements. The background color you choose sets the background color for the edit screen. |
| Current Statement | Specifies colors used to display the currently executing line. |
| Breakpoint Lines | Specifies colors used to display breakpoints (program lines where you temporarily stop program execution during debugging). |

The Normal Text option can be set so that program text is highlighted. The Current Statement and Breakpoint Lines options can be set so that they are highlighted, blinking, underlined, or any combination of the three. (Underlining is available only on systems with a Monochrome Display Adapter.)

Choose colors for Normal Text, Current Statement, and Breakpoint Lines, using either of the following methods:

- While the option is selected, type the first letter of the color you want. Note that the letter "B" represents both black and blue.

- While the option is selected, use the UP and DOWN keys to scroll through the color list until the name of the color you want appears in the box.

Color choices are useful only on a color monitor. On a monochrome monitor, only Black and White are in the list of background colors. If you choose White instead of Black as the background color, the display changes to reverse video.

The Display Options items control display of the following items:

| Option | Use |
| --- | --- |
| Scroll Bars | Toggles (turns on or off) the display of scroll bars in the view window. The scroll bars are useful only if you have a mouse. If you are not using a mouse, turning the scroll bars off gives you more space in the window for text. |
| Tab Stops | Sets the number of columns between tab positions. The default value is eight spaces. |

All the Display Options are on by default.

The "Prompt before saving file" check box controls whether QuickC automatically saves changes to the file you are working on if you do something that might result in a loss of changes (such as load or create a new file). If this check box is selected, QuickC displays a prompt asking if you want to save changes; you can choose the Yes command button to save changes or the No command button to discard them. If this check box is not selected, QuickC automatically saves changes without displaying a prompt.

# 5.4  Viewing Program Output: the Output Screen Command

The Output Screen command tells QuickC to display the program-output screen instead of the edit screen This command is typically used to look at output during program debugging.

After you choose this command, press any key to return to the edit screen.

The shortcut command for the Output Screen command is F4.

## 5.5   Opening or Closing the Error Window: the Errors Command

If errors occur during compilation, QuickC opens an error window at the bottom of the screen to display these errors. The Errors command tells QuickC to close the error window if is currently open or to open the error window if it is currently closed. A check mark appears next to this command on the menu when the error window is open.

See Section 7.3.4, "Finding Program Errors: the Next Error and Previous Error Commands," for more information about handling compilation errors.

# CHAPTER 6

## CREATING AND SAVING PROGRAMS

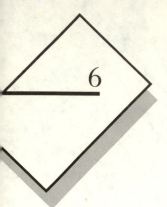

This chapter explains how to create and save programs with the Microsoft QuickC Compiler. First, it shows how modules are combined to form programs and describes the list of modules, known as the "program list," that can be maintained for each program. Then it shows how to use commands from the File menu to create, save, and print QuickC source files.

# 6.1 Programs and Modules: the Program List

A QuickC program consists of one or more C source files known as "modules." A program built from a single module is known as a "single-module program." A program built from more than one module is known as a "multiple-module program."

You can maintain a list of the modules that make up a QuickC program in a file known as a "program list." QuickC uses a program list to rebuild a program when any of its modules changes. This mechanism ensures that the program is always rebuilt using the most up-to-date versions of its modules.

## 6.1.1 Single-Module Programs

Single-module programs are the easiest to create. The usual process for creating a single-module program is:

1. Choose the New command (Section 6.2.1) from the File menu to create a new C source file, or choose the Open... command (Section 6.2.2) from the File menu to open an existing source file.

2. Enter program text using the editing keys and commands described in Chapter 7.

3. Compile, run, and debug the program using the commands described in Chapter 8.

You are not required to create a program list for a single-module program. If you do not create a program list, the program is created in memory, and no executable file is created on disk.

If the program calls standard C library routines, it can find definitions of most of these routines built into the QuickC programming environment. Table 6.1 lists the library routines that are built into QuickC, which are known collectively as the QuickC "core library."

**Table 6.1**

**C Library Routines Defined in QC.EXE[1]**

| | | | | |
|---|---|---|---|---|
| abort | _fmalloc | ltoa | rmdir | strncat |
| access | _fmsize | malloc | rmtmp | strncmp |
| atexit | fopen | memavl | sbrk | strncpy |
| atof | fprintf | memccpy | scanf | strnset |
| atoi | fputc | memchr | segread | strpbrk |
| atol | fputs | memcmp | setbuf | strrchr |
| bdos | fread | memcpy | setjmp | strrev |
| brk | free | _memmax | setmode | strset |
| calloc | _freect | memmove | setvbuf | strspn |
| chdir | fscanf | memset | signal | strstr |
| chmod | fseek | mkdir | sopen | strtok |
| clearerr | fstat | movedata | spawnl[2] | strupr |
| close | ftell | _msize | spawnle[2] | system |
| cputs | fwrite | _nfree | spawnlp[2] | tell |
| creat | getch | _nheapchk | spawnlpe[2] | time |
| dosexterr | getche | _nheapset | spawnv[2] | tmpfile |
| eof | getcwd | _nheapwalk | spawnvpe[2] | tmpnam |
| _exit | _getdate | _nmalloc | sprintf | tolower |
| exit | getenv | _nmsize | sscanf | toupper |
| _expand | gets | onexit | stackavail | tzset |
| fclose | gettime | open | strcat | ultoa |
| fflush | int86 | printf | strchr | ungetc |
| _ffree | int86x | putch | strcmp | unlink |
| fgets | intdosx | puts | strcmpi | vfprintf |
| _fheapchk | isatty | raise | strcpy | vprintf |
| _fheapset | itoa | read | strcspn | vsprintf |
| _fheapwalk | kbhit | realloc | strdup | write |
| filelength | longjmp | remove | stricmp | |
| flushall | lseek | rewind | strlwr | |

[1] The **halloc**, **hfree**, and **exec** family functions are defined within **QC.EXE**, but they cannot be called by programs running within the QuickC programming environment.

[2] These functions cannot be called with the **P_OVERLAY** mode flag by programs running within the QuickC programming environment.

The QuickC compiler generates an error if any functions in your program have the same names as functions defined in the QuickC core library.

If a program calls standard C library functions that are not listed in Table 6.1, you must do one of the following to make sure the compiler can find the definitions of these functions:

1. Create a Quick library containing the functions that are not listed (see Sections 10.1.1 and 10.1.3 for instructions). Then load this library when you start QuickC (Section 10.1.2). In this case, the missing function definitions are found in the Quick library.

2. Choose the Set Program List... command (Section 6.2.6) from the File menu to create a program list for the program. Then choose the Edit Program List... command (Section 6.2.8) to add the single module to the new program list and save the program list. In this case, the missing function definitions are found in the medium-model combined library **MLIBCE.LIB** on disk; see Section 6.1.4 for more information about how QuickC uses program lists.

## 6.1.2  Multiple-Module Programs

You are required to create a program list for a multiple-module program so that the QuickC compiler will know which modules to use when building the program. Use the following general procedure to create a multiple-module program:

1. Create, compile, and debug the source files that will make up the program using the following the steps:

   a. Choose the New command (Section 6.2.1) from the File menu to create a new source file, or choose the Open... command (Section 6.2.2) from the File menu to open an existing source file for editing.

   b. Enter text for the source file using the editing keys and commands described in Chapter 7.

   c. Choose the Compile... command (Section 8.1.4) from the Run menu to compile the source file and verify that it is free of syntax errors.

2. Choose the Set Program List... command (Section 6.2.6) from the File menu to create a program list for the program or load an existing file for editing.

3. Choose the Edit Program List... command (Section 6.2.8) to add modules to or subtract modules from the program list and then save the program list. Note that you can also add object files or stand-alone libraries (libraries with **.LIB** extensions) to a program list.

4. Repeat steps 1–3 as you develop additional program modules.

5. Compile, run, and debug the program using the commands described in Chapter 8.

When you compile a multiple-module program, QuickC checks the program list to see if any modules have been changed since the last time the program was compiled. If so, it recompiles the changed modules before rebuilding the program. This mechanism ensures that the program is always up to date with respect to its individual components.

The compiler saves the program list in a disk file with the same base name as the program and the extension **.MAK**. Outside of the QuickC environment, you can give the **.MAK** file as input to the **MAKE** utility to update the program. See Section 11.5 for more information about **.MAK** files.

---

*Note*

> Do not delete the **.MAK** file for a program that has a program list. If you copy a program that has a program list to a different directory, you must also copy the **.MAK** file to the new directory.

---

## 6.1.3   Working with Program Lists

The QuickC compiler makes it easy to create and edit program lists. The following list outlines the operations you can perform on a program list and the commands you use to perform these operations:

| Operation | Menu/Command |
|---|---|
| Create a program list | File/Set Program List... (Section 6.2.6) |
| Open an existing program list for editing | File/Set Program List... (Section 6.2.6) |
| View contents of the program list | File/Set Program List... (Section 6.2.6) or View/Source... (Section 5.1) |
| Display or edit a module in the program list | View/Source... (Section 5.1) |
| Edit and save the program list | File/Edit Program List... (Section 6.2.8) |
| Clearing the current program list from memory | File/New (Section 6.2.1), File/Clear Program List (Section 6.2.7), or File/Edit Program List... with the Clear List command button (Section 6.2.8) |

If you ever lose track of the program list that is currently in memory, remember that the name of the program list (without the **.MAK** extension) appears after the `Program List:` indicator on the status line at the bottom of the QuickC screen.

## 6.1.4   How QuickC Uses the Program List

The QuickC compiler performs the following steps when it compiles a single-module program with a program list or rebuilds a multiple-module program:

1. It recompiles any modules in the program list that have been updated since the last time the program was compiled. This creates updated object files on disk.

2. It creates a linker response file with the same last name as the program and the extension **.LNK**.

3. It invokes the linker, **LINK.EXE**. The linker links the object files created in step 1 with any other object files created from program modules and any object files or stand-alone libraries given in the program list, creating an executable file on disk. The linker looks for definitions of standard C-library routines in the following locations:

   - The core library that is built into the QuickC programming environment

   - The Quick library, if any, that is currently loaded

   - The stand-alone library **MLIBCE.LIB** on disk

   If the linker cannot find any of these routines, an error results and the program cannot be run.

4. The compiler reloads the newly created executable file into the QuickC environment, where the program can be run.

Note that the object files created in step 1, the linker-response file created in step 2, and the executable file created in step 3 are saved on disk. Other files may be saved on disk, depending on the options used to compile the program. For example, if you include debugging information in the program (see Section 8.1.4.3 for information on the Debug option), a map file is also saved.

To control the operation of the linker in step 2, you can specify, in the **.MAK** file, any of the linker options described in Sections 9.5.1–9.5.14. See Section 11.5.3 for instructions.

## 6.1.5   Common Questions About In-Memory Programs and Program Lists

The questions and answers in this section summarize information about in-memory programs, program lists, and Quick libraries.

QUESTION: I get unresolved-external errors when I try to compile programs in the QuickC environment. How can I solve these problems?

ANSWER: The most common reason for getting unresolved-external errors for an in-memory program is that the program calls standard C library routines that are not in the QuickC core library (see Table 6.1).

If your program uses standard library routines that are not listed in Table 6.1, employ either of the following methods:

- Create a single-module program list that includes the name of the current program (see Sections 6.2.6–6.2.8). In this case, the linker resolves external references using the medium-model combined library **MLIBCE.LIB** on disk.

- Build and load a Quick library containing the missing routines (see Sections 10.1.1–10.1.3). In this case, the functions in the Quick library resolve the external references.

QUESTION: If my programs use functions that are not listed in Table 6.1, when is it better to create and load a program list and when is it better to create and load a Quick library?

ANSWER: If you are running on a hard-disk system, it is usually easier to create a program list because this method saves the trouble of having to build a Quick library. Although the compiler must invoke the linker and go to the disk to find the functions that are not in the core library, the hard disk minimizes the amount of time needed for this process.

If you are running on a floppy-disk system, it is usually preferable to create and load a Quick library containing the missing functions. This is because all of the functions that the program needs can be found in memory, either in the core library or in the Quick library, and there is no need to access the disk.

QUESTION: How do I create a new program list?

ANSWER: Choose the Set Program List... command (Section 6.2.6) from the File menu, and give the name you have chosen for the new program list in the File Name text box. Usually, this is the base name of the program, with the extension **.MAK**. If this program list does not exist, QuickC asks if you want to create it; choose the Yes command button. QuickC automatically executes the Edit Program List... command (Section 6.2.8) so that you can add modules to the new program list. After you have finished adding modules to the program list, choose the Save List command button to save the new list.

QUESTION: How can I easily move between modules in a program list?

ANSWER: Choose the Source command from the View menu and select the module you want to edit.

QUESTION: How do I remove a program list from memory once I've loaded it?

ANSWER: Choose the Clear Program List command from the File menu.

QUESTION: How do I create a Quick library?

ANSWER: See Section 10.1.1 for instructions. The basic procedure is to

1. Create a main program that calls the functions you want to put in the Quick library.

2. Compile this program with the **/c** and **/AM** compiler options.

3. Link the resulting file with the **QUICKLIB.OBJ** object file and the **/QU** linker option.

QUESTION: How can I include an existing object file or stand-alone library in an in-memory program?

ANSWER: Create a program list (Section 6.2.6) and add the object files or libraries to the program list (Section 6.2.8). Note that when you put a stand-alone library in the program list, the linker puts the complete contents of the library in the program.

QUESTION: Since the linker links the modules in a program list, is there a way to specify options to control linker operations?

ANSWER: Specify linker options (Sections 9.5.1–9.5.14) by using a macro named **LDFLAGS** in the **.MAK** file that contains the program list. See Section 11.5.3 for instructions.

# 6.2 Handling Source Files: the File Menu

The commands on the File menu are used to create new files, load existing files for editing, create and save program lists, save edited files, combine files, and print files.

When you select File on the menu bar, the File menu shown below in Figure 6.1 opens.

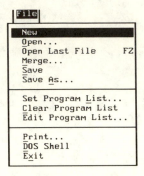

**Figure 6.1  The File Menu**

The commands on the File menu perform the following actions:

| Command | Action |
|---|---|
| New | Creates a new file. |
| Open . . . | Loads an existing file for editing. |
| Open Last File | Loads the most recently edited file and optionally saves the current file if it has been changed. The shortcut key for this command is F2. |
| Merge . . . | Copies a file from disk into the current file after the line on which the cursor is resting. |
| Save | Saves the file you were editing under its current name. |
| Save As... | Saves the file you were editing under a different name. |
| Set Program List... | Creates a new program list or loads an existing program list into the QuickC environment. |

| | |
|---|---|
| Clear Program List | Removes the current program list from memory. |
| Edit Program List... | Adds modules to or deletes modules from the current program list. |
| Print... | Prints selected text or the entire current file. |
| DOS Shell | Temporarily exits to DOS and later returns to QuickC. |
| Exit | Ends the QuickC session and exits to DOS. |

Sections 6.2.1–6.2.11 describe how to use each command on the File menu.

## 6.2.1 Creating New Programs: the New Command

The New command creates a new file in memory. This file may be any type of file, including a C source file, an include file, or a document. Assign a name to the file when you save it using the Save or Save As... command.

The New command also clears the current program list from memory. Use the Set Program List... command (Section 6.2.6) to create a program list for the new program.

## 6.2.2 Loading Files for Editing: the Open... Command

The Open... command loads an existing file for editing. You can also use the Open... command to list files that are in different directories on your system.

When you choose the Open... command from the File menu, the dialog box shown in Figure 6.2 opens.

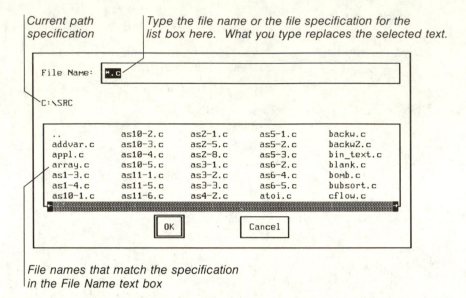

**Figure 6.2  The Open... Dialog Box**

Use the following options and displays in the dialog box to describe the file that you want to open:

| Option/Display | Use |
| --- | --- |
| File Name | Type the name of the file that you want to open. If you would rather choose this file from the list box, type a specification for the files that you want to appear in the list box. See Section 6.2.2.1, "Loading Files with Open...," and Section 6.2.2.2, "Listing Files with Open...," for more information. |
| (Path specification) | The current path specification appears between the File Name text box and the list box. |
| (List box) | Files that match the file and path specifications you typed appear in the File Name text box. Directory and file names are displayed alphabetically in columns. Names of directories are highlighted and appear in uppercase letters; file names appear in lowercase letters. |

If the file names do not fit in the box, press the RIGHT or LEFT key to move the reverse-video highlight to the edge of the box and scroll the list. If you are using a mouse, use the scroll bar at the bottom of the list box to scroll the list to the left or right. See Section 6.2.2.1, "Loading Files with Open...," and Section 6.2.2.2, "Listing Files with Open...," for more information.

OK                        Choose this command button to open the file you have selected.

Cancel                    Choose this command button to cancel the Open... command.

When the Open... dialog box first appears, the file specification `*.c` appears highlighted in the text box. All files in the current directory that have the extension `.C` appear in the list box.

## 6.2.2.1  Loading Files with Open...

You can specify the file you want to load in one of the following ways:

1.  Type the name of the file, then press ENTER. QuickC assumes the `.C` extension for all file names without extensions. If you want to load a file that has no extension, type a period (.) immediately after the file name.

2.  Press the TAB key to move the input focus to the list box and use the DIRECTION keys to move through the list box until the file you want to load is highlighted. Then press ENTER to load the file.

    You can also type the first letter of the name of the file you want to load. This moves the highlight to the first file name or directory name in the list that begins with that letter. For example, if you are looking for the file `PROG1.C`, typing `P` moves the input focus to the first file name beginning with "P."

3.  Using the mouse, double-click the file name in the list box.

## 6.2.2.2  Listing Files with Open...

You can use the text box on the Open... dialog box to list the contents of any directory on your system.

In the list box, file names appear in lowercase letters, and directory names appear in highlighted uppercase letters. The entry ".." in the upper-left corner of the list box represents the directory immediately above the current directory. When you enter a directory in the text box, or select a directory from the list box, QuickC lists the files in that directory. (When you select or enter a file name, the file is loaded into memory.) You can use the DOS wild-card characters (? and *) to list groups of files.

### 6.2.3 Opening the Last Edited File: the Open Last File Command

The Open Last File command loads the file you were most recently editing. If you have not saved changes to the current file, QuickC asks if you want to save it before loading the new file. If you have not edited other files since you started QuickC, no new file is loaded.

If you are editing two source files, this command makes it easy to move back and forth between the two. After you save one source file and load a second source file for editing, the first source file becomes the "last file" edited. To reload this previously saved file for editing, simply choose Open Last File or press the F2 shortcut key again.

### 6.2.4 Merging Files: the Merge... Command

The Merge... command inserts a file beginning after the line on which the cursor is resting in the edit window. When you select Merge... from the File menu, the dialog box shown in Figure 6.3 opens.

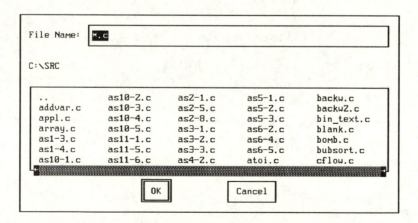

**Figure 6.3 The Merge... Dialog Box**

The options in the Merge... dialog box are the same as the options in the Open... dialog box. See Section 6.2.2 for more information.

## 6.2.5 Saving Files: the Save and Save As... Commands

The Save and Save As... commands save the file you are editing in a disk file. Use the Save command to save the file under its original name or the Save As... command to change the file name. If you are saving a new, unnamed file, you can use either command to specify the file name. When you choose the Save As... command, the dialog box shown in Figure 6.4 opens.

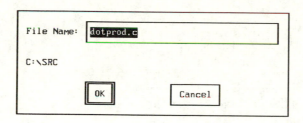

**Figure 6.4  The Save As... Dialog Box**

The Save As... dialog box has the following options and displays:

| Option/Display | Use |
| --- | --- |
| File Name | If you are saving a new, unnamed file, enter the file name in the text box. If you are saving a file that already has a name, the file name appears in the text box. To use the same file name, just press ENTER. To change the file name, begin typing. What you type replaces the old name. |
| (Path specification) | The current path specification appears between the File Name text box and the command buttons. |
| OK | Choose this command button to save the file with the name given in the text box. |
| Cancel | Choose this command button to cancel the Save As... command and return to the editor. |

### 6.2.6 Creating and Loading Program Lists: the Set Program List... Command

The Set Program List... command creates a new program list or loads an existing program list into the QuickC environment.

When you choose the Set Program List... command, a dialog box similar to the Open... dialog box (Figure 6.2) appears, except that the file specification in the File Name list box is *.mak. (Recall that program lists are saved in files with extensions of **.MAK**.) You can choose a **.MAK** file for editing or display the **.MAK** files in any directory on your system, just as you do for the Open... command; see Sections 6.2.2.1–6.2.2.2 for details. If you choose an existing **.MAK** file for editing, use the Edit Program List... command to make the changes to the file.

If you give the name of a nonexistent **.MAK** file, QuickC asks if you want to create the file. If you respond with "Yes," QuickC automatically opens the dialog box for the Edit Program List... command so that you can add modules to the new program list.

After you load a program list, the name of the program list appears after the Program List: indicator on the status line.

When you compile, the Build Program and Rebuild All command buttons affect only the modules in this program list, not the source file you are editing.

### 6.2.7 Clearing the Current Program List: the Clear Program List Command

The Clear Program List command clears the current program list from memory. The Program List: indicator in the status line is changed to read <none> to indicate that no program list is currently in memory. Until you load a new program list with the Set Program List... command, the QuickC compiler assumes that any source files you compile are single-module files that are not part of a program list.

### 6.2.8 Editing the Program List: the Edit Program List... Command

The Edit Program List... command maintains the list of modules that comprise a program.

When you select Edit Program List... from the File menu, or after you create a new program list with the Set Program List... command, the dialog box shown in Figure 6.5 opens.

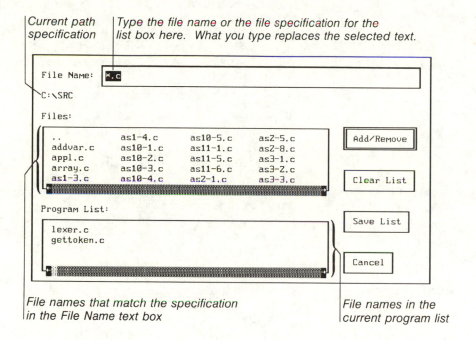

Figure 6.5 The Edit Program List... Dialog Box

Use the following options and displays in the Edit Program List... dialog box to specify the program list you want to change and the changes you want to make:

| Option/Display | Use |
| --- | --- |
| File Name | Type the name of the **.MAK** file containing the program list you want to edit, or type a specification for the files that you want to list in the list box. You can use the Edit Program List... command in the same way you use the Open... command to list files on the current drive or in the current directory; see Section 6.2.2.1, "Loading Files with Open...," and Section 6.2.2.2, "Listing Files with Open...," for details. |

(Path specification)    The current path specification appears between the File Name text box and the command buttons.

Files    This list box shows all disk files that match the file and path specifications you have given in the File Name text box. When you select a file name in the list box, choose the Add/Remove command button to add the file to, or delete the file from, the program list. You can select files from the list box or display files in different directories just as you do for the Open... command on the File menu. See Section 6.2.2.1, "Loading Files with Open...," and Section 6.2.2.2, "Listing Files with Open...," for details.

Program List    This list box shows all modules associated with the program list that is currently loaded. Choose files to be deleted from the program list the same as you choose files for the Open... command; see Section 6.2.2.1, "Loading Files with Open...," for details.

Add/Remove    Choose this command button to add the selected file to the program list or remove it from the list. If the file is not already in the program list, it is added to the list. If the file is already in the program list, it is deleted from the list. The program list is not actually changed until you choose the Save List command button.

Clear List    Choose this command button to remove all modules from the current program list.

Note that this command button removes all modules from the program list whether or not you choose the Save List command button; the Cancel command button does not restore the original program list.

Save List    Choose this command button to save all changes to the program list in the **.MAK** file for the program.

Cancel    Choose this command button to cancel the Edit Program List... command.

Use the following procedure to edit the program list:

1.  Select the Edit Program List... command from the File menu.

2.  Choose the directory from which you want to add files to the program list. See Section 6.2.2.1, "Loading Files with Open...," and Section 6.2.2.2, "Listing Files with Open...," for instructions.

3.  Choose a file from the Files list box to be added to or deleted from the list.

4.  Press ENTER.  If the file you chose is not in the Program List list box, QuickC adds it. If it is already in the Program List list box, QuickC removes it from that list box. The dialog box remains on the screen.

5.  Repeat steps 4–5 until the Program List box contains the files you want.

6.  Type ALT+S to save the program list and update the program **.MAK** file, or type ALT+C to clear the program list. The dialog box disappears from the screen.

Press ESC or choose the Cancel command button at any time to cancel the Edit Program List... command.

## 6.2.9  Printing Files: the Print. . . Command

The Print... command prints either the file you are editing or selected text from that file. Files are printed without page breaks or headings.

To use this command, your printer must be connected to LPT1. (Alternatively, you can use the DOS **MODE** command to redirect LPT1 to COM1.)

When you choose the Print... command from the File menu, the dialog box shown in Figure 6.6 opens.

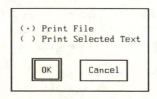

**Figure 6.6  The Print... Dialog Box**

You can select either of the following print options:

| Option | Use |
| --- | --- |
| Print File | Prints the contents of the file you are editing |
| Print Selected Text | Prints only the text selected (highlighted) in the view window |

While the file is printing, a dialog box with a Cancel command button appears on the screen. To stop printing, simply press ESC or SPACEBAR.

## 6.2.10   Temporarily Returning to DOS: the DOS Shell Command

The DOS Shell command lets you temporarily return to the DOS command level, where you can execute other programs and DOS commands. QuickC remains in memory. Note that you should not delete **.MAK** files, C source files, or files in the current program list before you return to QuickC.

QuickC needs to be able to find the **COMMAND.COM** file before it can execute the DOS Shell command. QuickC first looks in the directory given in the **COMSPEC** environment variable, then in the current directory. See your DOS user documentation for more information about **COMMAND.COM** and **COMSPEC**.

To return to QuickC from the DOS command level, execute the DOS **EXIT** command.

## 6.2.11   Leaving QuickC: the Exit Command

The Exit command removes QuickC from memory and then returns you to DOS.

If you have been editing a file but have not saved it, a prompt asks you if you want to save the program. To save the program, press ENTER or click the Yes button with the mouse. If the program has no name, the Save As... dialog box appears.

To return to the system without saving the file, type n or click the No button with the mouse.

# CHAPTER 7

# EDITING SOURCE FILES

The program editor built into the QuickC programming environment provides a powerful, flexible set of keyboard and menu commands for editing source files. Most QuickC editing operations require only a single keystroke or a single key sequence using the ALT, CTRL, or SHIFT key. Using the QuickC editor, you can quickly perform editing operations such as moving the cursor; selecting, inserting, copying, and deleting text; and opening new lines in the source file.

*Note*

If you have used the MicroPro WordStar® program, you will find that many of the QuickC editing commands are the same as the commands used in WordStar.

This section describes how to enter and edit program text using the QuickC editor commands and the Edit and Search menus.

- Section 7.1 presents the keyboard and mouse editing commands.
- Sections 7.2 and 7.3 describe the commands on the two editing menus, Edit and Search.

# 7.1   Editing with the Keyboard and Mouse

When you want to edit text, simply follow these steps:

1. Move the cursor to the beginning of the text you want to edit.
2. Select the text you want to edit. Press the SHIFT key plus any cursor-movement key to select text.
3. Edit the selected text.

## 7.1.1   Using QuickC Editing Keys

Table 7.1 describes the keyboard commands that move the cursor, select text, and perform editing functions.

### Table 7.1
### QuickC Editing Keys

| To Move the Cursor: | Press: |
| --- | --- |
| Up/down one line | UP or CTRL+E / DOWN or CTRL+X |
| Right/left one character | RIGHT or CTRL+D / LEFT or CTRL+S |
| Left one character (delete character) | BACKSPACE or CTRL+H |
| Right/left one word | CTRL+RIGHT or CTRL+F / CTRL+LEFT or CTRL+A |
| To beginning/end of the line | HOME or CTRL+Q S / END or CTRL+Q D |
| To top/bottom of the screen | CTRL+Q E / CTRL+Q X |
| To beginning/end of the file | CTRL+HOME or CTRL+Q R / CTRL+END or CTRL+Q C |
| To next error | SHIFT+F3 |
| To previous error | SHIFT+F4 |

| To Scroll: | Press: |
| --- | --- |
| Up/down one line | CTRL+W / CTRL+Z |
| Up/down one window | PGUP or CTRL+R / PGDN or CTRL+C |
| Left/right one window | CTRL+PGUP / CTRL+PGDN |

| To Select Text: | Press: |
| --- | --- |
| Character | SHIFT+LEFT / SHIFT+RIGHT |
| Current line and line above/below | SHIFT+UP / SHIFT+DOWN |
| Word | SHIFT+CTRL+LEFT / SHIFT+CTRL+RIGHT |
| Screen | SHIFT+PGUP / SHIFT+PGDN |
| To beginning/end of the file | SHIFT+CTRL+HOME / SHIFT+CTRL+END. |

| To Insert: | Press: |
| --- | --- |
| Text from the Clipboard (see Section 7.2) | SHIFT+INS |
| Line above the current line | CTRL+N |

**Table 7.1** *(continued)*

| To Insert: | Press: |
| --- | --- |
| Tab at the current cursor position | TAB or CTRL+I |
| Tab at the beginning of each selected line (when one or more lines are selected) | TAB |
| Control character | CTRL+P, followed by CTRL+character |

| To Delete: | Press: |
| --- | --- |
| Character where cursor is resting | DEL or CTRL+G |
| Word | CTRL+T |
| Current line, saving in Clipboard (see Section 7.2) | CTRL+Y |
| To end of line | CTRL+Q Y |
| Selected text | SHIFT+DEL |
| Selected text, not saving in Clipboard | DEL |
| Character left of cursor | BACKSPACE or CTRL+H |

| To Copy: | Press: |
| --- | --- |
| Selected text, saving in Clipboard (see Section 7.2) | CTRL+INS |

| To Tab: | Press: |
| --- | --- |
| All selected text right/left | TAB / SHIFT+TAB |

| To Break a Line: | Press: |
| --- | --- |
| At the current location | ENTER |

## 7.1.2  Using Insert and Overtype Modes

The QuickC editor operates in one of two modes: insert mode or overtype mode. When the editor is in "insert" mode, typed characters are inserted to the left of the cursor. When the editor is in "overtype" mode, typed characters overwrite the characters on the current line.

Use the INS key or the CTRL+V key sequence to toggle the editor between insert mode and overtype mode. When overtype mode is on, the cursor becomes a block.

In insert mode, the editor inserts a typed character at the cursor position. In overtype mode, the editor replaces the character under the cursor with the character you type. Insert mode is the default mode.

### 7.1.3   Using Place Markers in Text

If you are working on different parts of a large file, you can set place markers at different places in the file, then jump to each place marker when you need to work on that part of the file again. You can set up to four place markers, numbered 0 through 3, in any source file. To use place markers:

- Press CTRL+K *n* to set place-marker number *n*.
- Press CTRL+Q *n* to move the cursor to place-marker number *n*.

### 7.1.4   Matching Braces

The QuickC editor provides a simple solution to a common problem in editing C source files: finding the matching left or right brace ({ }), bracket ([ ]), angle bracket (< >), or parenthesis (( )). To find a matching brace, bracket, angle bracket, or parenthesis, follow these steps:

1. Move the cursor to the brace, bracket, angle bracket, or parenthesis you want to match.
2. Press CTRL+] or CTRL+[.

### 7.1.5   Editing with the Mouse

Using the mouse, you can move the cursor and select text quickly, then use the keyboard to perform the desired editing function.

To move the cursor with the mouse, position the mouse pointer where you want the cursor and click the left button.

Table 7.2 describes ways to select text with the mouse.

**Table 7.2**

**Selecting Text with a Mouse**

| To Select: | Do This: |
|---|---|
| A character | Point to the character to the right of the character you want to select, press the left button, and drag the pointer left over the character or characters you want to select. Dragging right selects the character the cursor is on. |
| A word | Double-click the word. |
| A line | Point to the first column of the line, press the left button, drag the highlight down one line and release the button. Dragging up selects the line above the cursor. |
| Several lines | Point to the first line you want to select, then press the left button and drag the highlight up or down through the lines you want to select. |

If you make a mistake while selecting text, click the selected text to cancel the selection.

## 7.2   Editing Commands: the Edit Menu

Figure 7.1 shows the Edit menu. The commands in the Edit menu let you delete, move, or copy text from your program and undo modifications to the current line.

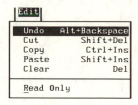

**Figure 7.1  The Edit Menu**

Use the following commands from the Edit menu to edit the contents of your source file:

| Command | Action |
| --- | --- |
| Undo | Reverses any changes to the current line. The shortcut key sequence for this command is ALT+BACKSPACE. |
| Cut | Deletes the selected text and places it in the Clipboard. The "Clipboard" is a temporary storage area that the QuickC editor uses to hold copied or deleted text. The shortcut key for this command is SHIFT+DEL. |
| Copy | Copies the selected text and places it in the Clipboard, leaving the copied text in its original location. The shortcut key sequence for this command is CTRL+INS. |
| Paste | Inserts text from the Clipboard into the file you are editing. The shortcut key sequence for this command is SHIFT+INS. |
| Clear | Removes the selected text but does not put it in the Clipboard. The shortcut key sequence for this command is DEL. |
| Read Only | Places the editor in read-only mode and prevents changes to the current file. |

Sections 7.2.1–7.2.3 describe the Edit menu commands in detail.

## 7.2.1  Undoing Edits: the Undo Command

The Undo command reverses changes to the current line. You can restore a line as long as the cursor is on it. When you move the cursor off the line, the changes are permanent.

Undo is turned off until the current line is modified. When these commands are turned off, no letter is highlighted in the command name on the menu. If you choose Undo while it is turned off, nothing happens.

You cannot use Undo to restore lines deleted with the CTRL+Y key sequence. Use CTRL+Q L or CTRL+INS instead.

## 7.2.2 Deleting and Inserting Text: the Cut, Copy, Paste, and Clear Commands

Use the Cut, Copy, Paste, and Clear commands to move, copy, delete, or insert text in the source file you are editing.

The Cut, Copy, and Clear commands all affect the currently selected text. For various editing tasks, use combinations of the following commands:

- Use the Cut command, along with the Paste command (see below), to move text to a different place in the file. The Cut command deletes the selected text and places it in the Clipboard. The previous contents of the Clipboard are deleted.

- Use the Copy command to copy text to a different place in the file. The Copy command leaves the selected text in place and copies it to the Clipboard. The previous contents of the Clipboard are deleted.

- Use the Clear command to remove text from the file. The Clear command deletes the selected text but does not place it in the Clipboard.

---

*Note*

If you are moving text to a different place in the file, it is safest to use the Paste command immediately after you select Cut or Copy. This will ensure that you don't accidentally remove the text you are moving from the Clipboard.

---

Until text is selected, the Cut, Copy, and Clear commands are turned off; no letter is highlighted in the command name on the menu. If you choose any of these commands while they are turned off, nothing happens.

The Paste command inserts text from the Clipboard. One handy use for this command is to replace text that you have selected in the view window: when you choose Paste, the contents of the the Clipboard replace the selected text. If no text is selected, the Paste command inserts the contents of the Clipboard to the left of the cursor. You can paste the same information from the Clipboard as many times as you want. If no text is in the Clipboard, Paste is turned off.

To insert text from the Clipboard, follow these steps:

1. Move the cursor to the place you want the text inserted. The text is inserted to the left of the cursor. If you want to replace text with the contents of the Clipboard, select the text to be replaced.

2. Choose Paste from the Edit menu.

Text remains in the Clipboard until you end your QuickC session. (The New and Open... commands don't erase the Clipboard.) If you run out of memory during compilation, erase the Clipboard by copying something small into it, such as a single character.

### 7.2.3   Setting Read-Only Mode: the Read Only Command

The Read Only command turns read-only mode on and off. When the editor is in read-only mode, no changes can be made to the currently loaded file; an R appears on the status line and a check mark appears next to the Read Only command on the Edit menu.

This command is useful during debugging. Ordinarily, if you accidentally change the file during debugging, a prompt asks if you want to recompile the program before proceeding with program execution. Selecting the Read Only command prevents you from making such accidental changes to the file.

## 7.3   Searching For and Replacing Text: the Search Menu

Figure 7.2 shows the Search menu. You can find specific parts of your program by using commands from the Search menu.

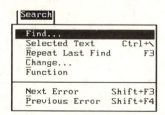

**Figure 7.2  The Search Menu**

The commands in the Search menu perform the following actions:

| Command | Action |
|---------|--------|
| Find... | Finds the first occurrence of the text you specify. The shortcut key sequence for this command is CTRL+\ or CTRL+Q F. |
| Selected Text | Finds text you selected from the view window. The shortcut key sequence for this command is CTRL+\. |
| Repeat Last Find | Finds the next occurrence of the text you specified in a previous search command. The shortcut key for this command is F3; the shortcut key sequence is CTRL+L. |
| Change... | Finds specified text and replaces it with different text. The shortcut key sequence for this command is CTRL+Q A. |
| Function | Finds a specified function during debugging. |
| Next Error | Finds the source line containing the next error. The shortcut key sequence for this command is SHIFT+F3. |
| Previous Error | Finds the source line containing the previous error. The shortcut key sequence for this command is SHIFT+F4. |

Searches begin at the cursor and "wrap around" the top of the view window to the starting point of the search. All the commands on the Search menu search for the text you last specified in a search command, unless you specify otherwise.

The following sections describe the Search menu commands in detail.

## 7.3.1 Finding Text: the Find..., Selected Text, and Repeat Last Find Commands

The QuickC editor provides the following ways to search for text:

- Select the Find... command and specify the text you are searching for.

- Select the text in the view window and search for it using the Selected Text command.

- Search for the next instance of the same text using the Repeat Last Find command.

Sections 7.3.1.1–7.3.1.4 describe these commands.

### 7.3.1.1   The Find... Command

Use the Find... command to search for a character, a word, or groups of characters and words in your program. The shortcut key sequence for this command is CTRL+Q F; in cases where no text is currently selected, another shortcut key sequence is CTRL+\ .

When you choose the Find... command, the Find... dialog box shown in Figure 7.3 opens.

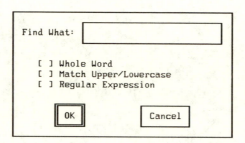

**Figure 7.3  The Find... Dialog Box**

The following list explains the options on the Find... dialog box:

| Option | Use |
| --- | --- |
| Find What | Choose this text box to highlight the text you last searched for. If you are searching for different text, type the text you are searching for. |
| Whole Word | Choose this text box to find the specified text only if it is surrounded by spaces, punctuation marks, or other characters not considered parts of a word. Characters considered as part of a word include uppercase letters ($\mathbf{A}$–$\mathbf{Z}$), lowercase letters ($\mathbf{a}$–$\mathbf{z}$), digits ($\mathbf{0}$–$\mathbf{9}$), and the underscore (_), which is commonly used in variable declarations. For example, if define is the specified text, the Whole Word option will locate #define but not define_terms. |

Match Upper/Lowercase | Choose this check box if you want to find only instances of the specified text that match exactly. For example, if DEFINE is the specified text, the Match Upper/Lowercase option will find DEFINE but not define.

Regular Expression | Choose this check box if you want to use special characters to generalize the text you are searching for. See Section 7.3.1.4, "Special Characters in Regular Expressions," for a list of regular expressions.

OK | Choose this command button to start the search for the next occurrence of the specified text.

Cancel | Choose this command button to cancel the selections in the Find... dialog box and return to the view window.

If the text isn't found, a box appears that says Match Not Found. To remove the box and continue, either press ENTER or SPACEBAR, or click the OK command box with the mouse.

## 7.3.1.2 Finding Selected Text: the Selected Text Command

Another way to search for text in a program is to use the Selected Text command. Instead of typing the text you want to search for, you can simply highlight the text you want to search for in the view window. Follow these steps to use the Selected Text command:

1. Select the text you wish to search for. Selected text must be on a single line.

2. Choose the Selected Text command from the Search menu.

The highlight moves to the next occurrence of the selected text. If no text is selected, this command behaves the same as the Find... command. The shortcut key sequence for Selected Text is CTRL+\ .

## 7.3.1.3 The Repeat Last Find Command

The Repeat Last Find command searches for the text specified in the most recent Find..., Selected Text, or Change command. The shortcut key for Repeat Last Find is F3; the shortcut key sequence is CTRL+L.

### 7.3.1.4  Special Characters in Regular Expressions

If you select the Regular Expressions check box in the Find... dialog box, you can use the the following characters to specify text patterns in searches for text on a line:

| Character | Meaning |
|-----------|---------|
| Period (.) | Matches any single character. |
| Caret (^) | Matches text that appears at the beginning of a line. |
| Dollar sign ($) | Matches text that appears at the end of a line. The dollar sign must appear at the end of the text being searched for. |
| Asterisk (*) | Matches zero or more repetitions of the character preceding the asterisk. For example, _* finds any sequence of one or more underscores. |
| Brackets ([ ]) | Matches sets of the characters specified within the brackets. To match a right-bracket character, type it immediately after the left bracket that delimits the set of characters. The following special characters may be used inside brackets: |

| Character | Use |
|-----------|-----|
| Caret (^) | Matches any character *except* those specified within the brackets. Must be the first character within brackets to be treated as a special character. |
| Dash (–) | Matches characters in ASCII order between the characters on either side of the dash, including the delimiting characters. |

| Character | Meaning |
|-----------|---------|
| Backslash (\) | Characters preceded by a backslash lose their special meanings and are treated literally. For example, to match a dollar sign instead of using the dollar sign to represent the end of the line, type \$. |

Note that using special characters in search text uses additional memory.

■   **Examples**

The following examples illustrate the uses of special characters in regular expressions:

```
I*J
```

```
I\*J
```

In the example above, the first regular expression matches such combinations as `IJ`, `IIJ`, and `IIIJ`. The second regular expression matches only `I*J`. The backslash is necessary because the asterisk (`*`) is a special character in regular expressions.

```
x[-+/*]y
```

In the example above, the regular expression matches `x+y`, `x-y`, `x/y`, or `x*y`, but not `x=y` or `xzy`.

```
[A-Za-z ]
```

The regular expression above matches any uppercase letter, lowercase letter, or space.

```
[^0-9]
```

The regular expression above matches any character other than a digit.

```
[]#![@%]
```

The regular expression above matches either a left or a right bracket, or any of the other characters delimited by the first left bracket and the last right bracket. The first right bracket is not treated as a special character, since it appears immediately after the initial left bracket.

```
\[[0-9]*\]
```

The regular expression above matches strings of numbers that appear within brackets.

## 7.3.2 Replacing Text:
## the Change... Command

Use the Change... command to search for text and replace it with
different text. The shortcut key sequence for this command is CTRL+Q A.
When you choose the Change... command, the dialog box shown in Figure
7.4 opens.

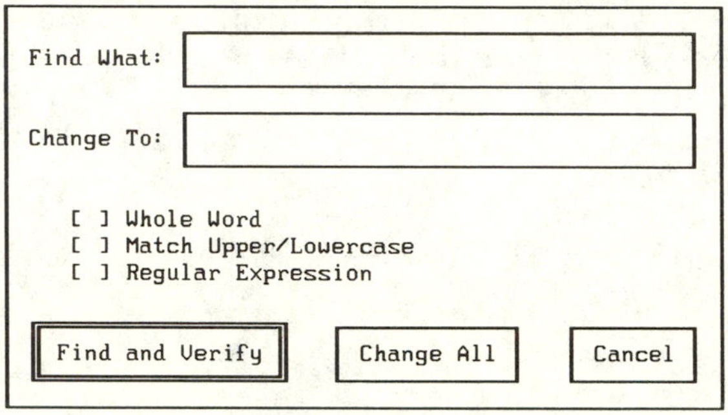

```
┌───────────────────────────────────────────────────┐
│                                                    │
│   Find What:  ┌─────────────────────────────────┐  │
│               │                                 │  │
│               └─────────────────────────────────┘  │
│                                                    │
│   Change To:  ┌─────────────────────────────────┐  │
│               │                                 │  │
│               └─────────────────────────────────┘  │
│                                                    │
│                                                    │
│          [ ] Whole Word                            │
│          [ ] Match Upper/Lowercase                 │
│          [ ] Regular Expression                    │
│                                                    │
│   ┌─────────────────┐  ┌──────────────┐  ┌────────┐│
│   │ Find and Verify │  │  Change All  │  │ Cancel ││
│   └─────────────────┘  └──────────────┘  └────────┘│
└───────────────────────────────────────────────────┘
```

**Figure 7.4  The Change... Dialog Box**

The Find What, Whole Word, Match Upper/Lowercase, Regular Expression, and Cancel options have the same uses as they have in the Find...
command; see Section 7.3.1.1, "The Find... Command," and Section
7.3.1.4, "Special Characters in Regular Expressions," for details. The following list describes the remaining options in the Change... dialog box:

| Option | Use |
|---|---|
| Change To | Type the replacement text in this text box. |
| Find and Verify | Select this command button if you want to confirm each change before the QuickC editor makes it. When you select this command button, the editor finds the text, then displays three more command buttons: Change, Skip, and Cancel. These command buttons are shown below: |

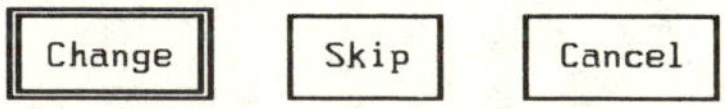

```
┌──────────┐   ┌────────┐   ┌──────────┐
│  Change  │   │  Skip  │   │  Cancel  │
└──────────┘   └────────┘   └──────────┘
```

Select the Change command button to make the change; select the Skip command button to leave the text as it is and search for the next occurrence of the specified text; or select the Cancel command button to stop the search and return to the view window.

Change All                    Select this command button if you want to replace all occurrences of the specified text without having to confirm each change.

---

*Note*

If you use the Change command to change text, you cannot undo your changes with the Undo command from the Edit menu.

---

### 7.3.3  Finding Functions: the Function Command

The Function command finds the entry point of a given function in the file you are editing. Before you use this command, compile the current source file with the Debug option selected.

When you choose the Function command, the dialog box shown in Figure 7.5 appears.

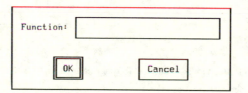

**Figure 7.5  The Function Dialog Box**

Type the function name in the Function text box. If you have selected a function name, that name automatically appears in the text box. Then select the OK command button to find that function, or select the Cancel command button to cancel the command.

## 7.3.4 Finding Program Errors: the Next Error and Previous Error Commands

Use the Next Error and Previous Error commands to quickly find and correct syntax errors in your programs. The shortcut key sequence for Next Error is SHIFT+F3; the shortcut key sequence for Previous Error is SHIFT+F4.

If your program has compilation errors, QuickC creates a list of these errors in order of appearance and opens a window at the bottom of the screen to display the errors. For each error that it displays, QuickC indicates how many errors are in the list and where the error falls in the list. For example, if a program has generated six errors and the fourth error is being displayed, the message (4 of 6) appears after the error message.

If you choose Next Error while QuickC is displaying the last error in the list, a beep indicates that it is at the end of the list. If you choose Next Error a second time, QuickC displays the first error in the list. Similarly, if you choose Previous Error while QuickC is displaying the first error in the list, a beep indicates that it is at the beginning of the list. If you choose Previous Error a second time, QuickC displays the last error in the list.

The Next Error command moves the cursor to the line in the program that caused the next error in the list and displays the corresponding error message in the error window. Similarly, the Previous Error command moves the cursor to the line that caused the previous error in the list and displays the previous error message. If the error occurred in an include file, the QuickC editor displays the include file and moves the cursor to the line in the include file that caused the error.

---

*Note*

Error messages may appear without text if there is insufficient memory to load the error-message text.

---

The QuickC compiler saves the first 26 errors during compilation. Thus, you may still get errors after you have corrected all of the errors that QuickC displays for a single compilation.

See Appendix D of this manual for lists and descriptions of QuickC error messages.

# CHAPTER 8

## COMPILING, RUNNING, AND DEBUGGING PROGRAMS

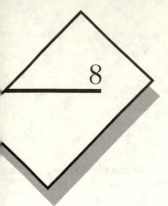

The compiler and debugger included with Microsoft QuickC provide powerful, flexible development tools that will help you get programs up and running—fast. This chapter will show you how to

- Compile and execute QuickC programs
- Choose compile-time and run-time options for programs
- Create object and executable files on disk
- Control program execution during debugging

# 8.1  Compiling and Running Programs: the Run Menu

You compile and execute programs with commands from the Run menu, shown in Figure 8.1.

**Figure 8.1  The Run Menu**

The commands in the Run menu perform the following actions:

| Command | Action |
| --- | --- |
| Start | Compiles and runs the program currently being edited or defined by the current program list. The shortest key sequence for this command is SHIFT+F5. |
| Restart | Resets the program so that the first statement in the **main** program is the next statement to be executed. |
| Continue | Resumes execution of a stopped program. If you have edited the program, this command allows you to recompile it before resuming execution. The shortcut key for this command is F5. |

| Compile... | Sets compile-time options for the program, compiles the program, and creates either a program that can be run within the QuickC environment or an object or executable file on disk. |
| Set Runtime Options... | Sets run-time options for the program including stack size, default-data-segment size, and values to be passed to the program through the *argv* and *argc* arguments to the **main** function. |

Sections 8.1.1–8.1.5 describe the commands on the Run menu.

## 8.1.1  Running Programs: the Start Command

The Start command runs the program you are editing or the program defined by the program list, beginnning with the first statement in the **main** program. If you have changed any modules since the last time you compiled the program, this command automatically recompiles these modules and recreates the program.

## 8.1.2  Getting Programs Ready to Rerun: the Restart Command

The Restart command resets the program so that the first statement in the **main** program is the next statement to be executed. This command is useful if you want to restart program execution after any of the following:

- You have been single-stepping through the program during debugging. (See Section 8.2.2 for information about the QuickC commands that perform single-stepping.)

- The program has temporarily stopped at a breakpoint. (See Section 8.2.1.2 for information about breakpoints).

- The program has completed execution normally.

After a Restart command, the next Start or Continue command executes the first statement in the **main** program. A Restart command does not actually start program execution.

During debugging, use this command after you have edited the program to correct errors and then recompiled.

### 8.1.3 Continuing Program Execution: the Continue Command

The Continue command resumes execution of a stopped program, beginning with the statement following the most recently executed statement. Use this command after executing a statement during single-stepping or after the program has stopped for a breakpoint.

If you have changed the program, QuickC automatically recompiles the program before continuing execution.

### 8.1.4 Controlling Compile-Time Options: the Compile... Command

The Compile... command compiles the source file in the view window or the modules in the current program list. Use the options of this command to control how the program will behave after it is compiled.

When you select Compile... from the Run menu the dialog box shown in Figure 8.2 opens.

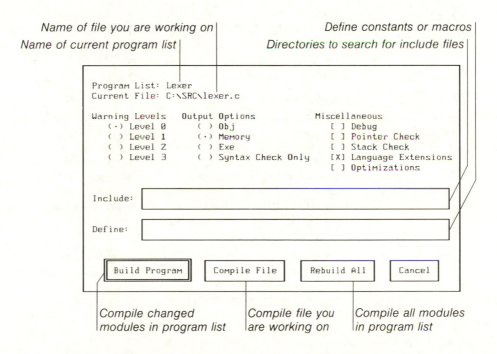

Figure 8.2 The Compile... Dialog Box

Sections 8.1.4.1–8.1.4.10 describe the options of this command and the effects these options have on program behavior.

These options are saved in the **QC.INI** file, so that the default options used at the end of a QuickC session are used as the defaults for the next QuickC session. Also, for multiple-module programs and single-module programs that have a program list, the options used to compile the program are saved in the **.MAK** file that contains the program list. This ensures that these options are used if you rebuild the program within the QuickC environment or use the **MAKE** utility to update the program outside the QuickC environment.

### 8.1.4.1  Suppressing Compiler Warnings: the Warning Levels Options

Choose one of the Warning Levels circular buttons to suppress compiler warning messages. Compiler warning messages are any messages beginning with the prefix C4; see Section D.1.3 for a full listing of these messages. Warnings indicate potential problems, rather than actual errors.

The Warning Levels options have the following effects:

| Option | Effect |
| --- | --- |
| Level 0 | Turns off all warning messages. This option is useful when you compile programs that deliberately include questionable statements. |
| Level 1 | Causes the compiler to display most warning messages. This option is the default. |
| Level 2 | Causes the compiler to display an intermediate level of warning messages. These warnings may or may not indicate serious problems. They are generated when, for example, functions do not have a declared return type; **return** statements are missing from functions with non-**void** return types; and data conversions occur that would cause loss of data or precision. |
| Level 3 | Displays the highest level of warning messages, including warnings about using non-ANSI features and extended keywords, and calling functions before function prototypes appear in the program. |

Note that the descriptions of the warning messages in Appendix D, "Error-Message Reference," indicate the warning level that must be set (that is, the number for the appropriate Warning Levels option) in order for the message to appear.

### 8.1.4.2 Choosing Output-File Format: Output Options

Choose one of the Output Options circular buttons to specify what kind of file is created when you compile the source file you are editing or the modules in the current program list. The following list describes these options:

| Option | Use |
| --- | --- |
| Obj | Creates an object file on disk with the same base name as the source file you are editing plus the extension **.OBJ**. |
| Memory | Creates a program that can be run within the QuickC environment. If you do not choose one of the output options, Memory is the default. |
| Exe | Creates an executable file on disk with the same base name as the current program plus the extension **.EXE**. This executable file cannot be run under QuickC, but it can be run, like any other program, from the DOS command level. |
| Syntax Check Only | Checks the syntax of the program and displays diagnostic messages for any errors found, but does not create an object or executable file. |

### 8.1.4.3 Preparing for Debugging: the Debug Option

Choose the Debug check box if you want to debug your program within QuickC. The Debug option produces a program containing full symbolic-debugging information for use with in-memory debugging.

If you choose this option and then choose the Build Program or Rebuild All command button (Section 8.1.4.10), the linker creates a map file on disk containing the debugging information. This file has the same base name as the program and the extension **.MAP**. See Section 9.5.10 for information about map files and their formats.

If you choose the Exe output option with the Debug option, the executable file you create is suitable for debugging using the Microsoft® CodeView® window-oriented debugger.

### 8.1.4.4 Using "Smart Pointers": the Pointer Check Option

The Pointer Check check box protects your program from common pointer errors that do not otherwise cause run-time errors. When you choose Pointer Check, the QuickC compiler generates run-time code that verifies that pointer values address program data before the pointers are used. If not, QuickC displays a run-time error in the error window.

Pointer checking can prevent errors that might overwrite QuickC or DOS code or data and cause QuickC or DOS to stop running. As a result, the use of this option is strongly recommended during program development.

Note that the Pointer Check option may significantly slow program execution. An alternative to using Pointer Check is to turn pointer checking on or off only for selected pointers, leaving the default (see below) for the remaining pointers in the module. When you want to turn on pointer checking, put the following line before the declaration of the pointer you want to check:

**# pragma check_ pointer (on)**

This line turns on pointer checking for all pointers that follow it in the source file, not just the pointers on the following line. To turn off pointer checking, insert the following line:

**# pragma check_ pointer (off)**

If no argument is given for the **check_ pointer** pragma, pointer checking reverts to the behavior specified by the Pointer Check option: turned on if the Pointer Check option is turned on, or turned off otherwise. The interaction of the **check_ pointer** pragma with the Pointer Check option is explained in greater detail in Table 8.1.

Table 8.1

Using the check_ pointer Pragma

| Syntax | Compiled with Pointer Check? | Action |
|---|---|---|
| # pragma check_ pointer() | Yes | Turns on checking for pointers that follow |
| # pragma check_ pointer() | No | Turns off checking for pointers that follow |
| # pragma check_ pointer(on) | Yes or no | Turns on pointer checking for pointers that follow |
| # pragma check_ pointer(off) | Yes or no | Turns off pointer checking for pointers that follow |

### 8.1.4.5 Checking for Stack Overflow: the Stack Check Option

Choose the Stack Check check box if you want QuickC to verify that your program has enough stack space at run time and to return a diagnostic message if it does not.

Stack checking is performed by routines known as "stack probes." A stack probe is called on entry to a function to verify that there is enough room in the program stack to allocate local variables required by the function. The stack probe is called at every function entry point. It generates a stack-overflow message if it finds that the required stack space is not available. Since stack checking can catch errors that otherwise might halt the operation of QuickC or DOS, the use of Stack Check during program development is strongly recommended.

When stack checking is turned off, stack-probe routines are not called, and stack overflow may occur without being diagnosed (that is, no error message is displayed). However, programs that do not include the stack-checking code are smaller and faster than programs that do.

Use the **check_stack** pragma when you want to turn stack checking on or off for selected routines only, leaving the default (see below) for the remaining routines in the module. When you want to turn on stack checking, put the following line before the definition of the function that you want to check:

# pragma check_ stack (on)

This line turns on stack checking for all routines that follow it in the source file, not just for the routines on the following line. To turn off stack checking, insert the following line:

# pragma check_ stack (off)

If no argument is given for the **check_stack** pragma, stack checking reverts to the behavior specified by the Stack Check option line: turned on if the Stack Check option is turned on, or turned off otherwise. The interaction of the **check_stack** pragma with the Stack Check option is explained in greater detail in Table 8.2.

**Table 8.2**

**Using the check_stack Pragma**

| Syntax | Compiled with Stack Check? | Action |
|---|---|---|
| # pragma check_ stack() | Yes | Turns on stack checking for routines that follow |
| # pragma check_ stack() | No | Turns off stack checking for routines that follow |
| # pragma check_ stack(on) | Yes or no | Turns on stack checking for routines that follow |
| # pragma check_ stack(off) | Yes or no | Turns off stack checking for routines that follow |

It is a good practice to choose the Stack Check option unless you are sure that your program does not exceed the available stack space. For example, you may not need this option for programs that make very few function calls, that have only modest local variable requirements, or that do no recursion.

### 8.1.4.6 Using Microsoft Extensions to C: the Language Extensions Option

Choose the Language Extensions check box if you want to use the extensions to the ANSI C standard that are offered in the Microsoft QuickC Compiler. These extensions include the following:

- The **cdecl**, **far**, **fortran**, **near**, and **pascal** keywords

- Use of casts to produce lvalues, as in the following example:

```
int *p;
((long *)p)++;
```

- Use of the trailing comma (,) rather than a comma followed by ellipsis dots (,...) in function declarations to indicate variable-length argument lists, such as

```
int printf(char *,);
```

- Benign **typedef** redefinitions within the same scope, as in the following example:

```
typedef int INT;
typedef int INT;
```

- Use of mixed character and string constants in an initializer, such as those in the code below:

```
char arr[6] = {'a', 'b', "cde"};
```

- Use of bit fields with base types other than **unsigned int** or **signed int**

---

*Note*

The **far** keyword cannot be used to declare data items for in-memory programs, even if the Language Extensions option is selected. However, it can be used to declare pointers to data items.

---

Do not choose the Language Extensions option if you will be compiling with compilers that do not recognize Microsoft's extensions to the C language. Turning Language Extensions off causes extended keywords to be treated as simple identifiers and the other extensions listed above to be considered as illegal constructions.

When language extensions are disabled, the compiler automatically defines the identifier **NO_EXT_KEYS**. In the include files provided with the run-time library, this identifier is used with #**ifndef** preprocessor directives to control use of the **cdecl** keyword in library-function prototypes. For an example of this conditional compilation, see the include file named **stdio.h**.

### 8.1.4.7 Creating Faster Programs: the Optimizations Option

Choose this check box to optimize your program for execution speed. The optimizations performed include constant folding, auto-enregistering, and automatic generation of 80286 instructions.

Programs compiled with this option may be slightly larger than programs compiled without it, but they execute faster.

### 8.1.4.8 Searching for Include Files: the Include Text Box

If you want to search for include files in directories other than those given in the **INCLUDE** environment variable, type one or more search paths separated by commas (,) in the Include text box. The compiler searches the directory or directories you type, in the order you type them, before it searches the standard places given in the **INCLUDE** environment variable. The directories are searched in the order you give them.

If QuickC cannot find an include file in the directories you type in the text box or in the directories given by the **INCLUDE** variable, the compiler displays an error message and stops processing. In this case, you must recompile the program and tell QuickC where to find the missing include file, using either the **INCLUDE** variable or the Include text box.

### 8.1.4.9 Defining Constants and Macros: the Define Text Box

Use the Define text box to define a constant or macro for your source file. Type one or more constant or macro definitions of the following form, separated by commas (,):

*identifier=string*

In each definition, *identifier* is the name of the constant or macro and *string* is its value or meaning. If you leave out both the equal sign and *string*, the given constant or macro is assumed to be defined, and its value is set to 1. For example, SET is sufficient to define a macro named SET with a value of 1.

The Define option is especially useful if you use it with #**if** and #**ifdef** directives to perform conditional compilation of source files.

If you give the equal sign with an empty string, the given constant or macro is considered defined, and its definition is the empty string. Such a definition effectively removes all occurrences of the identifier from the source file. For example, to remove all occurrences of REGISTER, use the following option:

```
REGISTER=
```

Note that the identifier register is still considered to be defined, since case is significant in names.

Typing macro and constant definitions in the Define text box has the same effect as using a **#define** preprocessor directive at the beginning of your source file or a **/D** option on the **QCL** command line. The identifier is defined in the source file being compiled until either an **#undef** directive removes the definition or the end of the file is reached.

If an identifier defined in the Define text box is also defined within the source file, the definition given in the text box is used until the identifier is redefined in the source file.

■ **Example**

```
#if !defined(RELEASE)
        _nheapchk();
#endif
```

This example calls a function to check the near heap unless the constant RELEASE is defined. While the program is under development, you can leave RELEASE undefined and perform heap checking to find bugs. Then, when you have found all of the bugs in the program, define RELEASE so that the program will run faster.

### 8.1.4.10  Compile Command Buttons

The command buttons on the Compile dialog box tell QuickC whether to compile the source file you are editing or the modules in the current program list. Select any of the following command buttons:

| Command Button | Use |
| --- | --- |
| Build Program | Recompiles all modules in the current program list that have been changed since the last time you rebuilt the program, then rebuilds the program. See Section 6.1.4 for a detailed description of this procedure. The resulting object files, linker-response file, executable file, and (if the Debug option is turned on) map file are saved on disk. If no program list is present, compiles the source file you are currently editing. |

| | |
|---|---|
| Compile File | Compiles the source file you are currently editing. |
| Rebuild All | Recompiles all modules in the current program list, whether or not they have been changed since the last time you rebuilt the program, then rebuilds the program. See Section 6.1.4 for a detailed description of this procedure. The resulting object files, linker-response file, executable file, and (if the Debug option is turned on) map file are saved on disk. If no program list is present, compiles the source file you are currently editing. |
| Cancel | Cancels compilation and returns you to the view window. |

## 8.1.5   Controlling Run-Time Options: the Set Runtime Options... Command

The Set Runtime Options... command controls various aspects of a program's behavior at run time. These options go into effect the next time the program is started or restarted.

When you select Set Runtime Options... from the File menu the dialog box shown in Figure 8.3 opens.

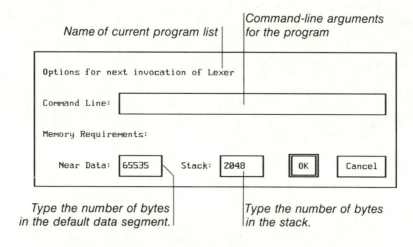

Figure 8.3  The Set Runtime Options... Dialog Box

The following list describes the options in the Set Runtime Options... dialog box:

| Option | Use |
|---|---|
| Command Line | Type the arguments you would type after the program name if you ran the program from the DOS command level. These arguments are passed to the program through the standard *argv* and *argc* arguments to the C **main** function. |
| Near Data | To reduce the amount of memory allocated for the default data segment (64K by default), type the number of bytes, in decimal, to be allocated. The default data segment contains all initialized global and static program data except data explicitly declared with the **far** keyword. You may want to reduce the size of this segment if your program does not use much data that would go in the default segment, but does use a large amount of data (for example, large arrays) that would be allocated in other data segments. See Appendix B, "Working with QuickC Memory Models," for more information about allocation of data. See Appendix C, "Interfacing C with Assembly Language," for more information about the default data segment and the other segments used by the Microsoft QuickC Compiler. |
| Stack | To use a stack size other than the default (2K), type the number of bytes, in decimal, in the Stack text box. The largest stack size you can request is 64K. You may want to increase the stack size if your program gets stack-overflow diagnostic messages. Conversely, if your program uses the stack very little, you may want to decrease the size of your program by reducing the stack size. |

## 8.2  Debugging Programs

The Microsoft QuickC Compiler contains powerful debugging features
that make it easy to isolate errors in program logic. For example, use the
debugger to trace and single-step program execution, set breakpoints, and
examine the values of variables and expressions.

### 8.2.1  General Debugging Procedure

Use the following general procedure to debug a program within the
QuickC programming environment:

1.  Compile the program with the Debug option in the Compile dialog
    box turned on.

2.  Turn on any debugging features such as breakpoints, watch expres-
    sions, or screen swapping by using the keyboard or Debug menu
    commands described in Section 8.2.3.

3.  Run your program by using the keyboard commands described in
    Section 8.2.2 or the Start, Restart, and Continue commands on the
    Run menu. Observe the order in which statements and functions
    are executed, the changes made to watch variables, and the pro-
    gram output.

4.  Edit your program as needed to correct errors you found in step 3.
    Then recompile your program, again choosing the Debug option
    from the Compile menu.

5.  If you need to change any of the debugging information, go back to
    step 2. Otherwise, go back to step 3 and rerun your program.

6.  Repeat steps 3–5 until your program runs correctly.

#### 8.2.1.1  Adding Watch Expressions

When you add a watch expression, QuickC opens a window, known as a
"watch window," at the top of the screen and displays the values of watch
expressions in the window. During program execution, QuickC continu-
ously displays the values of watch expressions, changing them at each
point in the program where the corresponding program variables change.
Unexpected changes in the value of a watch expression may indicate program errors.

Select the Add Watch command from the Debug menu to add a watch
expression. Use the Delete Last Watch command from the Debug menu, or

type SHIFT+F2, to delete the last-added watch expression. Use these commands together to view the values of local variables while tracing through the functions in which these variables are defined, then delete the watch expressions for these variables after exiting the function.

Select the Delete All Watch command from the Debug menu to delete *all* watch expressions.

### 8.2.1.2  Setting Breakpoints

"Breakpoints" are set at particular lines in the program. Setting a breakpoint tells QuickC to stop program execution temporarily at that line in the program. Breakpoints are often used in conjunction with watch expressions: set breakpoints at lines in the program where you suspect bugs, then check the watch expressions at these points for unexpected values.

To toggle a breakpoint on or off, move the cursor to the line where you want to toggle the breakpoint. Then either press F9 or select the Toggle Breakpoint command from the Debug menu. To delete *all* breakpoints, select the Clear All Breakpoints command from the Debug menu. (See Section 8.2.3.5, "Controlling Breakpoints," for more information on the Clear All Breakpoints command.)

## 8.2.2  Debugging Keyboard Commands

QuickC provides the following single-keystroke debugging commands:

| Command To: | Key |
| --- | --- |
| Execute the next program statement; trace through function | F8 |
| Execute the next program statement; trace around function | F10 |
| Execute the program to the current cursor position | F7 |
| Display the output screen | F4 |

To execute the program to the line where the mouse pointer is pointing, click that line with the right-hand mouse button.

## 8.2.3  Debugging Commands: the Debug Menu

Figure 8.4 shows the Debug menu.

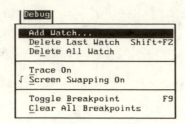

**Figure 8.4  The Debug Menu**

The commands in the Debug menu perform the following actions:

| Command | Action |
|---|---|
| Add Watch... | Adds one or more new watch expressions to the watch window. |
| Delete Last Watch | Deletes the most recently added watch expression from the watch window. The shortcut key sequence for this command is SHIFT+F2. |
| Delete All Watch | Deletes all watch variables from the watch window. |
| Trace On | Toggles program tracing on or off. |
| Screen Swapping On | Toggles screen swapping on or off. |
| Toggle Breakpoint | Turns a breakpoint on or off on the line where the cursor is resting. The shortcut key for this command is F9. |
| Clear All Breakpoints | Clears all breakpoints from the current program. |

Sections 8.2.3.1–8.2.3.5 describe the commands on the Debug menu.

### 8.2.3.1  Adding Watch Expressions: the Add Watch... Command

Use the Add Watch... command to add one or more watch variables to the watch window at the top of the view window.

When you choose Add Watch... from the Debug menu, the dialog box shown in Figure 8.5 opens.

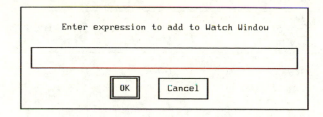

**Figure 8.5  The Add Watch... Dialog Box**

Type one or more watch expressions in the text box. If you type more than one expression, type a semicolon at the end of each expression.

A watch expression may be any of the following:

- A variable

- A C expression consisting of variables combined with parentheses (( )), brackets ([ ]), the structure-member operator (.), the structure-pointer operator (−>), or the indirection operator (∗)

- An entire structure or array

Note that math operators are not allowed in watch expressions.

To display the value of a watch variable using a different output format, type a comma, followed by a format character, after the watch-variable name. Table 8.3 lists these format characters, along with examples of output that would appear for sample values stored in memory.

**Table 8.3**

**Format Specifiers for Watch Variables**

| Character | Output Format | Watch Value | Displayed Value |
|---|---|---|---|
| d | Signed decimal integer | 40000 | 40000 |
| i | Signed decimal integer | 40000 | 40000 |
| u | Unsigned decimal integer | 40000 | 40000 |
| o | Unsigned octal integer | 40000 | 116100 |

## Table 8.3 (continued)

| Character | Output Format | Watch Value | Displayed Value |
|---|---|---|---|
| x | Hexadecimal integer | 40000 | 9c40 |
| f | Signed value in floating-point decimal format with six decimal places | 3./2. | 1.500000 |
| e | Signed value in scientific-notation format with up to six decimal places (trailing zeros and decimal point are truncated) | 3./2. | 1.500000e+000 |
| g | Signed value with floating-point decimal format (**f**) or scientific-notation format (**e**), whichever is more compact | 3./2. | 1.5 |
| c | Single character | 65 | A |
| s | Characters printed up to the first null character | "String" | String |

If no format specifier is given, the QuickC debugger uses the default format specifier for the type of the watch variable. For structures, each field is displayed with the default format specifier for the field type. Single- and double-precision real numbers are displayed by using the **g** format specifier.

The prefix **h** can be used with the integer format specifiers (**d**, **o**, **u**, and **x**) to specify a two-byte integer. The prefix **l** can be used with the same types to specify a four-byte integer. For example, if the value of a watch variable is 100,000, the  ld  specifier produces the output  100000. However, the  hd  specifier evaluates only the low-order two bytes, producing the output  -31072.

Format specifiers for watch variables work the same way as format specifiers for the **printf** families of library functions. As a result, specifying a watch variable of one type and a format specifier of a different type does *not* implicitly cast the watch variable to the type of the format specifier. Instead, the bit pattern at the memory location represented by the watch variable appears as if it represented an item of the same type as the format specifier. For example, if a variable of type **int** has the value 4, and if you display it with the **f** format specifier, the displayed value will be "0.00000" rather than "4.00000." This value is displayed because, in floating-point format, the bit pattern "00000100" format represents a number with such a small exponent that the number is effectively 0.

You are not restricted to viewing the contents of a watch variable. If you type more than one format character after a watch-variable name, each format character represents a memory location *after* the location of the watch variable. The QuickC debugger displays the value stored at each of these memory locations, using the format given by the format character.

After you type the watch expressions in the text box, choose the OK command button to add these expressions to a watch window or the Cancel command button to cancel the Add Watch... command.

Note that a watch expression is undefined if it is not defined for the function currently being executed (that is, if it is out of scope).

■ **Examples**

```
watchvar,f
```

The example above displays the value of the watch variable `watchvar` in floating-point decimal format with six decimal places.

```
watchvar,dulx10c
```

This second example displays the value of the watch variable `watchvar` in signed-decimal format. The values of the twelve memory locations following the address of `watchvar` are also displayed, in the formats shown below:

- An unsigned decimal number
- A long hexadecimal number
- Ten characters

### 8.2.3.2 Deleting Watch Variables: the Delete Last Watch/All Watch Commands

The Delete Last Watch command deletes the most recently added watch expression from the watch window. If you added more than one watch expression with a single Add Watch... command, only the last expression given in the text box is deleted. The shortcut key sequence for this command is SHIFT+F2.

The Delete All Watch command deletes all watch expressions and closes the watch window.

### 8.2.3.3  Controlling Tracing: the Trace On Command

The Trace On command toggles program tracing on or off. A check appears next to this command on the Debug menu when tracing is turned on.

If you choose the Start or Continue command from the Run menu when tracing is turned on, the program executes up to the next breakpoint, highlighting each currently executing statement. If the next executing statement is in another module, that module is displayed in the view window.

When tracing is turned off, the currently executing statement is not highlighted. Execution proceeds immediately to the first breakpoint, which is the first statement that is highlighted.

### 8.2.3.4  Controlling Screen Swapping: the Screen Swapping On Command

The Screen Swapping On command toggles screen swapping on or off. A check appears next to this command on the Debug menu when screen swapping is turned on.

If screen swapping is on, the QuickC screen disappears and is replaced by the program-output screen at each step of program execution; consequently, flickering is constant.

If screen swapping is off, the output screen appears only if the program performs an output operation using an output or graphics function. This removes the flickering effect that results from having screen swapping on.

### 8.2.3.5  Controlling Breakpoints: the Toggle Breakpoint and Clear All Breakpoints Commands

The Toggle Breakpoint and Clear All Breakpoints commands control the use of breakpoints during debugging.

The Toggle Breakpoint command turns a breakpoint on or off on the line where the cursor is resting. If a breakpoint is currently set, the command turns the breakpoint off; if a breakpoint is not set, the command sets one. The shortcut key for this command is F9.

Lines where breakpoints are set have the colors and other attributes given by the Breakpoint Lines option in the Options... dialog box from the View menu.

The Clear All Breakpoints command removes all breakpoints from the program being debugged.

## 8.2.4 Tracing Between Functions: the Calls Menu

Selecting the Calls menu displays a list of the functions that have been called. You can use the list to display a function. You can also use the list to execute a program up to a particular function.

For example, selecting the Calls menu while the CFLOW.C program is running might produce the display shown in Figure 8.6.

**Figure 8.6  The Calls List Display**

When the Calls list is displayed, you can use the mouse or the DIRECTION keys and the ENTER key to select one of the functions. QuickC displays the function and places the cursor on the next statement that will be executed when control returns to the calling function.

If you have accidentally traced into a function and want to get out of that function immediately, follow these steps:

1. Open the Calls menu.

2. Use the UP and DOWN keys to highlight the name of the function from which you called the function you are tracing through, and press ENTER.

3. Press F7.

The QuickC debugger returns you to the point immediately after the point from which you called the function.

# PART 3

# THE QUICKC TOOL KIT

# PART 3

◇ THE QUICKC TOOL KIT

The Microsoft QuickC Compiler is not just an integrated programming environment; it also includes several powerful programming tools that complement the integrated environment. This section shows how to use these tools, which include

- The **QCL** compiler driver, which creates object and executable files on disk from C source files
- The **LINK** overlay linker, which combines object files and stand-alone libraries into executable files or Quick libraries
- The **LIB** library manager, which combines object files into stand-alone libraries
- The **MAKE** program-maintenance utility, which automatically updates programs whenever a program module is updated

# CHAPTER 9

# COMPILING AND LINKING PROGRAMS

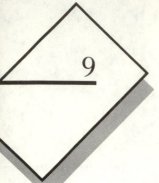

Once you have mastered the QuickC programming environment, you can gain extra control over how programs will work by compiling and linking them outside the environment. You might want to do this for any of the following reasons:

- To create source programs using your own editor

- To compile programs that cannot be compiled within the QuickC programming environment

- To use different memory models in the programs that you create

- To change the default naming or function-calling conventions for your programs

- To generate specialized instructions for an 80286 processor when you compile your program

- To create listings showing output from the C preprocessor or showing program segments, in order of appearance

The Microsoft QuickC Compiler includes a program named **QCL** that can compile and link programs outside of the QuickC environment. The following chapter shows how to use **QCL** and the Microsoft Overlay Linker, **LINK**. It is organized as shown below:

| Sections | Contents |
| --- | --- |
| 9.1–9.1.2 | Describe the compiling and linking process. Read this section if you are new to Microsoft language products; otherwise, turn to Section 9.2. |
| 9.2–9.3 | Explain how to compile and link programs using a single **QCL** command line and describe files and options you can give as input to the **QCL** command. |
| 9.4–9.7 | Explain how to compile and link in two steps: by compiling with **QCL**, then linking with **LINK**. These sections describe information that **QCL** passes to **LINK** and list files and options you can give as input to the **LINK** command. |

# 9.1   The Compiling and Linking Process

The following procedure is used to create a stand-alone program from a C source file outside of the QuickC programming environment:

1. Each source file in the program is compiled, creating an object file.

2.  The object files are linked with one or more stand-alone libraries (libraries with **.LIB** extensions) to form an executable file. The linker resolves external references in the object files before it creates the executable file. (That is, it makes sure that all function calls in the object files match up with functions in the libraries or with functions in other object files.)

Sections 9.1.1 and 9.1.2 describe two methods that you can use to compile and link programs. Figure 9.1 illustrates these methods.

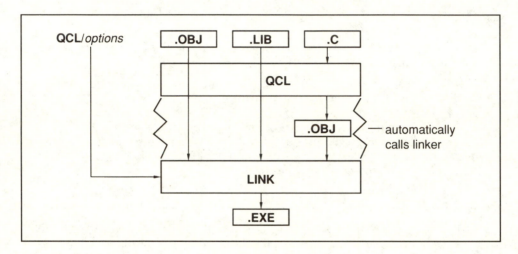

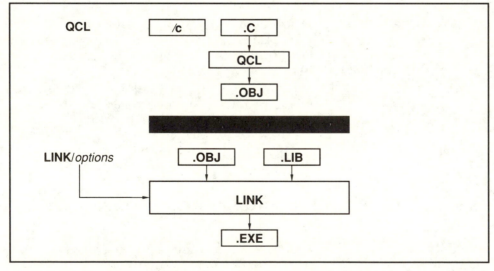

**Figure 9.1  Compiling and Linking Programs**

### 9.1.1  Using a Single QCL Command Line

You can compile and link programs using a single **QCL** command line. Specifically, the same command line can be used to specify source files to be compiled, object files and libraries to be linked, and options that control the compiler and linker. **QCL** compiles any source files you specify, then passes any object-file names, library names, and linker options to the linker, which then links the object files and libraries to produce an executable file.

### 9.1.2  Using the QCL and LINK Commands

As an alternative, you can compile first with **QCL** and the **/c** option, then use the **LINK** command to invoke the linker explicitly. The advantage of using this method is that you do not need to use a single command line to give the linker all the information it needs; the **LINK** command prompts you for any information that you do not give. See Sections 9.4.2.1–9.4.2.4 for instructions for using the **LINK** command.

## 9.2  One-Step Compiling and Linking: the QCL Command

To compile and link with the **QCL** command, your DOS environment should be set up as summarized below. For a full description, see Section 1.3.1.6 (for hard-disk users) or Section 1.3.2.4 (for floppy-disk users).

- If you are using a hard-disk system, use the DOS **CD** command to make the directory with your source file the current directory.

- If you are using a floppy-disk system, insert the disk containing your source program in drive B and your copy of the Product distribution disk in drive A. Make drive B the current drive. When you run **QCL**, type the drive name A: immediately before the **QCL** command, with no intervening spaces. During the compiling/linking process, you will be prompted to swap in drive A your working copy of the Work distribution disk and the disk containing the appropriate stand-alone library.

The **QCL** command has the following format:

**QCL** [[*option*]]... *file*... [[*option*|*file*]]... [[**/link** [[*lib*... *link-opt*...]]]]

The information you enter on the **QCL** command line is explained in the following list:

| Entry | Meaning |
| --- | --- |
| *option* | A **QCL** option; see Sections 9.3.1–9.3.13 for descriptions. For a quick overview of the commonly used options, type<br><br>QCL /HELP<br><br>and press ENTER. |
| *file* | The name of a source or object file that you want to process, or the name of a library that you want to pass to the linker for processing. You must give at least one file name. See Sections 9.2.1.1–9.2.1.3 for information about specifying file names to the **QCL** command. |
| *lib* | The name of a stand-alone library that you want to pass to the linker for processing. See Section 9.4.2.3 for more information about specifying stand-alone libraries. |
| *link-opt* | One or more of the linker options described in Sections 9.5.1–9.5.14; the **QCL** command passes these options to the linker for processing. Ordinarily, you do not need to give linker options unless you want the linker to perform a special operation such as linking with a specified library, changing the program stack size, creating a map file, or including debugging information in the executable file. |

You can give any number of options, file names, and stand-alone-library names on the **QCL** command line, as long as the command line does not exceed 128 characters.

## 9.2.1  Specifying File Names

The **QCL** command makes certain assumptions about the files you specify, based on the path names and extensions you use for the files. The following sections describe these assumptions and other rules you should follow in specifying file names to **QCL**.

### 9.2.1.1  Uppercase and Lowercase Letters

You can use any combination of uppercase and lowercase letters for file names, just as in DOS. (Note that **QCL** options *are* case sensitive.)

## 9.2.1.2   File-Name Extensions

A DOS file name has two parts: the "base name," which includes every-thing before the period (.); and the "extension," which includes the period and up to three characters following the period. The extension identifies the type of the file.

The **QCL** command uses the extension of each file name to determine how to process the corresponding file, as explained in the following list:

| Extension | Processing |
|---|---|
| .C | **QCL** assumes the file is a C source file and compiles it |
| .OBJ | **QCL** assumes the file is an object file and passes it to the linker for linking |
| .LIB | **QCL** assumes the file is a stand-alone library and passes it to the linker for linking with the generated object files and the object files given on the command line |
| Any other extension or no extension | **QCL** assumes the file is an object file and passes it to the linker for linking |

■   **Example**

The command line

```
QCL A.C B.C C.OBJ D
```

compiles the files A.C and B.C, creating object files named A.OBJ and B.OBJ. These object files are then linked with C.OBJ and D.OBJ to form an executable file named A.EXE (since the base name of the first file on the command line is A). Note that the extension .OBJ is assumed for D since no extension is given on the command line.

## 9.2.1.3   Path Names

Any file name can include a full or partial path name. A full path name starts with the drive name; a partial path name has one or more directory names before the file name, but does not include a drive name.

Giving a path name allows you to specify files in different paths as input to **QCL** and allows you to create files on different drives or in different directories on the current drive.

For output files (such as object or executable files) that you create with **QCL**, you can give a path name ending in a backslash (\) to create the file in that path. When it creates the file, **QCL** uses the default name for the file.

If you do not give a full or partial path name, **QCL** assumes that the source and object files you specify are in the current working directory, where it creates all output files.

## 9.3 Controlling Compilation with QCL Options

Options to the **QCL** command consist of either a forward slash (/) or a dash (−) followed by one or more letters. (In this manual, forward slashes are used for options, although in error messages dashes are used.)

---

*Important*

> **QCL** options are case sensitive. For example, /**W** and /**w** are two different options.

---

Options can appear anywhere on the **QCL** command line. Unless otherwise stated, a **QCL** option applies to the files that follow it on the command line and does not affect files preceding it on the command line.

All **QCL** options are compatible with the Microsoft C Optimizing Compiler, Version 5.0.

■ **Common Options in the CL Environment Variable**

If you are recompiling a given set of files more than once, or if you use the same set of options when you compile, the **CL** environment variable can save you from having to retype the files and options on the command line each time you recompile. Use the DOS **SET** command as shown below to define the value of **CL**:

**SET CL**= [[*option|file*]... [[/**link**[*link-libinfo*]]]]

This variable is also useful if you usually give a large number of files and options when you compile: since the files and options that you define with this variable are not counted in the 128-character limit for the command line, you can define the files and options you use most often with the **CL** variable and then give on the command line only the files and options you need for specific purposes.

The information you define with **CL** is treated as if it appeared before the information you give on the **QCL** command line. For example, if you use a command sequence of the form

```
SET CL=/Fm TEST1.C /link LIB1.LIB /PAC
```

```
QCL /Zi TEST2.C /link LIB2.LIB /ST0xC00
```

the effect would be the same as entering

```
QCL /Fm TEST1.C /Zi TEST2.C /link LIB1.LIB /PAC
LIB2.LIB /ST0xC00
```

Note that if you have defined a file or option with **CL**, you generally cannot turn off the definition from the command line. You must reset the **CL** environment variable and omit the file or option that you do not want to use.

Since options defined in the environment are treated as if they appeared before options given on the command line, they affect any files given on the command line. However, you can override the effect of an option defined in the environment by explicitly giving a different option on the command line. In cases where one option is defined in the environment and a conflicting option is given on the command line, the command-line option takes precedence for any files that follow it on the command line.

■   **QCL Options and Object Files**

Most **QCL** options apply only to the compilation process and do not affect object files given on the command line. See Table 9.2 in Section 9.3.2 for a list of the **QCL** options that affect the linking process.

■ **Examples**

```
SET CL=FILE1.C FILE2.C
QCL FILE3.OBJ
```

In the example above, the **CL** environment variable tells the **QCL** command to compile and link the source files FILE1.C and FILE2.C. The **QCL** command

```
QCL FILE1.C FILE2.C FILE3.OBJ
```

would then have the same effect as the first command line.

```
SET CL=/Za
```

```
QCL FILE1.C /Ze FILE2.C
```

The example above illustrates how to turn off the effects of a **CL** option defined in the environment. In this example, the **CL** environment variable is set to the **/Za** option, described in Section 9.3.1, which tells the compiler not to recognize Microsoft extensions to the C language. This option causes Microsoft-specific keywords to be treated as ordinary identifiers rather than reserved words. The **CL** command specifies the inverse option, **/Ze**, which tells the compiler to treat language extensions as reserved words. Since the effect is the same as compiling with the command line

```
QCL /Za FILE1.C /Ze FILE2.C
```

FILE1.C is compiled with language extensions turned off and FILE2.C is compiled with language extensions enabled.

## 9.3.1 Environment Options

A number of **QCL** options have the same effects as options in the Compile dialog box. Table 9.1 shows these **QCL** options, the corresponding Compile options and the sections where these options are discussed, and the effect of each **QCL** option.

**Table 9.1**

**QCL Options and Compile Dialog Box Options**

| QCL Option | Compile Option | Effect |
|---|---|---|
| /c | Obj button on | Creates an object file on disk |
| /D *identifier*[[= [[*string*]]]] | Define text box (8.1.4.9) | Defines symbolic constants or macros. The /D option allows up to 16 definitions if language extensions are turned off (/Za compiler option or Language Extensions circular button in the environment) or up to 17 definitions if they are enabled. |
| /Gs | Stack Check check box off (8.1.4.5) | Disables stack probes |
| /I*directory* | Include text box (8.1.4.8) | Tells the compiler which paths to search for include files. Each /I option specifies a different directory. |
| /Ot | Optimizations check box on (8.1.4.7) | Optimizations favor execution time over code size. |
| /Ox | Optimizations check box on (8.1.4.7) and Stack Check check box off (8.1.4.5) | Performs maximum optimization of programs. This option also turns on loop optimizations; see Section 9.3.13 for more information about loop optimizations. |
| /W[[{ 0|1|2|3} ]] | Warning Level button on (8.1.4.1) | Sets the warning level for warning messages |
| /Za | Language Extensions check box off (8.1.4.6) | Disables Microsoft extensions to the ANSI C standard |

**Table 9.1** *(continued)*

| QCL Option | Compile Option | Effect |
|---|---|---|
| /Zd | Debug check box on (8.1.4.3) | Produces an object file containing line-number records corresponding to the line numbers of the source file. Useful when you want to pass an object file to the **SYMDEB** symbolic debugger. This debugger can use the line numbers to refer to program locations; however, it cannot refer to local symbols in your programs. |
| /Zi | Debug check box on (8.1.4.3) | Puts information needed for debugging in object file; allows file to be used with QuickC debugging or Microsoft CodeView symbolic debugger. To use the program with QuickC debugging, the **/Zi** option must be given with the **/Zd** and **/Zq** options. |
| /Zq | Debug check box on (8.1.4.3) | Generates interrupts needed for QuickC debugging. |
| /Zr | Pointer Check check box on (8.1.4.4) | Checks for null pointers or out-of-range far pointers |
| /Zs | Syntax Check Only button on (8.1.4.2) | Checks program syntax only; does not create an object file |

See Section 8.1.4 for more information about the effects of these options.

## 9.3.2  Options to Control Linking

Several **QCL** options affect the linking process rather than the compilation process. These options have the same effects as prompts, command-line fields, or options of the **LINK** command. Table 9.2 shows these **QCL** options, the corresponding **LINK** features, and their effects.

**Table 9.2**

**QCL and LINK Options**

| QCL Option | LINK Option | Effect |
|---|---|---|
| /F *hexnum* | /STACK:*number* | Sets the program stack size (see Section 9.5.11) |
| /Fe[[*exefile*]] | Run File prompt or *exefile* field | Names the executable file (see Section 9.4.2.2) |
| /Fm[[*mapfile*]] | List File prompt, *mapfile* field, or /MAP option | Creates a map file showing program segments, in order (see Section 9.5.10). The /Fm option allows you to rename the map file, if desired. |

## 9.3.3  Listing the Compiler Options (/HELP)

■   **Option**

**/HELP**
**/help**

This option displays a list of the most commonly used compiler options. **QCL** processes all information on the line containing the **/help** option, and displays the command list.

This option is not case sensitive: any combination of uppercase and lowercase letters is acceptable. For example, **/hELp** is a valid form of this option.

## 9.3.4  Naming the Object File (/Fo)

■  **Option**

*/Foobjfile*

The **/Fo** option gives different names to object files or, if you specify a path name, creates them in a different directory.

Keep the following rules in mind when using this option:

- The *objfile* argument must appear immediately after the option, with no intervening spaces.

- Each **/Fo** option applies to the next source file that appears on the command line after the option.

You are free to supply any name and any extension you like for *objfile*. However, it is recommended that you use the conventional **.OBJ** extension because the linker and the **LIB** library manager use **.OBJ** as the default extension when processing object files.

If you do not give a complete object-file name with the **/Fo** option (that is, if you do not give an object-file name with a base and extension or if you give a path name with no file name), **QCL** names the object files according to the following rules:

- If you give an object-file name without an extension (such as TEST), **QCL** automatically appends the **.OBJ** extension.

- If you give an object-file name with a blank extension (such as TEST.), **QCL** leaves the extension blank.

- If you give a path name with no file name, **QCL** creates the object file in the directory with the given path and gives it the base name of the first source file on the command line plus the **.OBJ** extension. In this case, the path name must end with a backslash (\) so that **QCL** does not mistake the path name for a file name.

■  **Examples**

```
QCL /FoB:\OBJECT\ FILE1.C
```

In the example above, the source file FILE1.C is compiled; the resulting object file is named FILE1.OBJ (by default). The directory specification B:\OBJECT\ tells **QCL** to create FILE1.OBJ in the directory named \OBJECT on drive B.

```
QCL /Fo\OBJECT\ FILE1.C FILE2.C /Fo\SRC\NEWFILE3.OBJ FILE3.C
```

In the example above, the first **/Fo** option tells the compiler to create, in the \OBJECT directory, the object files FILE1.OBJ (created as a result of compiling FILE1.C) and FILE2.OBJ (created as a result of compiling FILE2.C). The second **/Fo** option tells the compiler to create the object file named NEWFILE3.OBJ (created as a result of compiling FILE3.C) in the \SRC directory.

## 9.3.5  Memory-Model (/A) and Floating-Point (/FP) Options

Two important options that you specify with the **QCL** command are the following:

1.  The memory model used for your program
2.  The way your program handles floating-point-math operations

The memory model defines the rules that the compiler will use to set up the program's code and data segments in memory. **QCL** offers the memory-model options described in Table 9.3.

**Table 9.3**

**Memory Models**

| CL Option | Memory Model | Data Segments | Code Segments |
|---|---|---|---|
| **/AS** | Small | One | One |
| **/AM** | Medium | One | One code segment for each module |
| **/AC** | Compact | Multiple data segments; data items must be smaller than 64K | One |
| **/AL** | Large | Multiple data segments; data items must be smaller than 64K | One code segment per module |

Generally, memory models with multiple code segments can accommodate larger programs than can memory models with one code segment, and memory models with multiple data segments can accommodate more data-intensive programs than can memory models with one data segment. However, programs with multiple code or data segments are usually slower than programs with a single code or data segment.

By default, the Microsoft QuickC Compiler uses the medium memory model for programs compiled within the QuickC environment and the small memory model for programs compiled with the **QCL** command. (For more information about using and adjusting memory models, see Appendix B, "Working with QuickC Memory Models.")

The **QCL** command includes the following options that allow you to choose how the program you are compiling will handle floating-point-math operations:

| Option | Effect |
| --- | --- |
| **/FPi** | Handles floating-point-math operations with software that emulates the functionality of an 8087 or 80287 math coprocessor. A coprocessor is not required to run programs compiled with this option, although these programs run successfully on systems with coprocessors. This option is the default. |
| **/FPi87** | Handles floating-point-math operations by generating instructions for an 8087 or 80287 math coprocessor. This option reduces the size of programs that will always be run on systems with a coprocessor. |

The floating-point and memory-model options you choose determine the name of the stand-alone library that **QCL** places in the object file it creates. If you plan to link with that library, you do not need to give the linker a library name. Table 9.4 shows each combination of memory-model and floating-point options and the corresponding library name that **QCL** embeds in the object file.

**Table 9.4**

**QCL Options and Default Libraries**

| Floating-Point Option | Memory-Model Option | Default Library |
|---|---|---|
| /FPi87 | /AS | SLIBC7.LIB |
|  | /AM | MLIBC7.LIB |
|  | /AC | CLIBC7.LIB |
|  | /AL | LLIBC7.LIB |
| /FPi | /AS | SLIBCE.LIB |
|  | /AM | MLIBCE.LIB |
|  | /AC | CLIBCE.LIB |
|  | /AL | LLIBCE.LIB |

## 9.3.6 Using the 8086 or 80286 Processor (/G0, /G2)

■ **Options**

/G0  Enables instruction set for 8086/8088 processor (default)
/G2  Enables instruction set for 80286 processor

If you have an 80286 processor, you can use the **/G2** option to enable the 80286 instruction set for your program. By default, the Microsoft QuickC Compiler uses the 8086/8088 instruction set. Although it is usually advantageous to compile with **/G2** if your machine has an 80286 processor, you are not required to do so. Programs compiled with the **/G2** option cannot run on a machine with an 8088 or 8086 processor. However, programs compiled without the **/G2** option and programs explicitly compiled with the **/G0** option can run on a machine with an 80286 processor.

## 9.3.7 Controlling the Preprocessor

The **QCL** command provides several options that control the operation of the C preprocessor. You can define macros and manifest (symbolic) constants from the command line, change the search path for include files, and stop compilation of a source file after the preprocessing stage to produce a preprocessed source-file listing.

### 9.3.7.1 Removing Definitions of Predefined Identifiers (/U, /u)

■ **Options**

/U *identifier*  Removes definition of a predefined identifier
/u              Removes definitions of all predefined identifiers

The Microsoft QuickC Compiler defines four identifiers that are useful in writing portable programs. Use these identifiers to conditionally compile parts of a program, depending on the processor, operating system, and memory model being used. The predefined identifiers and their functions are listed below:

| Identifier | Function |
|---|---|
| MSDOS | Always defined. Identifies target operating system as DOS. |
| M_I86 | Always defined. Identifies target machine as a member of the 8086 family. |
| M_I86$m$M | Always defined. Identifies memory model, where $m$ is either **S** (small model), **C** (compact model), **M** (medium model), or **L** (large model). Memory models are discussed in Appendix B, "Working with QuickC Memory Models." |
| NO_EXT_KEYS | Defined only when language extensions are turned off (that is, when the program is compiled with the Language Extensions circular button off or with the **/Za** compiler option). |

The **/U** (for "undefine") option turns off the definition of the given predefined identifiers. One or more spaces may separate the **/U** and *identifier*. You can specify more than one **/U** option on the same command line.

The **/u** option turns off all four definitions.

You may want to remove definitions of predefined identifiers in the following cases:

- If you want to give more than the maximum number of definitions on the command line. You can give 16 definitions if language extensions are turned off or 17 otherwise.

- If you want to use a predefined identifier to represent something different in your program.

For each definition of a predefined identifier you remove, you can substitute a definition of your own on the command line. If you remove the definitions of all four predefined identifiers, you can specify up to 20 command-line definitions. However, because DOS limits the number of characters you can type on a command line, the number of definitions you can specify in practice is probably less than 20.

■ **Example**

```
QCL /UMSDOS /UM_I86 WORK.C
```

This example removes the definitions of two predefined identifiers. Note that the /U option must be given twice to do this.

### 9.3.7.2 Producing a Preprocessed Listing (/P, /E, /EP)

■ **Options**

/P Writes preprocessed output to a file
/E Writes preprocessed output to standard output; includes # **line** directives
/EP Writes preprocessed output to a file and standard output

The **/P**, **/E**, and **/EP** options produce listings of preprocessed files. These options allow you to examine the output of the C preprocessor. All three options suppress compilation; no object file or map file is produced, even if you specify an **/Fo** or **/Fm** option on the **QCL** command line.

A preprocessed listing file is identical to the original source file except that all preprocessor directives are carried out, macro expansions are performed, and comments are removed.

The following list explains how each option handles preprocessed output:

| Option | Output Handling |
|--------|-----------------|
| /P | Writes the preprocessed listing to a file with the same base name as the source file, but with an .I extension. |

/E    Copies the preprocessed listing to the standard output (usually your terminal); DOS redirection can be used to save the listing in a disk file. This option also places a #**line** directive at the beginning and end of each included file and around lines removed by preprocessor directives that specify conditional compilation. This option is useful when you want to resubmit the preprocessed listing for compilation. The #**line** directives renumber the lines of the preprocessed file so that errors generated during later stages of processing refer to the original source file rather than to the preprocessed file.

/EP    Combines features of the /**E** and /**P** options: preprocesses the file and copies it to the standard output, but does not add #**line** directives.

### ■  Examples

```
QCL /P MAIN.C
```

This example creates the preprocessed file MAIN.I from the source file MAIN.C.

```
QCL /E ADD.C > PREADD.C
```

The command above creates a preprocessed file with inserted #**line** directives from the source file ADD.C. The output is redirected to the file PREADD.C.

```
QCL /EP ADD.C
```

The command above produces the same preprocessed output as the second example, but without the #**line** directives. The output appears on the screen.

### 9.3.7.3  Preserving Comments (/C)

### ■  Option

/C

The /**C** (for "comment") option preserves comments during preprocessing.

If this option is not given, the preprocessor strips comments from a source file, since they do not serve any purpose in later stages of compiling.

This option is valid only if the **/E**, **/P**, or **/EP** option is also used.

■  **Example**

```
QCL /P /C SAMPLE.C
```

This example produces a listing named SAMPLE.I. The listing file contains the original source file, including comments, with all preprocessor directives expanded or replaced.

### 9.3.7.4  Searching for Include Files (/X)

■  **Option**

**/X**

The **/X** option tells the compiler not to search for include files in the "standard places" defined by the DOS environment variable **INCLUDE**. This option lets you change the order in which the compiler searches for include files without changing the compiler environment you normally use.

The **/X** option is often used in conjunction with the **/I** option, which tells the compiler to search directories other than the standard places for include files. For more information about specifying directories other than the standard places for include files, see Section 8.1.4.1, "Suppressing Compiler Warnings: The Warning Levels Options," and Section 9.3.1, "Environment Options."

■  **Example**

```
QCL /X MAIN.C
```

In the example above, the compiler looks for include files only in the current working directory, since the **/X** option tells **QCL** to consider the list of standard places empty.

## 9.3.8   Preparing for Debugging (/Zi, /Zd)

■   **Options**

/Zi   Creates object file for in-memory debugging/CodeView debugger
/Zd   Creates object file with limited debugging information

The **/Zi** option produces an object file containing full symbolic-debugging information for use with the debugger built into the QuickC environment or with the CodeView symbolic debugger. This object file includes full symbol-table information and line numbers.

The **/Zd** option produces an object file containing line-number records corresponding to the line numbers of the source file. The **/Zd** option is useful in cases where you want to reduce the size of an executable file that you will be debugging with the CodeView debugger, and you do not need to use the expression evaluator during debugging.

■   **Example**

```
QCL /Zi TEST.C
```

This command produces an object file named TEST.OBJ that contains line numbers corresponding to the line numbers of TEST.C.

## 9.3.9   Packing Structure Members (/Zp)

■   **Options**

**/Zp[[{ 1|2|4} ]]**
**# pragma pack([[{ 1|2|4} ]])**

When storage is allocated for structures, structure members are ordinarily stored as follows:

- Items of type **char** or **unsigned char**, or arrays containing items of these types, are byte aligned.

- Structures are word aligned; structures of odd size are padded to an even number of bytes.

- All other types of structure members are word aligned.

To conserve memory, you may want to store structures more or less compactly. The **/Zp** option and the **pack** pragma control how structure data are "packed" into memory. Note that, on some processors, the **/Zp** option may slow program execution because of the time required to unpack structure members when they are accessed. For example, on an 8086 processor, this option can reduce efficiency if members with **int** or **long** type are packed in such a way that they begin on odd-byte boundaries.

Use the **/Zp** option to specify the same packing for all structures in a module. When you give the **/Zp**[*n*] option, where *n* is 1, 2, or 4, each structure member after the first is stored on an *n*-byte boundary, depending on the option you choose. If you use the **/Zp** option without an argument, structure members are packed on one-byte boundaries.

Use the **pack** pragma when you want to specify packing other than the packing specified on the command line for particular structures. Give the **pack**(*n*) pragma, where *n* is 1, 2, or 4, before the declarations of structures that you want to pack differently. To reinstate the packing given on the command line, give the **pack**() pragma with no arguments.

Table 9.5 shows the interaction of the **/Zp** option with the **pack** pragma.

**Table 9.5**

**Using the pack Pragma**

| Syntax | Compiled with /Zp Option? | Action |
| --- | --- | --- |
| # **pragma pack**() | Yes | Reverts to packing specified on the command line for structures that follow |
| # **pragma pack**() | No | Reverts to default packing for structures that follow |
| # **pragma pack**(*n*) | Yes or no | Packs the following structures to the given byte boundary until changed or turned off |

■   **Example**

```
QCL /Zp PROG.C
```

This command causes all structures in the program PROG.C to be stored without extra space for alignment of members on **int** boundaries.

## 9.3.10  Suppressing Default-Library Selection (/Zl)

■  **Option**

**/Zl**

Ordinarily **QCL** places the name of the default library, **SLIBCE.LIB**, in the object file. This mechanism allows the linker to automatically find the appropriate library to be linked with the object file.

The **/Zl** option tells the compiler not to place the default library name in the object file. As a result, the object file is slightly smaller.

The **/Zl** option is useful when you are using the **LIB** utility (described in Section 10.2) to build a stand-alone library. You can compile the object files you are putting in the library with **/Zl** to remove the library names before you combine them. Although the **/Zl** option saves only a small amount of space for a single object file, the total amount of space saved is significant in a library containing many object modules.

■  **Example**

```
QCL ONE.C /Zl TWO.C
```

The example above creates the following two object files:

- An object file named `ONE.OBJ` that contains the name of the C library **SLIBCE.LIB**
- An object file named `TWO.OBJ` that contains no default-library information

When `ONE.OBJ` and `TWO.OBJ` are linked, the default-library information in `ONE.OBJ` causes the given library to be searched for any unresolved references in either `ONE.OBJ` or `TWO.OBJ`.

## 9.3.11  Controlling the Calling Convention (/Gc)

■  **Options**

**/Gc**
**fortran**
**pascal**
**cdecl**

The **fortran**, **pascal**, and **cdecl** keywords and the **/Gc** option control the function-calling and function-naming conventions that your programs use so that they can call and be called by functions written in Microsoft Pascal, FORTRAN, and BASIC.

## 9.3.12   Setting the Data Threshold

■   **Option**

/Gt[*number*]

The **/Gt** option causes all data items whose size is greater than or equal to *number* bytes to be allocated in a new data segment. When *number* is specified, it must follow the **/Gt** option immediately, with no intervening spaces. When *number* is omitted, the default threshold value is 256. When the **/Gt** option is omitted, the default threshold value is 32,767.

---

*Note*

You can use the **/Gt** option only if you are creating a compact- or large-model program, since small- and medium-model programs have only one data segment.

---

## 9.3.13   Optimizing Loops (/Ol)

■   **Option**

/Ol

The **/Ol** option tells the compiler to perform loop optimizations. When you choose this option, the compiler automatically places frequently used loop variables in registers to speed program execution.

This option is turned on implicitly when you compile with the **/Ox** (maximum optimization) option.

## 9.4   Separate Compiling and Linking: QCL and LINK

With the Microsoft QuickC Compiler you can link in several different ways. Sections 9.4.1–9.4.2 describe these methods. For each method, you specify the following information to the linker:

- The object files you are linking

- The names of the libraries you are linking with, if different from the default

- The name of the executable file, if you want to rename it or use an extension other than **.EXE**

- The name of the map file, if you want to create one

- The linker options, if any, that you are using to control the linking process

To compile and link in two discrete steps, use the **QCL** command to compile source files without linking the resulting object files. Simply specify the **/c** option and give only the names of source files on the **QCL** command line. Then link the resulting object files with the appropriate libraries and linker options in a separate step.

### 9.4.1   Linking with the QCL Command

To link with the **QCL** command, use this command syntax:

**QCL** [[*option...*]] *objfile...* [[*lib...*]] **/link** *link-option... lib...*

As described in Section 9.2, the **QCL** command bypasses compiling and invokes the linker if you give only object-file names on the command line. **QCL** passes the linker the object-file names, library names, and linker options you specify.

### 9.4.2   Linking with the LINK Command

If you are linking in a separate step, the alternative to using **QCL** is to invoke the linker directly by using the **LINK** command. Do this after compiling with **QCL** and the **/c** option.

To link with the **LINK** command, your DOS environment should be set up as summarized below. For a full description, see Section 1.3.1.6 (for hard-disk users) or Section 1.3.2.4 (for floppy-disk users).

- If you are running **LINK** on a hard-disk system, use the DOS **CD** command to make the directory with the object files you are linking the current directory.

- If you are running **LINK** on a floppy-disk system, the disk containing your object files should be in drive B, and your working copy of the Work distribution disk in drive A. Make drive B the current drive. When you run **LINK**, type the drive name A: immediately before the **LINK** command, with no intervening spaces. During the linking process, you will be prompted to swap your working copy of the disk containing the appropriate stand-alone library in drive A.

You can give the **LINK** command the input it needs in one of the following ways:

| Method | Instructions |
|---|---|
| Give input on the command line | Use a command line of the following form: <br><br> **LINK** *objfile*... [[,[*exefile*]] [,[*mapfile*][,[*lib*]... ]]]] [*link-opt*]... [;] <br><br> The command line cannot be longer than 128 characters. |
| Respond to prompts | Type <br><br> LINK <br><br> and respond to the following prompts: <br><br> `Object Modules [.OBJ]:`<br>`Run File [`*basename*`.EXE]:`<br>`List File [NUL.MAP]:`<br>`Libraries [.LIB]:` <br><br> To give more files for any prompt, type a plus sign (+) at the end of the line. The prompt reappears on the next line, and you can continue typing input for the prompt. |
| Create a response file | Set up a file with responses to **LINK** command prompts, known as a "response file," then type a **LINK** command of the form <br><br> **LINK** @ *filename* <br><br> where *filename* is the name of the response file. You can append linker options to any response or give options on one or more separate lines. The responses must be in the same order as the **LINK** prompts discussed above. You can also enter the name of a response file after any linker prompt, or at any position in the **LINK** command line. |

Table 9.6 shows the input you must give on the **LINK** command line, or in response to each prompt.

**Table 9.6**

**Input to the LINK Command**

| Field | Prompt | Input |
|-------|--------|-------|
| *objfile* | Object Modules | One or more object files that you are linking, separated by plus signs or spaces. You can also specify libraries in this field; in this case, all object modules in the library are linked with the other object files given in this field. |
| *exefile* | Run File | Name of the executable file you are creating, if you want to give it a name or extension other than the default. You should always use the files to have this extension. |
| *mapfile* | List File | Name of the file containing a symbol map listing, if you are creating one. You can also give one of the following DOS device names to direct the map file to that device: **AUX** for an auxiliary device, **CON** for the console (terminal), **PRN** for a printer device, or **NUL** for no device (so that no map file is created). See Section 9.5.10 for a sample map file and information about its contents.[1] |
| *lib* | Libraries | One or more stand-alone libraries, or directories to be searched for stand-alone libraries, separated by plus signs or spaces. You can give up to 32 libraries in response to the Libraries prompt; any additional libraries are ignored. See Section 9.4.2.3 for rules for specifying library names to the linker. |
| *link-opt* | Give options after any response | Any of the linker options described in Sections 9.5.1–9.5.14. Specify linker options anywhere on the command line. |

[1]You can also create a map file with the **QCL /Fm** option (Section 9.3.2) or the **LINK /MAP** option (Section 9.5.10).

### 9.4.2.1   Default Information for LINK

You can choose defaults for information that **LINK** needs in any of the following ways:

| Type of Default | How to Choose |
|---|---|
| Command Line | Omit the file name or names before the entry and type only the required comma. The only exception to this is the default for the *mapfile* entry: if you use a comma as a placeholder for this entry, **LINK** *will* create a map file. |
| Prompt | Simply press ENTER. |
| All remaining entries | Type a semicolon after the applicable entry or prompt. (Note that you are required to give at least one object-file name as input.) |

The following list shows the defaults that **LINK** uses for executable files, map files, and libraries:

| File Type | Default |
|---|---|
| Executable | Base name of the first object file given, plus the **.EXE** extension. To rename the executable file, give only the new base name; if you give a file name with no extension, **LINK** automatically appends the **.EXE** extension. |
| Map | The special file name **NUL.MAP**, which tells **LINK** *not* to create a map file. To create a map file, give only the base name; if you give a file name with no extension, **LINK** automatically appends the **.MAP** extension. |
| Libraries | Libraries named in the given object files. The library names placed in the object files depend on the floating-point and memory-model options that were given when the source files were compiled; see Table 9.4 for a list of the default names. If you specify a library other than the default library, give only the base name; if you give a library name with no extension, **LINK** automatically appends the **.LIB** extension. See Section 9.4.2.3 for information about specifying libraries other than default libraries. |

■ **Examples**

```
STDEV SQROOT EXP
/PAUSE /MAP
STDVLST
MATHFN.LIB
```

217

This response file tells **LINK** to load the three object modules STDEV, SQROOT, and EXP. The executable file, STDEV.EXE, and the map file, STDVLST.MAP, are produced. The /PAUSE option causes **LINK** to pause before producing the executable file so that you can swap disks if necessary. The /MAP option tells **LINK** to include public symbols and addresses in the map file. **LINK** also links any needed routines from the library file, MATHFN.LIB. See the discussion of the **/PAUSE** option in Section 9.5.2 and the discussion of the **/MAP** option in Section 9.5.10.

```
LINK STDEV+SQROOT+EXP, ,STDVLIST, MATHFN.LIB
```

In the example above, **LINK** loads and links the object modules STDEV.OBJ, SQROOT.OBJ, and EXP.OBJ, searching for unresolved references in the library file MATHFN.LIB. By default, the executable file is named STDEV.EXE. A map file called STDVLIST.MAP is also produced.

```
LINK

Object Modules [.OBJ]: STDEV SQROOT EXP INP+
Object Modules [.OBJ]: READDATA+GRAPH+PRINT+
Object Modules [.OBJ]: REPORT
Run File [STDEV.EXE]: ;
```

The example above illustrates how to continue any prompt by typing a plus sign (+) at the end of your response. The example above links all of the given object files, then creates an executable file. Since a semicolon is typed as a response to the Run File prompt, the executable file is given the default name: the base name of the first object file given (STDEV) plus the **.EXE** extension. The defaults are also used for the remaining prompts; as a result, no map file is created, and the default libraries named in the object files are used for linking.

### 9.4.2.2  Specifying Files to LINK

Most of the rules for specifying file names to **LINK** are the same as the rules for specifying file names to **QCL**: uppercase and lowercase letters can be used interchangeably, and file names can include path names to tell the linker to look for files or create files in the given path. However, the **LINK** command does not recognize wild-card characters in file names.

### 9.4.2.3  Specifying Libraries to LINK

Ordinarily, you do not need to give the linker a stand-alone-library name. When the **QCL** command creates object files, it places in each object file the name of the correct stand-alone library for that object file. **QCL** determines which library name is appropriate based on the memory-model and floating-point options you give on the **QCL** command line, as described in Table 9.4 (Section 9.3.5). When the object file is passed to the linker, the linker looks for a library with the same name as the name in the object file and links the object file with that library automatically.

To link object files with stand-alone libraries other than the defaults, you must tell the linker which libraries to link with. You can give the library names in any of the following places:

- On the **QCL** command line. Library names appearing before **/link** must have **.LIB** extensions; library names appearing after **/link** may have blank extensions or no extensions.

- In the fourth field of the **LINK** command line.

- In response to the Libraries prompt of the **LINK** command.

The linker searches libraries you specify to resolve external references before it searches default libraries.

You might want to link with a stand-alone library other than the default if you want to do any of the following:

- Link with additional stand-alone libraries. For example, if you did not include graphics functions in the libraries built by the **SETUP** program, you must link graphics programs with the stand-alone library **GRAPHICS.LIB** in addition to the default library.

- Link with libraries in different paths.

  If you give a complete path name for the library, the linker looks only in that path for the library. Otherwise, it looks in the following locations, in the order shown:

  1. The current working directory.

  2. Any paths or drives that you give where you would ordinarily give library names. These paths or drives may be given after the **/link** option on the **QCL** command line, in the fourth field of the **LINK** command line, or in response to the Libraries prompt of the **LINK** command.

  3. The locations given by the **LIB** environment variable.

- Ignore the library named in the object file; for example, if you want to link with uncombined libraries as described in Section 1.4. In this case, you must give the linker option **/NOD** in addition to specifying the library you want to use for linking. See Section 9.5.7 for more information about the **/NOD** option.

■ **Example**

```
QCL STDEV SQROOT EXP /link C:\TESTLIB\ NEWLIBV3
```

This example links three object modules to create an executable file named STDEV.EXE. The linker searches NEWLIBV3.LIB before searching the default libraries to resolve references. To locate NEWLIBV3.LIB and the default libraries, the linker searches the current working directory, then the C:\TESTLIB\ directory, and finally, the locations given by the **LIB** environment variable.

### 9.4.2.4 LINK Memory Requirements

**LINK** uses available memory for the linking session. If the files to be linked create an output file that exceeds available memory, **LINK** creates a temporary disk file to serve as memory. **LINK** creates the temporary file in the directory specified by the **TMP** environment variable. For example, if the **TMP** variable is set to C:\TEMPDIR, then **LINK** puts the temporary file in C:\TEMPDIR. If no **TMP** environment variable is defined, or if the directory specified by **TMP** does not exist, then **LINK** puts the temporary file in the current working directory.

The temporary file is handled in one of the following ways, depending on the DOS version:

1. When running on DOS Version 3.0 or later, **LINK** uses a DOS system call to create a temporary file with a unique name.

2. When running on a version of DOS prior to 3.0, **LINK** creates a temporary file named **VM.TMP**.

When **LINK** creates a temporary disk file, you will see the message

```
Temporary file tempfile has been created.
Do not change diskette in drive, letter
```

Here, *tempfile* is ".\" followed by either **VM.TMP** or a name generated by DOS, and *letter* is the drive containing the the temporary file.

If the drive named *letter* is a floppy-disk drive, the message Do not change diskette in drive also appears. If it appears, do not remove the disk from the drive until the linking session ends. If you remove the disk, linker operations will be unpredictable, and you may see the following message:

```
L1087: unexpected end-of-file on scratch file
```

If you see this message, rerun the linker session.

The temporary file that **LINK** creates is a working file only. **LINK** deletes it at the end of the session.


# 9.5   Using Linker Options

All linker options begin with the linker's option character, the forward slash (/). Case is not significant in linker options; for example, **/NOI** and **/noi** are equivalent.

To save space and effort, abbreviate linker options. However, be sure that your abbreviation is unique so that the linker can determine which option you want. (The minimum legal abbreviation for each option is indicated in the syntax of the option.) For example, several options begin with the letters "NO"; therefore, abbreviations for those options must be longer than "NO" to be unique. You cannot use "NO" as an abbreviation for the **/NOIGNORECASE** option, since the linker cannot tell which of the options beginning with "NO" you intend. The shortest legal abbreviation for this option is **/NOI**.

Abbreviations must begin with the first letter of the option and must be continuous through the last letter typed. No gaps or transpositions are allowed.

Some linker options take numeric arguments. A numeric argument can be any of the following:

- A decimal number in the range 0 to 65,535. (Note that commas do not appear in numeric arguments.)

- An octal number from 0 to 0177777. A number is interpreted as octal if it starts with "0." For example, the number 10 is a decimal number, but the number 010 is an octal number, equivalent to 8 in decimal.

- A hexadecimal number from 0 to 0xFFFF. A number is interpreted as hexadecimal if it starts with 0x or 0X. For example, 0x10 is a hexadecimal number, equivalent to 16 in decimal.

Linker options affect all files in the linking process, regardless of where the options are specified.

## 9.5.1  Viewing the Options List (/HE)

■  **Option**

/HE[LP]

Use the **/HE** option to display a list of the available linker options.

## 9.5.2  Pausing during Linking (/PAU)

■  **Option**

/PAU[SE]

The **/PAU** option tells the linker to pause in the link session and display a message before it writes the executable (**.EXE**) file to disk. This allows you to insert a new disk to hold the executable file.

If you specify the **/PAU** option, **LINK** displays this message before it creates the executable file:

```
About to generate .EXE file
Change diskette in drive letter and press <ENTER>
```

The *letter* is the current drive. **LINK** resumes processing when you press ENTER.

---

*Note*

Do not remove the disk containing the newly created list file or the disk used for the temporary file.

If a temporary file is created on the disk you plan to swap, press CTRL+C to terminate the linking session. Rearrange your files so that the temporary file and the executable file can be written to the same disk. Then try linking again.

---

## 9.5.3 Displaying Linker-Process Information (/I)

■ **Option**

**/I[NFORMATION]**

This option is useful if you want to determine the locations of the object
files being linked and the order in which they are linked. It displays information about the linking process, including each phase of linking and the
names of the object files being linked.

■ **Example**

```
**** PASS ONE ****
HTOI.OBJ(htoi.c)
**** LIBRARY SEARCH ****
c:\lib\MLIBCE.LIB(chkstk)
c:\lib\MLIBCE.LIB(crt0)
c:\lib\MLIBCE.LIB(printf)
c:\lib\MLIBCE.LIB(scanf)
        .
        .
        .
**** ASSIGN ADDRESSES ****
**** PASS TWO ****
HTOI.OBJ(htoi.c)
c:\lib\MLIBCE.LIB(chkstk)
c:\lib\MLIBCE.LIB(crt0)
c:\lib\MLIBCE.LIB(printf)
c:\lib\MLIBCE.LIB(scanf)
        .
        .
        .
**** WRITING EXECUTABLE ****

Segments              25
Groups                 1
Bytes in symbol table  16400
```

The example above shows a sample of the linker output when the **/I**
option is specified on the **LINK** command line.

### 9.5.4  Preventing Linker Prompting (/B)

■  **Option**

**/B[ATCH]**

The **/B** option tells the linker not to prompt you for a new path name whenever it cannot find a library or object file that it needs. When this option is used, the linker simply continues to execute without using the file in question.

Using the **/B** option may cause unresolved external references during linking. This option is intended primarily for users who use batch or **MAKE** files to link many executable files with a single command and do not want the linker to stop processing if it cannot find a required file.

This option does not prevent the linker from prompting for arguments that you do not give on the **LINK** command line.

### 9.5.5  Creating Quick Libraries (/Q)

■  **Option**

**/Q[UICKLIB]**

The **/Q** option tells the linker to combine the object files and libraries you specify into a Quick library. Quick libraries have extensions of **.QLB** rather than **.EXE** to distinguish them from executable files. When you start QuickC, you can give the **/l** option on the **QC** command line to load the Quick library.

When you create a Quick library, the file name **QUICKLIB.OBJ** must be first in the list of object files to be linked.

See Chapter 10, "Creating Quick Libraries and Stand-Alone Libraries," for more information about creating and loading Quick libraries.

## 9.5.6 Packing Executable Files (/E)

■ **Option**

**/E**[**XEPACK**]

The **/E** option removes sequences of repeated bytes (typically null characters) and optimizes the "load-time relocation table" before creating the executable file. The load-time relocation table is a table of references relative to the start of the program. Each reference changes when the executable image is loaded into memory and an actual address for the entry point is assigned.

Executable files linked with this option may be smaller and load faster than files linked without this option. However, you cannot debug packed programs with the debugger built into the QuickC programming environment or with the Microsoft CodeView window-oriented debugger.

## 9.5.7 Ignoring Default Libraries (/NOD)

■ **Option**

**/NOD**[**EFAULTLIBRARYSEARCH**]

The **/NOD** option tells the linker *not* to search any library specified in an object file to resolve external references.

In general, QuickC programs do not work correctly without the stand-alone libraries built by the **SETUP** program. Thus, if you use the **/NOD** option, you should give the name of the required stand-alone library explicitly.

## 9.5.8 Setting Maximum Number of Segments (/SE)

■ **Option**

**/SE**[**GMENTS**]:*number*

The **/SE** option controls the number of segments that the linker allows a program to have. The default is 128, but you can set *number* to any value (decimal, octal, or hexadecimal) in the range 1–3072 (decimal).

For each segment, the linker must allocate space to keep track of segment information. When you set the segment limit higher than 128, the linker allocates more space for segment information. For programs with fewer than 128 segments, you can minimize the amount of storage the linker needs by setting *number* to reflect the actual number of segments in the program. The linker displays an error message if this number is too high for the amount of memory the linker has available.

## 9.5.9  Setting the Maximum Allocation Space (/CP)

■  **Option**

/CP[ARMAXALLOC]:*number*

The **/CP** option sets the maximum number of 16-byte paragraphs needed by the program when it is loaded into memory to *number*, an integer in the range 1–65,535. The operating system uses this value when allocating space for the program before loading it. The Microsoft C start-up module cuts memory back to the larger of the following two values:

- 64K
- The amount of memory specified in this option

For programs with limited static data and heap usage, this option is unnecessary.

## 9.5.10  Creating a Map File (/M, /LI)

■  **Option**

/M[AP][:*number*]

/LI[NENUMBERS]

The **/M** and **/LI** options create a map file. A map file lists the segments of a program in their order of appearance in the load module. A sample map file is shown below:

```
Start  Stop   Length Name            Class
00000H 01E9FH 01EA0H _TEXT           CODE
01EA0H 01EA0H 00000H C_ETEXT         ENDCODE
  .
  .
  .
```

The information in the `Start` and `Stop` columns shows the 20-bit address (in hexadecimal) of each segment, relative to the beginning of the load module. The load module begins at location zero. The `Length` column gives the length of the segment in bytes. The `Name` column gives the name of the segment, and the `Class` column gives information about the segment type. See your DOS programmer's documentation for information about groups, segments, and classes.

The starting address and name of each group appears after the list of segments. A sample group listing is shown below:

```
Origin     Group
01EA:0     DGROUP
```

In the example above, `DGROUP` is the name of the data group. **DGROUP** is the only group used by programs compiled with the Microsoft QuickC Compiler.

If you link with the **/LI** option, the map file shows the line numbers of your source program and the address associated with each line number, as shown in the following example:

```
Line numbers for HTOI.OBJ(htoi.c) segment _TEXT

    2 0000:0010     4 0000:0019     5 0000:0023     6 0000:0031
    7 0000:0047    10 0000:004B    12 0000:0054    13 0000:005A
   14 0000:005F    16 0000:0067    17 0000:0070    18 0000:0078
   19 0000:007D    20 0000:008A    21 0000:008D    22 0000:008F
   23 0000:0095    25 0000:009A    26 0000:009D    28 0000:00A5
   29 0000:00C2    30 0000:00C5    32 0000:00CA    33 0000:00D2
   36 0000:00D6    38 0000:00DF    40 0000:00E9    42 0000:0107
   43 0000:010F
```

If you link with the **/M** option, the map file contains two lists of global symbols: the first sorted in ASCII-character order by symbol name and the second by symbol address. The notation `Abs` appears next to the names of absolute symbols (symbols containing 16-bit constant values that are not associated with program addresses).

Each list can contain a maximum of 2048 sorted symbols. You can give the *number* argument with the **/M** option to list more symbols sorted by address. The *number* argument can be any decimal, octal, or hexadecimal number between 0 and 65,535 (decimal), inclusive; however, in practice, the number of sorted symbols is limited by the amount of near heap space. If you give a *number* argument, the `Publics by Name` list does not appear in the map file.

```
Address                 Publics by Name

01EA:0096               STKHQQ
0000:1D86               _brkctl
01EA:04B0               _edata
01EA:0910               _end
.
.
.
01EA:00EC               __abrkp
01EA:009C               __abrktb
01EA:00EC               __abrktbe
0000:9876     Abs       __acrtmsg
0000:9876     Abs       __acrtused
.
.
.
01EA:0240               ___argc
01EA:0242               ___argv

Address                 Publics by Value

0000:0010               _main
0000:0047               _htoi
0000:00DA               _exp16
0000:0113               __chkstk
0000:0129               __astart
0000:01C5               __cintDIV
.
.
.
```

Many of the global symbols that appear in the map file are symbols used internally by the Microsoft QuickC Compiler. These symbols usually begin with one or more leading underscores or end with QQ.

The addresses of the external symbols are in the *frame:offset* format, showing the location of the symbol relative to zero (the beginning of the load module).

For both the **/LI** and the **/M** options the map file gives the program entry point, as shown in the following example:

```
Program entry point at 0000:0129
```

You can also create a map file by giving the **/Fm** option on the **QCL** command line, by giving a map-file name on the **LINK** command line, or by giving a map-file name in response to the List File prompt. These methods do not allow you to increase the number of symbols sorted by address.

## 9.5.11  Controlling the Stack Size (/ST)

■  **Option**

**/ST[ACK]**:*number*

The **/ST** option specifies the size of the stack for your program, where *number* is any positive decimal, octal, or hexadecimal value up to 65,535 (decimal) representing the size, in bytes, of the stack. Give octal or hexadecimal numbers by using the usual C format, octal numbers beginning with "0" and hexadecimal numbers beginning with "0x".

If you do not specify this option, the start-up routine in the stand-alone C library sets the default stack size to 2K.

If you get a stack-overflow message, you may need to increase the size of the stack. In contrast, if your program uses the stack very little, you can save some space by decreasing the stack size.

This option has the same effect as the **/F** option of the **QCL** command.

■  **Example**

```
LINK FACT.OBJ EXP.OBJ,,, /STACK:0xC00
```

This example sets the stack size to C00 hexadecimal (3K decimal) for the program created by linking the `FACT.OBJ` and `EXP.OBJ` object files.

## 9.5.12  Translating Far Calls (/F, /NOF)

■  **Options**

**/F[ARCALLTRANSLATION]**

**/NOF[ARCALLTRANSLATION]**

The **/F** linker option tells the linker to optimize far calls to procedures that lie in the same segment as the caller. This option results in slightly faster, more compact programs.

When you specify the **/F** linker option, the linker optimizes 32-bit calls to procedures in the same segment as the calling procedure. Since the segment addresses of the calling and called procedures are the same, only a 16-bit call is required. If the **/F** linker option is given, the linker removes the far call and replaces it with code that first places the contents of the **CS** register on the stack, then makes a near call. The called procedure still returns with a far (32-bit) return instruction. However, because both the code segment (stored in **CS**) and the near address are on the stack, the far return is done correctly. The linker also adds a **NOP** instruction; consequently, the five-byte far call is replaced by exactly five bytes of instructions.

Although the linker does not use far-call translation unless you explicitly ask for it, you can use the **/NOF** option to turn off far-call translation if, for example, you have given the **/F** linker option in the **CL** environment variable.

## 9.5.13  Packing Contiguous Segments (/PAC, /NOP)

■  **Options**

/PAC[KCODE][:number]

/NOP[ACKCODE]

The **/PAC** option tells the linker to group neighboring code segments. Code segments in the same group share the same segment address; all offset addresses are then adjusted upward as needed. As a result, many instructions that would otherwise have different segment addresses share the same segment address.

Used in conjunction with the **/F** linker option (described in Section 9.5.12), the **/PAC** option can reduce the size and improve the efficiency of medium-model programs.

If specified, *number* is the size limit of groups formed by **/PAC**. The linker stops adding segments to a particular group as soon as it cannot add a segment to the group without exceeding *number*. At that point, the linker starts forming a new group with the remaining code segments. If *number* is not given, the default is 65,530.

Although the linker does not pack neighboring segments unless you explicitly ask for it, you can use the **/NOP** option to turn off segment packing if, for example, you have given the **/PAC** option in the **CL** environment variable.

## 9.5.14   Other LINK Options

Not all options of the **LINK** command are suitable for use with QuickC programs. The following linker options can be used with Microsoft QuickC programs, but they are never required, since they request actions that the **QCL** command or the Microsoft QuickC Compiler performs automatically:

### /CO[DEVIEW]

Prepares an executable file to be debugged within the QuickC environment or by using the CodeView window-oriented debugger. If you are compiling and linking in separate steps, this option has an effect only if you are linking object files compiled with the **/Zi** option.

### /LI[NENUMBERS]

Creates a map file and includes the line numbers and associated addresses of the source program. If you are compiling and linking in separate steps, this option has an effect only if you are linking object files compiled with the **/Zd** option.

### /NOI[GNORECASE]

Tells the linker to distinguish between uppercase and lowercase letters; for example, the linker would consider ABC, abc, and Abc to be three separate names. If you want to link without using **/NOI**, you must invoke the linker in a separate step with the **LINK** command.

### /DO[SSEG]

Forces segments to be ordered using the defaults for Microsoft high-level language products. QuickC programs always use this segment order by default.

Do not use the following linker options when linking object files compiled with the Microsoft QuickC Compiler. They are suitable only for object files created by the Microsoft Macro Assembler (**MASM**).

### /DS[ALLOCATE]

Loads all data starting at the high end of the default data segment.

### /HI[GH]

Places the executable file as high in memory as possible.

### /NOG[ROUPASSOCIATION]

Tells the linker to ignore group associations when assigning addresses to data and code items.

**/O[VERLAYINTERRUPT]:***number*

Specifies an interrupt number other than 0x3F for passing control to overlays.

# 9.6   Controlling Stack and Heap Allocation

Programs compiled and linked under Microsoft C run with a fixed stack size (the default size is 2048 bytes). The stack resides above static data, and the heap uses whatever space is left above the stack. However, for some programs a fixed-stack model may not be ideal; a model where the stack and heap compete for space is more appropriate.

Linking with the *m***VARSTCK.OBJ** object files gives you such a model: when the heap runs out of memory, it tries to use available stack space until it runs into the top of the stack. When the allocated space in the stack is freed, it is once again made available to the stack. Note that the stack cannot grow beyond the last-allocated heap item in the stack or, if there are no heap items in the stack, beyond the size it was given at link time. Note also that while the heap can employ unused stack space, the reverse is not true: the stack cannot employ unused heap space.

You can change the model used to allocate heap space by linking your program with one of the *m***VARSTCK.OBJ** object files (where *m* is the first letter of the library you choose). These files are the small-, medium-, compact-, and large-model versions of a routine that allows the memory-allocation functions (**malloc**, **calloc**, **_expand**, **_fmalloc**, **_nmalloc**, and **realloc**) to allocate items in unused stack space if they run out of other memory.

When you link your program with one of the *m***VARSTCK.OBJ** files, do not suppress stack checking with the **#check_stack** pragma, or the **/Gs** or **/Ox** option. Stack overflow can occur more easily in programs that use this option, possibly causing errors that would be difficult to detect.

■   **Example**

```
QCL TEST.C SVARSTCK
```

This command line compiles `TEST.C` and then links the resulting object module with `SVARSTCK.OBJ`, the variable-stack object file for small-model programs.

# 9.7   Using Overlays

If you are not sure that a program will fit in available memory, you can direct **LINK** to create an overlaid version of the program. In an overlaid version of a program, specified parts of the program (known as "overlays") are loaded only if and when they are needed. These parts share the same space in memory. Only code is overlaid; data are never overlaid. Programs that use overlays usually require less memory, but they run more slowly because of the time needed to read the code from disk into memory.

Specify overlays by enclosing them in parentheses in the list of object files that you give the linker. Each module or combination of modules in parentheses represents one overlay. For example, you could give the following object-file list in the *objfiles* field of the **LINK** command line:

```
a + (b+c) + (e+f) + g + (i)
```

In this example, the modules  (b+c),  (e+f), and  (i)  are overlays. Whenever control passes to these modules, they are read into memory from disk. The  a  and  g  modules, and any modules drawn from the libraries, constitute the "resident part" (or "root") of your program.

Overlays are loaded into the same region of memory, so only one can be resident at a time. Duplicate names in different overlays are not supported, so each module can appear only once in a program.

The linker replaces calls from the root to an overlay, and calls from an overlay to another overlay with an interrupt (followed by the module identifier and offset). By default, the interrupt number is 63 (3F hexadecimal). You can use the **/O** linker option to change the interrupt number. The **/O** option should be used only by programs that use overlays and spawn another program using overlays. In this case, each program should use a separate overlay-interrupt number, meaning at least one of the programs should be linked with this option.

## 9.7.1   Restrictions on Overlays

You can overlay only modules to which control is transferred and returned by a standard 32-bit call/return instruction. However, calls to functions defined with the **near** keyword are 16-bit calls. This means that you cannot overlay modules containing near functions if other modules call those subroutines.

## 9.7.2  Overlay-Manager Prompts

The overlay manager is part of the standard libraries provided with the
Microsoft QuickC Compiler. If you specify overlays during linking, the
code for the overlay manager is automatically linked with the other
modules of your program.

When the executable file is run, the overlay manager searches for that file
whenever another overlay needs to be loaded. The overlay manager first
searches for the file in the current directory; then, if it does not find the
file, the manager searches the directories listed in the **PATH** environment
variable. When it finds the file, the overlay manager extracts the overlay
modules specified by the root program. If the overlay manager cannot find
an overlay file when needed, it prompts the user to enter the file name.

Even with overlays, the linker produces only *one* **.EXE** file. This file is
opened again and again, as long as the overlay manager needs to extract
new overlay modules.

For example, assume that an executable program called PAYROLL.EXE,
which does not exist in either the current directory or the directories
specified by **PATH**, uses overlays. If the user runs it by entering a complete path specification, the overlay manager displays the following message when it attempts to load overlay files:

```
Cannot find PAYROLL.EXE
Please enter new program spec:
```

The user can then enter the drive or directory, or both, where the program
PAYROLL.EXE is located. For example, if the file is located on drive B in
the directory \EMPLOYEE\DATA\ the user could enter either
B:\EMPLOYEE\DATA\ or simply \EMPLOYEE\DATA\ if the current drive
is B.

If the user later removes the disk in drive B and the overlay manager needs
to access the overlay again, it will not find PAYROLL.EXE. The following
message will be displayed:

```
Please insert diskette containing B:\EMPLOYEE\DATA\PAYROLL.EXE
in drive B: and strike any key when ready.
```

After the overlay file has been read from the disk, the overlay manager
displays the following message:

```
Please restore the original diskette.
Strike any key when ready.
```

# CHAPTER 10

# CREATING QUICK LIBRARIES AND STAND-ALONE LIBRARIES

Libraries are collections of routines that have been compiled or assembled to create a set of object modules that can be used by QuickC programs. The QuickC package provides tools for creating and maintaining two types of libraries, easily distinguishable by their characteristic file-name extensions:

| Extension | Function |
| --- | --- |
| **.QLB** | Generally referred to as a "Quick" library, this type of library, created with the **LINK** utility, is used for programs compiled and run within the QuickC programming environment. |
| **.LIB** | The **.LIB** extension characterizes a library created by the **LIB** library manager. These libraries are generally referred to as "stand-alone" libraries and have the same format as libraries shipped with other Microsoft high-level-language products. |

## 10.1   Quick Libraries

Quick libraries are used for programs that are compiled and run within the QuickC programming environment. Load a Quick library when you want to supplement the list of standard C library routines that are built into the QuickC programming environment.

### 10.1.1   Creating Quick Libraries

You can combine object files, stand-alone libraries, or any combination of the two into a Quick library. When you include a stand-alone library in a Quick library, all of the modules in that library become part of the Quick library.

Follow these steps to create a Quick library:

1.  Compile the C source files that you want to include in the library. Since modules in a Quick library must use the medium memory model, either compile from the QuickC programming environment and choose the Obj output option, or compile using the **/AM** option on the **QCL** command line.

2.  Invoke the linker, either from the **QCL** command line or by using the **LINK** utility. Give **QUICKLIB.OBJ** as the first object-file name on the command line or in response to the Object Files prompt. (**QUICKLIB.OBJ** is on the Libraries #1 distribution disk in the QuickC package.) Then give the names of the object files and stand-alone libraries you are combining. Give the name of

the Quick library as the name of the executable file on the command line, or in response to the Run File prompt. Specify the **/Q** linker option to create the Quick library.

■ **Example**

```
QCL QUICKLIB /AM CRCL.C ELPS.C LINE.C CRV.C /FeSHAPES.QLB /link /Q
```

The **QCL** command line above creates a Quick library named `SHAPES.QLB` from the source files `CRCL.C`, `ELPS.C`, `LINE.C`, and `CRV.C`.

## 10.1.2  Loading Quick Libraries

To load a Quick library when you start QuickC, use a command line of the following form:

**QC** /l*qlibname*

In this command line, *qlibname* is the base name of the Quick library (the name without the **.QLB** extension). If the Quick library has a different extension, you must give the file name with that extension.

Quick libraries, if used, must be loaded when you start the QuickC environment. You can load only one Quick library each time you start QuickC.

QuickC searches for the Quick libraries in the following locations, in the order shown:

1.  The path specified in the Quick-library name, if any.
2.  The current directory.
3.  The path specified by the **LIB** environment variable. (See your DOS user's guide for information about environment variables.)

■ **Example**

```
QC /lGRAPHICS.QLB
```

The command above loads the Quick library **GRAPHICS.QLB**, which contains the QuickC graphics functions. (This Quick library is provided as part of the QuickC package.)

### 10.1.3  Standard Library Routines in Quick Libraries

Table 6.1 in Section 6.1.1, "Single-Module Programs," lists the standard C library routines that are built into the QuickC environment. You can call these routines in your programs without loading a Quick library.

As you can see from Table 6.1, many of the standard C library routines are defined within the QuickC environment. However, if your program uses standard library routines that are not defined within the QuickC environment, you have several choices.

If your program uses library routines (for example, **getchar()**) that are implemented as macros, simply copy an #**include** directive for the appropriate header file into your source file.

If your program calls library functions, use the following procedure to create and load a Quick library containing these functions:

1.  Create a source file containing a **main** program that consists only of calls to the library routines that you want in the Quick library. For example, if you wanted to create a Quick library containing the BIOS-interface routines in the Microsoft C run-time library, you might create the following source file named **BIOS.C**:

    ```
    #include <bios.h>
    main()
    {
        _bios_serialcom();
        _bios_disk();
        _bios_equiplist();
        _bios_keybrd();
        _bios_memsize();
        _bios_printer();
        _bios_timeofday();
    }
    ```

    Note that the compiler may display warnings because no actual arguments are passed to the funtions in the program.

2.  Compile and link the source file as described in Section 10.1.1. In this example, you could use the **QCL** and **LINK** commands as shown below:

```
QCL /c /AM BIOS.C

LINK QUICKLIB.OBJ+BIOS.OBJ,BIOS.QLB, , /Q;
```

3. Load the resulting Quick library as usual. In this example, use the following command:

```
QC /lBIOS
```

# 10.2   Managing Stand-Alone Libraries: the LIB Utility

The Microsoft Library Manager, **LIB**, is used to manage the contents of stand-alone libraries. A stand-alone library is made up of "object modules"—that is, object files that have been combined to form a library. Unlike an object file, an object module does not exist independently of the library it belongs to, and it does not have a path name or extension associated with its file name. Use **LIB** to

- Combine object files to create a new library
- Add object files to an existing library
- Delete or replace the object modules of an existing library
- Extract object modules from an existing library and place them in separate object files
- Combine the contents of two existing libraries into a new library

Object files, stand-alone libraries, XENIX archives, Intel-style libraries, or any combination of these can be combined to form a stand-alone library. Stand-alone libraries are usually identified by their .LIB extension, though other extensions are allowed.

When updating an existing library, **LIB** performs all of its operations on a copy of the library. This mechanism ensures that you have a backup copy of any library you update.

## 10.2.1   Running LIB

If you are running **LIB** on a hard-disk system, use the DOS **CD** command to make the current directory that directory where you have stored the object files or libraries you are working with. If you are running **LIB** on a floppy-disk system, place your working copy of the Libraries #1 distribution disk in drive A and the disk containing the object files or libraries you are working with in drive B.

Give the **LIB** command the input it needs in one of the following ways:

- By giving the input on a command line of the form

  **LIB** *oldlib* [/**P**[**AGESIZE**]:*number*] [*commands*][,[*listfile*][,[*newlib*]]][;]

  The command line cannot be longer than 128 characters.

- By typing

  ```
  LIB
  ```

  and responding to the prompts

  ```
  Library name:
  Operations:
  List file:
  Output library:
  ```

  To give more files for any prompt, type an ampersand (**&**) at the end of the line. The prompt reappears on the next line, and you can continue typing your response to the prompt.

- By setting up a file with responses to **LIB** command prompts, known as a "response file," then typing a **LIB** command of the form

  **LIB** @ *filename*

  where *filename* is the name of the response file. The responses must be in the same order as the **LIB** prompts discussed above. You can also enter the name of a response file after any linker prompt, or at any position in the **LIB** command line.

Table 10.1 shows the input you give on the **LIB** command line, or in response to each prompt.

Table 10.1

Input to the LIB Command

| Field | Prompt | Input |
|-------|--------|-------|
| *oldlib* | Library name | Name of the library you are changing or creating. If this library does not exist, **LIB** asks if you want to create it. Type y to create a new library or n to terminate **LIB**. This message is suppressed if you type command characters, a comma, or a semi-colon after the library name. A semicolon tells **LIB** to perform a consistency check on the library; with the library and display, it displays a message if it finds errors in any library module. |
| **/P:***number* | **/P:***number* in response to "Library name" prompt | Sets the page size for the library to *number* bytes, where *number* is an integer power of 2 between 16 and 32,768, inclusive. See Section 10.2.5 for more information about the library page size. |
| *commands* | Operations | Command symbols and object files that tell **LIB** what changes to make in the library. |
| *listfile* | List file | Name of a cross-reference-listing file. No listing file is created if you do not give a file name. |
| *newlib* | Output library | Name of the changed library that **LIB** creates as output. If you do not give a new library name, the original, unchanged library is saved in a library file with the same name but with a **.BAK** extension replacing the **.LIB** extension. |

## 10.2.2 Defaults for LIB

Choose defaults in any of the following ways for the information that **LIB** needs:

- To choose the default for any command-line entry, omit the file name or names before the entry and type only the required comma. The only exception to this is the default for the *listfile* entry: if you use a comma as a placeholder for this entry, **LIB** *will* create a cross-reference-listing file.

- To choose the default for any prompt, press ENTER.

- To choose the defaults for all remaining command-line entries, or for all remaining prompts, type a semicolon (;) after those entries or prompts. The semicolon should be the last character on the command line.

The following list shows the defaults that **LIB** uses for cross-reference-listing files and output libraries:

| File | Default |
|------|---------|
| Cross-reference listing | The special file name **NUL**, which tells **LINK** *not* to create a cross-reference-listing file |
| Output library | The *oldlib* entry or the response to the "Library name" prompt |

## 10.2.3   Command Symbols

To tell **LIB** what changes you want to make to a library, type a command symbol (such as $+$, $-$, $-+$, *, or $-*$), followed immediately by a module name, object-file name, or library name. You can specify more than one operation, in any order.

The following list shows each **LIB** command symbol, the type of file name to specify with the symbol, and what the symbol does:

| Command | Meaning |
|---------|---------|
| $+${ *objfile*\|*lib*} | If given with an object-file name, the plus sign ($+$) adds the given object file to the input library and makes that object file the last module in the library. You can use a path name for the object-file name. Since **LIB** automatically supplies the **.OBJ** extension, you can omit the extension from the object-file name. |
| | If given with a library name, the plus sign ($+$) adds the contents of that library to the input library. The library name must have the **.LIB** extension. |
| $-$*module* | Deletes the given module from the input library. A module name has no path name and no extension. |

| | |
|---|---|
| −+*module* | Replaces the given module in the input library. Module names have no path names and no extensions. **LIB** deletes the given module, then appends the object file that has the same name as the module. The object file is assumed to have an **.OBJ** extension and to reside in the current working directory. |
| \**module* | Copies the given module from the library to an object file in the current working directory. The module remains in the library file. When **LIB** copies the module to an object file, it adds the **.OBJ** extension. You cannot override the **.OBJ** extension, drive designation, or path name given to the object file. However, you can later rename the file or copy it to whatever location you like. |
| −\**module* | Moves the given object module from the library to an object file. This operation is equivalent to copying the module to an object file, as described above, then deleting the module from the library. |

---

*Warning*

Library modules may contain calls to other library modules. If you extract library modules that call other library modules, the called modules are not extracted.

---

## ■ Examples

```
LIB LANG-+HEAP;
```

The example above uses the replace command symbol (−+) to instruct **LIB** to replace the HEAP module in the library LANG.LIB. **LIB** deletes the HEAP module from the library, then appends the object file HEAP.OBJ as a new module in the library. The semicolon at the end of the command line tells **LIB** to use the default responses for the remaining prompts. This means that no listing file is created and that changes are written to the original library file instead of to a new library file.

```
LIB LANG-HEAP+HEAP;
```

```
LIB LANG+HEAP-HEAP;
```

The examples above perform the same function as the first example in this section, but in two separate operations, using the add (+) and delete (−) command symbols. The effect is the same for these examples because delete operations are always carried out before add operations, regardless of the order of the operations in the command line. This order of execution prevents confusion when a new version of a module replaces an old version in the library file.

```
LIB FOR;
```

The example above causes **LIB** to perform a consistency check of the library file FOR.LIB. No other action is performed. **LIB** displays any consistency errors it finds and returns to the operating-system level.

```
LIB LANG,LCROSS.PUB
```

This example tells **LIB** to perform a consistency check of the library file LANG.LIB and then create a cross-reference-listing file that is named LCROSS.PUB.

```
LIB FIRST -*STUFF *MORE, ,SECOND
```

The example above instructs **LIB** to move the module STUFF from the library FIRST.LIB to an object file called STUFF.OBJ. The module STUFF is removed from the library in the process. The module MORE is copied from the library to an object file called MORE.OBJ; the module remains in the library. The revised library is called SECOND.LIB. It contains all the modules in FIRST.LIB except STUFF, which was removed by using the move command symbol (−*). The original library, FIRST.LIB, remains unchanged.

```
LIBFOR
+CURSOR+HEAP-HEAP*FOIBLES
CROSSLST
```

The contents of the above response file cause **LIB** to delete the module HEAP from the LIBFOR.LIB library file, extract the module FOIBLES and place it in an object file named FOIBLES.OBJ, and append the object files CURSOR.OBJ and HEAP.OBJ as the last two modules in the library. Finally, **LIB** creates a cross-reference-listing file named CROSSLST.

## 10.2.4   Cross-Reference-Listing Files

A cross-reference-listing file contains the following two lists:

1. An alphabetical list of all public symbols in the library.

   Each symbol name is followed by the name of the module in which it is referenced.

2. A list of the modules in the library.

   Under each module name is an alphabetical listing of the public symbols defined in that module.

■   **Example**

The examples here show parts of the cross-reference-listing file for the standard C library **MLIBCE.LIB**. In the part immediately below, the first and third columns show the public symbols in the library, and the second and fourth columns show the names of the modules where the symbols are referenced:

```
$$OVLINIT.........ovlm61          $i4_m10............ixtomx
$i8_implicit_exp..emfin           $i8_inpbas........emfin
$i8_input.........emfin           $i8_input_ws......emfin
$i8_m8............ixtomx          $i8_output........emfout
$i8_tpwr10........emtmul          $m4_i10...........ixtomx
$m8_i8............ixtomx          DOSCREATECSALIAS..apisim
DOSDEVCONFIG......apisim          DOSFREESEG........apisim
DOSGETMACHINEMODE..apisim         DOSSETVEC.........apisim
        .                 .               .                 .
        .                 .               .                 .
        .                 .               .                 .
```

In the second part of the listing, shown below, each module of the library is followed by the public symbols that appear in each module:

```
afhdiff           Offset: 00000010H  Code and data size: 41H
  __aFahdiff

anhdiff           Offset: 000000d0H  Code and data size: 3dH
  __aNahdiff

3_file            Offset: 00000190H  Code and data size: 11aH
  __iob              __iob2              __lastiob

access            Offset: 000002f0H  Code and data size: 1fH
  _access
                                     .
                                     .
                                     .
```

## 10.2.5  Setting the Library Page Size

The page size of a library affects the alignment of modules stored in the library. Modules in the library are always aligned to start at a position that is a multiple of the page size (in bytes) from the beginning of the file. The default page size for a newly created library is 16 bytes.

You can set a different library page size while you are creating a library or change the page size of an existing library by adding the following option after the *oldlib* entry on the **LIB** command line or after the name you type in response to the "Library name" prompt:

**/P[AGESIZE]**:*number*

The *number* specifies the new page size. It must be an integer value representing a power of 2 in the range 16 to 32,768.

The library page size determines the number of modules the library can hold; thus, increasing the page size allows you to include more modules in the library. However, the larger the page size, the larger the amount of wasted storage space in the library (on average, *pagesize*/2 bytes per module). In most cases you should use a small page size unless your library is very large.

The page size also determines the maximum size of the library. This limit is *number* * 65,536. For example, if you specify /P:16, the library must be smaller than one megabyte (16 * 65,536 bytes).

# CHAPTER 11

# AUTOMATING PROGRAM DEVELOPMENT WITH MAKE

The **MAKE** program-maintenance utility can help you develop programs containing more than one module. **MAKE** automatically updates a file whenever it is out of date with respect to other, related files. **MAKE** is especially useful in situations such as the following:

- In program development, **MAKE** can automatically update an executable file whenever any of the source or object files is altered.

- In library management, **MAKE** can automatically rebuild a library whenever any of the modules in the library is altered.

- In a networking environment, **MAKE** can automatically update a local copy of a program or file that is stored on the network whenever the master copy has been updated.

When you run **MAKE**, you must give it the name of a file. This file, known as a "**MAKE** description file," contains instructions that tell **MAKE** which files to update, which files must change before it performs the update, and what kind of updating to perform. A description file might contain the following data:

```
TEST.EXE: TEST.C TEST2.C
        QCL TEST.C TEST2.C
```

In this example, `TEST.EXE` is the file to be updated whenever either of the source files `TEST.C` or `TEST2.C` is altered. The actual updating is performed by the **QCL** command on the following line. See Section 11.1 for more information about description files.

The QuickC environment automatically builds a description file for programs that you compile within the environment.

Section 11.2 describes the information you can give with the description-file name on the **MAKE** command line, including **MAKE** options. Sections 11.3–11.4 describe more advanced features of the **MAKE** utility.

# 11.1   The Heart of MAKE:
## Description Files

The **MAKE** utility relies on "description files" to determine which files to update, when to update them, and what operations to perform. A **MAKE** description file consists of one or more "description blocks," each of which gives this information for a single file.

Section 11.1.1 shows how to create a simple description file consisting of a single description block.

Sections 11.1.1–11.1.2 explain the format of a description block, the rules to follow in setting one up, and guidelines for specifying description blocks in a description file.

Section 11.1.2 discusses the **MAKE** description files that the QuickC environment builds for programs created within the environment.

## 11.1.1   Building a MAKE Description File

To illustrate how the **MAKE** utility works, this section describes how to build a simple **MAKE** description file. Since a **MAKE** description file is a text file, you can use any text editor to create one.

In this example, assume that you want to update an executable file named UPDATE.EXE whenever any of its source files are changed. Assume further that the names of these source files are GETINPUT.C, FINDREC.C, and UPDATE.C. Use the following procedure to create a **MAKE** description file to update UPDATE.EXE automatically:

1.   Using the text editor, create a file named UPDATE. Although a **MAKE** description file can have any name, you may find it helpful to give the description file the same name (without an extension) as the file it maintains.

2.   Type the name of the file you are maintaining followed by a colon, as shown below. This file is known as the "outfile," since **MAKE** creates the updated version of the file as output. (Outfiles are sometimes known as "target files.")

     UPDATE.EXE :

3.   Following the colon, type the names of any files that, when changed, should cause the outfile to be updated. In this example, you want to update UPDATE.EXE whenever GETINPUT.C, FINDREC.C, or UPDATE.C is changed, so the line in the description file would look like this:

     UPDATE.EXE : UPDATE.C GETINPUT.C FINDREC.C

     The files to the right of the colon are known as "infiles" since **MAKE** uses them as input to determine whether or not to update the outfile. (Infiles are sometimes known as "dependent files.") Each infile is separated from the next by a space.

4.   Type a number sign (#) if you want to add a comment to any line in a **MAKE** description file. **MAKE** ignores any text between the

number sign and the next new-line character. For example, you might want to add a comment as shown below:

```
UPDATE.EXE: UPDATE.C GETINPUT.C FINDREC.C #UPDATE ROUTINE
```

5. If any of the infiles have changed, type the command you want to carry out. In this example, assume that you want to recompile and relink all of the infiles. The resulting description file would look like this:

```
UPDATE.EXE: UPDATE.C GETINPUT.C FINDREC.C #UPDATE ROUTINE
            QCL UPDATE.C GETINPUT.C FINDREC.C
```

If you want to add a comment before or after the command line, the comment must appear in column 1, as shown below:

```
UPDATE.EXE: UPDATE.C GETINPUT.C FINDREC.C # UPDATE ROUTINE
# RECOMPILE AND RELINK
            QCL UPDATE.C GETINPUT.C FINDREC.C
```

6. Save the description file and exit your text editor. Then type

```
MAKE
```

followed by the name of the description file and press ENTER. In this example, you would type

```
MAKE UPDATE
```

7. **MAKE** compares the last-modification dates of each of the infiles to the date of the outfile. If all of the infile dates are earlier than the outfile date, **MAKE** does nothing. If any infile date is later than the outfile date, **MAKE** recognizes that the outfile is out of date with respect to that infile and, therefore, carries out the command you have indicated. In this example, **MAKE** recompiles the source files and relinks the corresponding object files to recreate `UPDATE.EXE`.

## 11.1.2 Description Blocks

A description block has the following general form:

*outfile*: [[*infile*]]... [[*# comment*]]
[[*# comment*]]
    *command*
    [[*command*]]

   .

   .

   .

The following list defines the parts of a description block:

| Field | Meaning |
| --- | --- |
| *outfile* | Name of the file to be updated; may include drive or path specifications. Only one *outfile* is allowed. |
| *infile* | Names of files that, when any are changed, cause *outfile* to be updated; may include drive or path specifications. At least one space must separate one *infile* name from another. If you have more *infile* names than can fit on one line, type a backslash (\\), press RETURN, and then continue typing names on the next line. If no *infile* is given, then **MAKE** carries out the commands in the block automatically. |
| *command* | Command to be carried out if *outfile* is out of date with respect to an *infile*. Commands can be programs, batch commands, or DOS commands. You can give any number of commands, but each must begin on a new line and each must be preceded by at least one space or tab. |
| *comment* | A comment character (#) followed by one or more characters. **MAKE** ignores all characters that follow the comment character on the same line. So, if you want a comment to appear on the same line as *outfile*, you must place it after the *infile* name(s). If a comment appears on a line where a command is expected, the comment character must be the first character on the line; no leading spaces are allowed. |

*Note*

One way to remember the **MAKE** description-file format is to think of it in terms of an "if-then" form: if an *outfile* is out of date with respect to any *infile*, or if an *outfile* does not exist, then do *commands*.

You can give any number of description blocks in a description file. A blank line must appear between the last line of one description block and the first line of the next description block.

When you start **MAKE**, it reads the line in the first description block that names the outfile and infiles and then checks the modification dates of those files. If the modification date for any infile is later than the modification date for the outfile, if the outfile does not exist, or if no infiles are given, **MAKE** displays and executes the commands specified in the block. Otherwise, it skips to the next block, repeating this sequence for each block in the file.

If **MAKE** cannot find an infile, outfile, or command, it displays a diagnostic message. If the missing file is an outfile, **MAKE** continues running since, in many cases, the missing file is created by later commands. If the missing file is an infile or a command file, **MAKE** stops running.

**MAKE** also stops running and displays an exit code if any command in a block returns an error.

Since **MAKE** processes description blocks in their order of appearance in the description file, it is important that the description blocks appear in the order in which you want processing to proceed.

■   **Example**

```
MOD1.OBJ:      MOD1.C
        QCL /c MOD1.C

MOD2.OBJ:      MOD2.C
        QCL /c MOD2.C

EXAMPLE.EXE:  MOD1.OBJ MOD2.OBJ
        LINK MOD1+MOD2,EXAMPLE,EXAMPLE;
```

In the example above, the description blocks appear in the order in which the outfiles are updated or created. Thus, **MAKE** updates `MOD1.OBJ` and `MOD2.OBJ` (or creates them, if necessary) before it updates or creates `EXAMPLE.EXE`. After **MAKE** is run, any changes to the source files are reflected in `EXAMPLE.EXE`.

## 11.2   Running MAKE

■   **Syntax**

**MAKE** [[*options*]] [[*macrodefinitions*]] *filename*

If you are running **MAKE** on a hard-disk system, use the DOS **CD** command to make the current directory that directory which contains the description file and the files you are working with. If you are running on a floppy-disk system, place your working copy of the Libraries #1 distribution disk in drive A and the disk containing the description file and the files you are working with in drive B.

The **MAKE** command line allows you to give information in addition to the name of the description file. The following list describes the information you can give on the **MAKE** command line:

| Field | Meaning |
|---|---|
| *options* | One or more **MAKE** options. |
| *macrodefinitions* | One or more **MAKE** macro definitions. |
| *filename* | The name of a **MAKE** description file. This is usually the name of the program being maintained, without an extension. If you are updating a program named PROGRAM.C that was created within the QuickC environment, *filename* would be PROGRAM.MAK. |

The following list describes each option available with **MAKE** and how that option affects **MAKE**:

| Option | Action |
|---|---|
| /D | Displays the last modification date of each file as the file is scanned. |
| /I | Ignores exit codes (also called return or "error-level" codes) returned by programs that are called from the **MAKE** description file. |
| /N | "No-execution" mode: displays commands in the description file but does not execute these commands. This option is useful if you are debugging a **MAKE** description file. |
| /S | "Silent" mode: does not display lines as they are executed. |
| /X *filename* | Redirects error messages from **MAKE** or any of the programs run by **MAKE** to the given file. If *filename* is a dash (-), error messages are redirected to the standard output device. If this option is not given, error messages are sent to the standard error-output device. |

## 11.3   Using Macro Definitions with MAKE

One way to simplify definition files is to use macros. A "macro" is simply a name that you can substitute for other text in a **MAKE** description file. To change the text that the name represents, you only need to change it in the macro definition. The text is automatically updated everywhere else that the name is used.

You might want to use macros

- As the base names of source, object, and executable files under development. If the program name changes, you can change the base name in the macro definition; then the base name is changed automatically for the source, object, and executable files given in the description file.

- To specify a particular set of options for a command such as **QCL** or **LINK**. If the options change, you can change them throughout the description file simply by changing the macro definition.

### 11.3.1   Defining and Specifying Macros

A macro definition has the following general form:

*name= text*

After you define a macro, you can use it in the description file as shown below:

$(*name*)

Wherever the pattern $(*name*) appears in the description file, that pattern is replaced by *text*. The *name* is converted to uppercase; for example, the names `flags` and `FLAGS` are equivalent. If you define a macro name but leave *text* blank, or if you use a macro name that has not been defined, *text* will be a null string.

For *name*, you can also use any environment variable that is defined in the current environment. For example, if the environment variable **PATH** is defined in the current environment, the value of **PATH** replaces any occurrences of $(PATH) in the description file. (Note that using this macro does not redefine the value of **PATH** in the current environment.)

You can give macro definitions in either of the following places:

- Before any description block in a **MAKE** description file. Each macro definition must appear on a separate line. Any tab or space characters between *name* and the equal sign (=), or between the equal sign and *text*, are ignored. Any other tabs or spaces are considered part of *text*.

- On the **MAKE** command line.

To include tab or space characters in a macro definition on the command line, enclose the entire definition in double quotation marks (" ").

If the same *name* is defined in more than one place, the following order of precedence applies:

1. Command-line definition

2. Description-file definition

3. Environment definition

For example, if **PATH** is defined in the DOS environment and in a description file, **MAKE** uses the definition in the description file. If it is also defined on the **MAKE** command line, the command-line definition supersedes the other two definitions.

## ■ Example

Assume the existence of the following **MAKE** description file named COMPILE:

```
base=ABC
debug="/Zi"

$(base).EXE:        $(base).C
        QCL $(debug) $(base).C
```

In this description file, macro definitions are given for the names `base` and `debug`.

The `base` macro defines the base name of the object and executable files being maintained. **MAKE** replaces each occurrence of `$(base)` with the text ABC. If the program name changes, you would only have to replace ABC in the macro definition with the new program name to change the base name of the two files.

The `debug` macro tells the **QCL** command to create an executable file for the QuickC or CodeView debugger.

If you want to override one of the macro values in this description file, you can give a new macro definition on the **MAKE** command line, as shown in the following example:

```
MAKE base=DEF compile
```

This command-line definition of `base` overrides the definition of `base` in the description file. As a result, `base` is replaced with the text `DEF` instead of `ABC`.

If you do not want to create an executable file containing debugging information, you could run **MAKE** with the following command line:

```
MAKE debug= compile
```

Because macros defined on the command line have higher precedence than those defined in the description file, **MAKE** uses the command-line definition (a null string; note the white space between the equal sign and the **MAKE** description-file name) for the `$(debug)` macro. As a result, the **/Zi** switch does not appear on the **QCL** command line, and the executable file that is created does not include the information needed for debugging.

## 11.3.2   Using Macros within Macro Definitions

Macros can be used within macro definitions. For example, you could have the following macro definition in a **MAKE** description file named PICTURE:

```
LIBS=$(DLIB)\MLIBCE.LIB $(DLIB)\GRAPHICS.LIB
```

You could then run **MAKE** and specify the definition for the macro named `$(DLIB)` on the command line, as shown in the following example:

```
MAKE DLIB=C:\LIB PICTURE
```

In this case, every occurrence of the macro `$(DLIB)` in the description file would be expanded to `C:\LIB`; consequently, the definition of the LIBS macro in the description file would be expanded to the following:

```
LIBS=C:\LIB\MLIBCE.LIB C:\LIB\GRAPHICS.LIB
```

Be careful to avoid infinitely recursive macros such as the following:

```
A = $(B)
B = $(C)
C = $(A)
```

In the example above, if the macro $(B) has not been defined before the A = $(B) line, all of the other macros will be undefined as well.

### 11.3.3   Using Special Macros

**MAKE** recognizes the following special macro names and automatically substitutes the corresponding text for each:

| Name | Text Substituted |
|------|------------------|
| $* | Base name of the outfile |
| $@ | Complete outfile name |
| $** | Complete list of infiles |

■   **Example**

```
TEST.EXE: MOD1.OBJ MOD2.OBJ MOD3.OBJ
        LINK $**, $@;
        $*
```

In the **LINK** command in the example above, $** represents all of the infiles that correspond to the outfile TEST.EXE, and $@ specifies the complete name of TEST.EXE as the executable-file name on the **LINK** command line. The final line uses $* to specify the base name of TEST.EXE—that is, TEST—as the next command to be carried out. Therefore, this example is equivalent to the following:

```
TEST:EXE: MOD1.OBJ MOD2.OBJ MOD3.OBJ
        LINK MOD1.OBJ MOD2.OBJ MOD3.OBJ, TEST.EXE;
        TEST
```

## 11.4   Defining Inference Rules

Often you use **MAKE** to update one type of file when a file of another type is changed. For example, you often use **MAKE** to update object files when source files change, or to update executable files or libraries when source or object files change.

In cases such as these, you can define "inference rules" for **MAKE** to follow. These rules allow you to give a single **MAKE** command to convert *all* outfiles with a given extension to files with a different extension. For example, you can use inference rules to specify a single **QCL** command that changes any source file (which has an extension of .**C**) to an executable file (which has an extension of .**EXE**). Since **MAKE** looks for an applicable inference rule whenever no commands appear in a description block, you would not have to include the **QCL** command in all blocks in which you compile and link a file.

Inference rules have the following general form:

*.inextension.outextension* :
   *command*
   ⟦*command*⟧
   .
   .
   .

In this format, *command* specifies one of the commands that you must use to convert files with extension *inextension* to files with extension *outextension*. Using the earlier example of converting source files to executable files, you could define the following inference rule to compile and link all source files in the current directory to create object files:

```
.C.EXE:
    QCL $*.C
```

Giving an inference rule without a command has the effect of canceling an inference rule that has already been defined.

If **MAKE** finds a description block without any commands, it looks for an inference rule that matches both the outfile extension and the infile extension. If it finds such a rule, **MAKE** carries out any commands that are given in the rule.

You can include inference rules in either of the following places:

- In a **MAKE** description file.
- In a file named **TOOLS.INI**. This file is known as the "tools initialization file." A line beginning with the tag **[make]** must appear before any dependency rules in **TOOLS.INI**.

**MAKE** searches for dependency rules in the following order:

1. In the current description file.

2. In the **TOOLS.INI** file. **MAKE** looks for **TOOLS.INI** in the current drive and directory. If it cannot find this file, then **MAKE** looks for **TOOLS.INI** in the directory indicated by the **INIT** environment variable. If **MAKE** finds **TOOLS.INI**, it looks through the file for a line beginning with the tag **[make]**. It applies any appropriate inference rules following this line.

■  **Example**

Assume the following entry in the **TOOLS.INI** file:

```
[make]
.OBJ.LIB:
      LIB TEST.LIB +$*.OBJ;
```

Now assume the following description file:

```
EXAMPLE1.LIB:  EXAMPLE1.OBJ

EXAMPLE2.EXE:  EXAMPLE2.OBJ
      LINK /CO EXAMPLE2,,,LIBV3.LIB
```

The **TOOLS.INI** file defines an inference rule that executes the **LIB** command in the description file to update a library whenever a change is made in the corresponding object file. The file name in the inference rule is specified with the special macro name $* so that the rule applies to any file with the .OBJ extension.

When **MAKE** encounters a line containing an outfile and one or more infiles, it first looks for commands on the next line. If it does not find any commands, **MAKE** checks for a rule that may apply; in this case, it finds the rule defined in **TOOLS.INI**. **MAKE** applies the rule, replacing the $* macro with EXAMPLE1 when it executes the command; consequently, the **LIB** command becomes

```
LIB TEST.LIB +EXAMPLE1.OBJ;
```

When **MAKE** reaches the line containing the EXAMPLE2.EXE outfile, it does not search for a dependency rule, since a command is explicitly given for this outfile/infile relationship. Thus, in this case, **MAKE** links the object file EXAMPLE2.OBJ with the LIBV3.LIB library to create an executable file instead of adding EXAMPLE2.OBJ to the TEST.LIB library.

## 11.5   Using .MAK Files

If you create a program list for a program within the QuickC environment, QuickC automatically creates a **MAKE** description file for that program. The description file has the same base name as the program, with the extension **.MAK**. The description file allows QuickC to recompile and relink all of the modules that make up the program if any module in the program, or any include file specified in a program module, has been updated.

### 11.5.1   Using .MAK Files with MAKE

With minor changes, you can use the **MAKE** utility with a **.MAK** file to update a program outside the QuickC environment. Recall that a library with a **.LIB** extension must be present when you create a program outside of QuickC. If a Quick library was loaded in the QuickC environment at the time you compiled the program, the **.MAK** file will contain a comment line indicating the name of the Quick library.

Use this procedure when you update a program outside of QuickC:

1. Make a copy of the **.MAK** file under a different name so that QuickC can continue using the original.

2. Edit this copy, substituting the name of the appropriate stand-alone library name for the comment line that shows where the library name should go.

3. Run **MAKE** and give the name of the edited **.MAK** file for the program as input. **MAKE** automatically recompiles and relinks the program, which can be loaded into the the QuickC environment as usual.

### 11.5.2   Include File Dependencies

During program development, you will often centralize definitions of constants, macros, and external variables in an include file, then use the **#include** directive to include this code in different program modules. Using this mechanism, you need only update the common code contained in the include file, since the modules that include copies of the common code are automatically updated when you recompile them.

To make sure that a program is updated automatically when any of its include files has been changed, be sure to give include files among the infiles in the **.MAK** file. Although the QuickC compiler does not place include files in a **.MAK** file automatically, it does preserve any include files that you place in the **.MAK** file by using an editor.

When you load a program list in the QuickC environment by using the Set Program List command, any include files you have given in the **.MAK** file are included in the program list. The QuickC compiler uses the include file in the same way as any other file in the program list: if the include file has been updated since the last time the program was compiled, it recompiles the program.

■   **Example**

Assume that each module of a program named Lexer has an include file named `globals.h`, which resides in the `\INCLUDE` directory. Assume also that the first few lines of the `lexer.mak` file are

```
#
# Program: Lexer
#
        qcl -c  -WO -Zq -AM $*.c

lexer.obj : C:\SRC\lexer.c

gettoken.obj : C:\SRC\gettoken.c
        .
        .
        .
```

You can change the `lexer.mak` file as shown below to make sure that Lexer is updated whenever `globals.h` has been updated:

```
#
# Program: Lexer
#
        qcl -c  -WO -Zq -AM $*.c

lexer.obj : C:\SRC\lexer.c C:\INCLUDE\globals.h

gettoken.obj : C:\SRC\gettoken.c C:\INCLUDE\globals.h
        .
        .
        .
```

## 11.5.3   Specifying Linker Options

When the QuickC compiler compiles a program with a program list, it first compiles the modules in the program list, then links the resulting object files. You can control the linking process by specifying linker conditions in the **.MAK** file that contains the program list. Simply define a macro named **LDFLAGS** as shown below:

**LDFLAGS=** *link-opt ...*

The **LDFLAGS** macro is automatically included on the **LINK** command line in the **.MAK** file. Your definition must follow the rules outlined in Section 11.3.1.

The **LINK** options that you specify are used each time you recompile and relink the modules in the program list; they remain in use until you change the value of **LDFLAGS** in the **.MAK** file.

# APPENDIXES

| Ctrl | Dec | Hex | Char | Code |
|------|-----|-----|------|------|
| ^@ | 0 | 00 |  | NUL |
| ^A | 1 | 01 | ☺ | SOH |
| ^B | 2 | 02 | ☻ | STX |
| ^C | 3 | 03 | ♥ | ETX |
| ^D | 4 | 04 | ♦ | EOT |
| ^E | 5 | 05 | ♣ | ENQ |
| ^F | 6 | 06 | ♠ | ACK |
| ^G | 7 | 07 | • | BEL |
| ^H | 8 | 08 | ◘ | BS |
| ^I | 9 | 09 | ○ | HT |
| ^J | 10 | 0A | ◙ | LF |
| ^K | 11 | 0B | ♂ | VT |
| ^L | 12 | 0C | ♀ | FF |
| ^M | 13 | 0D | ♪ | CR |
| ^N | 14 | 0E | ♫ | SO |
| ^O | 15 | 0F | ☼ | SI |
| ^P | 16 | 10 | ► | DLE |
| ^Q | 17 | 11 | ◄ | DC1 |
| ^R | 18 | 12 | ↕ | DC2 |
| ^S | 19 | 13 | ‼ | DC3 |
| ^T | 20 | 14 | ¶ | DC4 |
| ^U | 21 | 15 | § | NAK |
| ^V | 22 | 16 | ▬ | SYN |
| ^W | 23 | 17 | ↨ | ETB |
| ^X | 24 | 18 | ↑ | CAN |
| ^Y | 25 | 19 | ↓ | EM |
| ^Z | 26 | 1A | → | SUB |
| ^[ | 27 | 1B | ← | ESC |
| ^\ | 28 | 1C | ∟ | FS |
| ^] | 29 | 1D | ↔ | GS |
| ^^ | 30 | 1E | ▲ | RS |
| ^_ | 31 | 1F | ▼ | US |

| Dec | Hex | Char |
|-----|-----|------|
| 32 | 20 |  |
| 33 | 21 | ! |
| 34 | 22 | " |
| 35 | 23 | # |
| 36 | 24 | $ |
| 37 | 25 | % |
| 38 | 26 | & |
| 39 | 27 | ' |
| 40 | 28 | ( |
| 41 | 29 | ) |
| 42 | 2A | * |
| 43 | 2B | + |
| 44 | 2C | , |
| 45 | 2D | - |
| 46 | 2E | . |
| 47 | 2F | / |
| 48 | 30 | 0 |
| 49 | 32 | 1 |
| 50 | 32 | 2 |
| 51 | 33 | 3 |
| 52 | 34 | 4 |
| 53 | 35 | 5 |
| 54 | 36 | 6 |
| 55 | 37 | 7 |
| 56 | 38 | 8 |
| 57 | 39 | 9 |
| 58 | 3A | : |
| 59 | 3B | ; |
| 60 | 3C | < |
| 61 | 3D | = |
| 62 | 3E | > |
| 63 | 3F | ? |

| Dec | Hex | Char |
|-----|-----|------|
| 64 | 40 | @ |
| 65 | 41 | A |
| 66 | 42 | B |
| 67 | 43 | C |
| 68 | 44 | D |
| 69 | 45 | E |
| 70 | 46 | F |
| 71 | 47 | G |
| 72 | 48 | H |
| 73 | 49 | I |
| 74 | 4A | J |
| 75 | 4B | K |
| 76 | 4C | L |
| 77 | 4D | M |
| 78 | 4E | N |
| 79 | 4F | O |
| 80 | 50 | P |
| 81 | 51 | Q |
| 82 | 52 | R |
| 83 | 53 | S |
| 84 | 54 | T |
| 85 | 55 | U |
| 86 | 56 | V |
| 87 | 57 | W |
| 88 | 58 | X |
| 89 | 59 | Y |
| 90 | 5A | Z |
| 91 | 5B | [ |
| 92 | 5C | \ |
| 93 | 5D | ] |
| 94 | 5E | ^ |
| 95 | 5F | _ |

| Dec | Hex | Char |
|-----|-----|------|
| 96 | 60 | ` |
| 97 | 61 | a |
| 98 | 62 | b |
| 99 | 63 | c |
| 100 | 64 | d |
| 101 | 65 | e |
| 102 | 66 | f |
| 103 | 67 | g |
| 104 | 68 | h |
| 105 | 69 | i |
| 106 | 6A | j |
| 107 | 6B | k |
| 108 | 6C | l |
| 109 | 6D | m |
| 110 | 6E | n |
| 111 | 6F | o |
| 112 | 70 | p |
| 113 | 71 | q |
| 114 | 72 | r |
| 115 | 73 | s |
| 116 | 74 | t |
| 117 | 75 | u |
| 118 | 76 | v |
| 119 | 77 | w |
| 120 | 78 | x |
| 121 | 79 | y |
| 122 | 7A | z |
| 123 | 7B | { |
| 124 | 7C | ¦ |
| 125 | 7D | } |
| 126 | 7E | ~ |
| 127 | 7F | ⌂ [†] |

† ASCII code 127 has the code DEL. Under DOS, this code has the same effect as ASCII 8 (BS). The DEL code can be generated by the CTRL-BKSP key.

| Dec | Hex | Char |
|-----|-----|------|
| 128 | 80 | Ç |
| 129 | 81 | ü |
| 130 | 82 | é |
| 131 | 83 | â |
| 132 | 84 | ä |
| 133 | 85 | à |
| 134 | 86 | å |
| 135 | 87 | ç |
| 136 | 88 | ê |
| 137 | 89 | ë |
| 138 | 8A | è |
| 139 | 8B | ï |
| 140 | 8C | î |
| 141 | 8D | ì |
| 142 | 8E | Ä |
| 143 | 8F | Å |
| 144 | 90 | É |
| 145 | 91 | æ |
| 146 | 92 | Æ |
| 147 | 93 | ô |
| 148 | 94 | ö |
| 149 | 95 | ò |
| 150 | 96 | û |
| 151 | 97 | ù |
| 152 | 98 | ÿ |
| 153 | 99 | Ö |
| 154 | 9A | Ü |
| 155 | 9B | ¢ |
| 156 | 9C | £ |
| 157 | 9D | ¥ |
| 158 | 9E | ₧ |
| 159 | 9F | ƒ |

| Dec | Hex | Char |
|-----|-----|------|
| 160 | A0 | á |
| 161 | A1 | í |
| 162 | A2 | ó |
| 163 | A3 | ú |
| 164 | A4 | ñ |
| 165 | A5 | Ñ |
| 166 | A6 | ª |
| 167 | A7 | º |
| 168 | A8 | ¿ |
| 169 | A9 | ⌐ |
| 170 | AA | ¬ |
| 171 | AB | ½ |
| 172 | AC | ¼ |
| 173 | AD | ¡ |
| 174 | AE | « |
| 175 | AF | » |
| 176 | B0 | ░ |
| 177 | B1 | ▒ |
| 178 | B2 | ▓ |
| 179 | B3 | │ |
| 180 | B4 | ┤ |
| 181 | B5 | ╡ |
| 182 | B6 | ╢ |
| 183 | B7 | ╖ |
| 184 | B8 | ╕ |
| 185 | B9 | ╣ |
| 186 | BA | ║ |
| 187 | BB | ╗ |
| 188 | BC | ╝ |
| 189 | BD | ╜ |
| 190 | BE | ╛ |
| 191 | BF | ┐ |

| Dec | Hex | Char |
|-----|-----|------|
| 192 | C0 | └ |
| 193 | C1 | ┴ |
| 194 | C2 | ┬ |
| 195 | C3 | ├ |
| 196 | C4 | ─ |
| 197 | C5 | ┼ |
| 198 | C6 | ╞ |
| 199 | C7 | ╟ |
| 200 | C8 | ╚ |
| 201 | C9 | ╔ |
| 202 | CA | ╩ |
| 203 | CB | ╦ |
| 204 | CC | ╠ |
| 205 | CD | ═ |
| 206 | CE | ╬ |
| 207 | CF | ╧ |
| 208 | D0 | ╨ |
| 209 | D1 | ╤ |
| 210 | D2 | ╥ |
| 211 | D3 | ╙ |
| 212 | D4 | ╘ |
| 213 | D5 | ╒ |
| 214 | D6 | ╓ |
| 215 | D7 | ╫ |
| 216 | D8 | ╪ |
| 217 | D9 | ┘ |
| 218 | DA | ┌ |
| 219 | DB | █ |
| 220 | DC | ▄ |
| 221 | DD | ▌ |
| 222 | DE | ▐ |
| 223 | DF | ▀ |

| Dec | Hex | Char |
|-----|-----|------|
| 224 | E0 | α |
| 225 | E1 | β |
| 226 | E2 | Γ |
| 227 | E3 | π |
| 228 | E4 | Σ |
| 229 | E5 | σ |
| 230 | E6 | µ |
| 232 | E7 | τ |
| 232 | E8 | Θ |
| 233 | E9 | θ |
| 234 | EA | Ω |
| 235 | EB | δ |
| 236 | EC | ∞ |
| 237 | ED | φ |
| 238 | EE | ∈ |
| 239 | EF | ∩ |
| 240 | F0 | ≡ |
| 241 | F1 | ± |
| 242 | F2 | ≥ |
| 243 | F3 | ≤ |
| 244 | F4 | ⌠ |
| 245 | F5 | ⌡ |
| 246 | F6 | ÷ |
| 247 | F7 | ≈ |
| 248 | F8 | ° |
| 249 | F9 | · |
| 250 | FA | · |
| 251 | FB | √ |
| 252 | FC | ⁿ |
| 253 | FD | ² |
| 254 | FE | ■ |
| 255 | FF | |

# APPENDIX B
# WORKING WITH
# QUICKC MEMORY MODELS

You can gain greater control over how your program uses memory by specifying the memory model for the program. Ordinarily, you do not need to specify a memory model except in the following cases:

- A program compiled within the QuickC environment has more than 64K of static data.

- A program compiled with the **QCL** command has more than 64K of code or more than 64K of static data.

In these cases, you have the following options:

1. If you are compiling with the **QCL** command, you can specify one of the other standard memory models (medium, compact, or large) using one of the **/A** options.

2. You can create a mixed-model program using the **near** and **far** keywords.

3. You can combine method 2 with method 1.

# B.1   Near and Far Addressing

The terms "near" and "far" are crucial to understanding the concept of memory models. These terms indicate how data can be accessed in the segmented architecture of the 8086 family of microprocessors (8086, 80186, and 80286).

DOS loads the code and data allocated by your program into "segments" in physical memory. Each segment is up to 64K long. Since separate segments are always allocated for the program code and data, the minimum number of segments allocated for a program is two. These two segments, required for every program, are called the default segments. The small memory model uses only the two default segments. The other memory models discussed in this chapter allow more than one code segment per program, or more than one data segment per program, or both.

In the 8086 family of microprocessors, all memory addresses consist of two parts:

1. A 16-bit number that represents the base address of a memory segment

2. Another 16-bit number that gives an offset within that segment

The architecture of the 8086 microprocessor is such that code can be accessed within the default code or data segment by using just the 16-bit offset value. This is possible because the segment addresses for the default segments are always known. This 16-bit offset value is called a "near address"; it can be accessed with a "near pointer." Since only 16-bit arithmetic is required to access any near item, near references to code or data are smaller and more efficient.

When data or code lie outside the default segments, the address must use both the segment and offset values. Such addresses are called "far addresses"; they can be accessed by using "far pointers" in a C program. Accessing far data or code items is more expensive in terms of program speed and size, but using them enables your programs to address all memory, rather than just a 64K piece.

The rest of this chapter deals with the various methods you can use to control whether your program makes near or far calls to access code or data.

## B.2   Using the Standard Memory Models

The libraries created by the **SETUP** program support four standard memory models. Using the standard memory models is the simplest way to control how your program accesses code and data in memory.

When you use the standard memory models, the compiler handles library support for you. The library corresponding to the memory model you specify is used automatically. Each memory model has its own library.

The advantage of using standard models for your programs is simplicity. In the standard models, memory management is specified by compiler options; since the standard models do not require the use of extended keywords, they are the best way to write code that can be ported to other systems (particularly systems that do not use segmented architectures).

The disadvantage of using standard memory models exclusively is that they may not produce the most efficient code. For example, if you have an otherwise medium-model program containing a large array that pushes the total data size for your program over the 64K limit for medium model, it may be to your advantage to declare the one array with the **far** keyword, while keeping the rest of the program medium model, as opposed to using the standard compact memory model for the entire program. For maximum flexibility and control over how your program uses memory, you can combine the standard-memory-model method with the **near** and **far** keywords, described in Section B.3.

The **/A** option for **QCL** is used to specify one of the four standard memory models (small, medium, compact, or large) at compile time. These memory-model options are discussed in the next four sections.

*Note*

In the following sections, which describe the different memory-model addressing conventions, it is important to keep in mind two common features of all five models:

1. No *single* source module can generate 64K or more of code.

2. No *single* data item can exceed 64K.

## B.2.1   Creating Small-Model Programs

■   **Option**

**/AS**

The small-model option tells the compiler to create a program that occupies the two default segments—one for code and one for data.

Small-model programs are typically C programs that are short or have a limited purpose. Since code and data for these programs are each limited to 64K, the total size of a small-model program can never exceed 128K. Most programs fit easily into this model.

By default, both code and data items in small-model programs are accessed with near addresses. You can override the defaults for data and code by using the **far** keyword.

The **QCL** command creates small-model programs automatically if you do not specify a memory model. The **/AS** option is provided for completeness; you never need give it explicitly.

Figure B.1 illustrates how memory is set up for the small memory model.

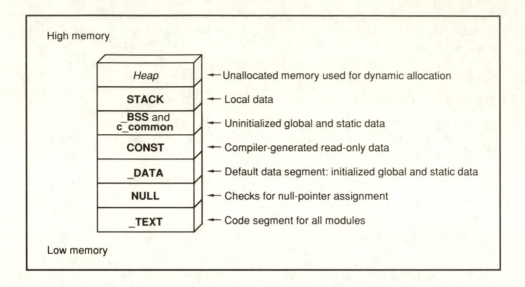

High memory

| Heap | ← Unallocated memory used for dynamic allocation |
| STACK | ← Local data |
| _BSS and c_common | ← Uninitialized global and static data |
| CONST | ← Compiler-generated read-only data |
| _DATA | ← Default data segment: initialized global and static data |
| NULL | ← Checks for null-pointer assignment |
| _TEXT | ← Code segment for all modules |

Low memory

**Figure B.1  Memory Map for Small Memory Model**

## B.2.2  Creating Medium-Model Programs

■  **Option**

**/AM**

The medium-model option provides a single segment for program data and multiple segments for program code. Each source module is given its own code segment.

Medium-model programs are typically C programs that have a large number of program statements (more than 64K of code), but a relatively small amount of data (less than 64K). Program code can occupy any amount of space and is given as many segments as needed; total program data cannot be greater than 64K. The medium model provides a useful trade-off between speed and space, since most programs refer more frequently to data items than to code.

Since programs compiled within the QuickC environment always use the medium memory model, you should give this option in cases where you use the **QCL** command to compile a module for use within the QuickC environment.

Figure B.2 illustrates how memory is set up for the medium memory model.

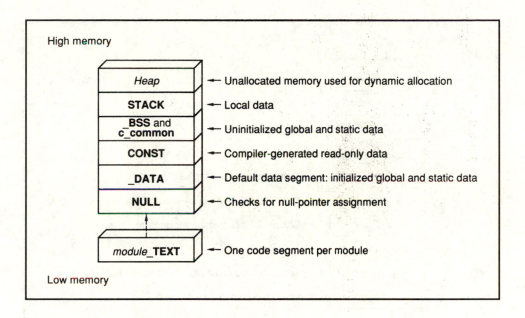

**Figure B.2  Memory Map for Medium Memory Model**

## B.2.3   Creating Compact-Model Programs

■   **Option**

/AC

The compact-model option directs the compiler to allow multiple segments for program data, but only one segment for the program code.

Compact-model programs are typically C programs that have a large amount of data, but a relatively small number of program statements. Program data can occupy any amount of space and are given as many segments as needed.

By default, code items in compact-model programs are accessed with near addresses, and data items are accessed with far addresses. You can override the default by using the **near** keyword for data and the **far** keyword for code.

Figure B.3 illustrates how memory is set up for the compact memory model.

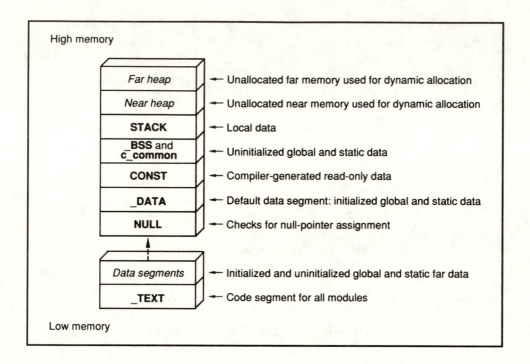

| | |
|---|---|
| Far heap | ← Unallocated far memory used for dynamic allocation |
| Near heap | ← Unallocated near memory used for dynamic allocation |
| STACK | ← Local data |
| _BSS and c_common | ← Uninitialized global and static data |
| CONST | ← Compiler-generated read-only data |
| _DATA | ← Default data segment: initialized global and static data |
| NULL | ← Checks for null-pointer assignment |
| Data segments | ← Initialized and uninitialized global and static far data |
| _TEXT | ← Code segment for all modules |

**Figure B.3  Memory Map for Compact Memory Model**

*Note*

Note that in medium and compact models, **NULL** must be used carefully in certain situations. **NULL** actually represents a null data pointer. In memory models where code and data pointers are the same size, it can be used with either. However, in memory models where code and data pointers are different sizes, this is not the case. Consider the following example:

```
void func1(char *dp)
{
.
.
.
}

void func2(char (*fp)(void))
{
.
.
.
}

main()
{
func1(NULL);
func2(NULL);
}
```

This example passes a 16-bit pointer to both func1 and func2 if compiled in medium model, and a 32-bit pointer to both func1 and func2 if compiled in compact model, unless prototypes are added to the beginning of the program to indicate the types, or an explicit cast is used on the argument to func1 (compact model) or func2 (medium model).

## B.2.4  Creating Large-Model Programs

■   **Option**

**/AL**

The large-model option allows the compiler to create multiple segments, as needed, for both code and data.

Large-model programs are typically very large C programs that use a large amount of data storage during normal processing.

By default, both code and data items in large-model programs are accessed with far addresses. You can override the default by using the **near** keyword for data and code.

Figure B.4 illustrates how memory is set up for the large memory model.

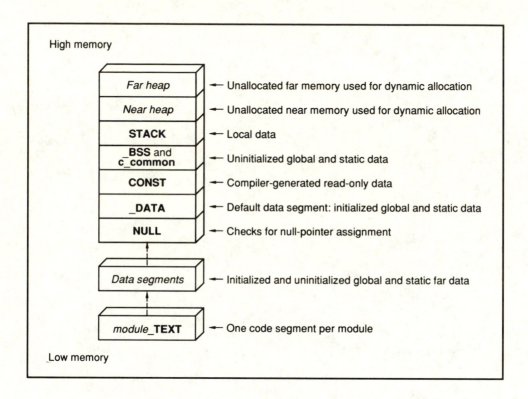

**Figure B.4 Memory Map for Large Memory Model**

# B.3 Using the near and far Keywords

One limitation of the predefined memory-model structure is that, when you change memory models, all data and code address sizes are subject to change. However, the Microsoft QuickC Compiler lets you override the default addressing convention for a given memory model and access items with a near or far pointer. This is done with the **near** and **far** keywords. These special type modifiers can be used with a standard memory model to overcome addressing limitations for particular data or code items, or to optimize access to these items, without changing the addressing conventions for the program as a whole. Table B.1 explains how the use of these keywords affects the addressing of code or data, or pointers to code or data.

**Table B.1**

**Addressing of Code and Data Declared with near and far**

| Keyword | Data | Function | Pointer Arithmetic |
|---------|------|----------|--------------------|
| **near** | Resides in default data segment; referenced with 16-bit addresses (pointers to data are 16 bits) | Assumed to be in current code segment; referenced with 16-bit addresses (pointers to functions are 16 bits) | Uses 16 bits |
| **far** | May be anywhere in memory—not assumed to reside in current data segment; referenced with 32-bit addresses (pointers to data are 32 bits) | Not assumed to be in current code segment; referenced with 32-bit address (pointers to functions are 32 bits) | Uses 16 bits |

*Note*

The **near** and **far** keywords are not a standard part of the C language; they are meaningful only for systems that use a segmented architecture similar to that of the 8086 microprocessors. Keep this in mind if you want your code to be ported to other systems.

In the Microsoft QuickC Compiler, the words **near** and **far** are C keywords by default. To treat these keywords as ordinary identifiers, you must do one of the following:

- For programs compiled within the QuickC environment, compile with the Language Extensions option turned off.

- For programs compiled with the **QCL** command, give the **/Za** option at compile time.

These options are useful if you are compiling programs with compilers in which **near** and **far** are not keywords—for instance, if you are porting a program in which one of these words is used as a label. See Section 8.1.4.6, "Using Microsoft Extensions to C: the Language Extensions Option," for further information about the use and effects of the Language Extensions and **/Za** options.

## B.3.1   Library Support for near and far

When using the **near** and **far** keywords to modify addressing conventions for particular items, you can usually use one of the standard libraries (small, compact, medium, or large) with your program. However, you must use care when calling library routines. In general, you cannot pass far pointers, or the addresses of far data items, to a small-model library routine. (Some exceptions to this statement are the library routines **halloc** and **hfree**, and the **printf** family of functions.) Of course, you can always pass the *value* of a far item to a small-model library routine. For example:

```
long far time_val;

time(&time_val);                    /* Illegal */
printf("%ld\n", time_val);          /* Legal */
```

If you use the **near** or **far** keyword, it is strongly recommended that you use function prototypes with argument-type lists to ensure that all pointer arguments are passed to functions correctly. See Section B.3.4, "Pointer Conversions," for more information.

## B.3.2   Declaring Data with near and far

The **near** and **far** keywords modify either objects or pointers to objects. When using them to declare data or code (or pointers to data or code), keep the following rules in mind:

- The keyword always modifies the object or pointer immediately to its right. In complex declarators, think of the **far** keyword and the item immediately to its right as being a single unit. For example, in the declarator

```
char far* *p;
```

p is a pointer (whose size depends on the memory model specified) to a far pointer to **char**. See the *Microsoft C Language Reference* for complete rules for using special keywords in complex declarations.

- If the item immediately to the right of the keyword is an identifier, the keyword determines whether the item will be allocated in the default data segment (**near**) or a separate data segment (**far**). For example,

```
char near a;
```

allocates a as an item of type **char** with a near address.

- If the item immediately to the right of the keyword is a pointer, the keyword determines whether the pointer will hold a near address (16 bits) or a far address (32 bits). For example,

```
char far *p;
```

allocates p as a far pointer (32 bits) to an item of type **char**.

- The **far** keyword cannot be used to declare data items in programs that will be run within the QuickC environment. However, it can be used to declare pointers to data items. For example,

```
int far item;
```

is illegal for in-memory programs, but

```
int far *item;
```

is legal.

## ■ Examples

The examples in this section show data declarations using the **near** and **far** keywords.

```
char a[3000];                    /* small-model program */
char far b[30000];
```

The first declaration in the example above allocates the array a in the default data segment. By contrast, the array b in the second declaration may be allocated in any far data segment. Since these declarations appear in a small-model program, array a probably represents frequently used data that were deliberately placed in the default segment for fast access. Array b probably represents seldom-used data that might make the default data segment exceed 64K and force the programmer to use a larger memory model if the array were not declared with the **far** keyword. The second declaration uses a large array because it is more likely that a programmer would want to specify the address allocation size for items of substantial size.

```
char a[3000];                  /* large-model program */
char near b[3000];
```

In the example above, access speed would probably not be critical for array a. Even though it may or may not be allocated within the default data segment, it is always referenced with a 32-bit address. Array b is explicitly allocated near to improve speed of access in this memory model (large).

```
char *pa;                      /* small-model program */
char far *pb;
```

The pointer pa is declared as a near pointer to an item of type **char** in the example above. The pointer is near by default since the example appears in a small-model program. By contrast, pb is allocated as a far pointer to an item of type **char**; pb could be used to point to, and step through, an array of characters stored in a segment other than the default data segment. For example, pa might be used to point to array a in the first example, while pb might be used to point to array b.

```
char far * *pa;                /* small-model program */
char far * *pa;                /* large-model program */
```

The pointer declarations in the example above illustrate the interaction between the memory model chosen and the **near** and **far** keywords. Although the declarations for pa are identical, in a small-model program pa is declared as a near pointer to an array of far pointers to type **char**, while in a large-model program, pa is declared as a far pointer to an array of far pointers to type **char**.

```
char far * near *pb;           /* any model */
char far * far *pb;
```

In the first declaration in the example above, pb is declared as a near pointer to an array of far pointers to type **char**; in the second declaration, pb is declared as a far pointer to an array of far pointers to type **char**. Note that, in this example, the **far** and **near** keywords override the model-specific addressing conventions shown in the example preceding the example above; the declarations for pb would have the same effect, regardless of the memory model.

## B.3.3 Declaring Functions with the near and far Keywords

The rules for using the **near** and **far** keywords for functions are similar to those for using them with data, as listed below:

- The keyword always modifies the function or pointer immediately to its right. See Section 4.3.3, "Declarators with Special Keywords," of the *Microsoft C Language Reference* for more information about rules for evaluating complex declarations.

- If the item immediately to the right of the keyword is a function, then the keyword determines whether the function will be allocated as near or far. For example,

  ```
  char far fun( );
  ```

  defines `fun` as a function called with a 32-bit address and returning type **char**.

- If the item immediately to the right of the keyword is a pointer to a function, then the keyword determines whether the function will be called using a near (16-bit) or far (32-bit) address. For example,

  ```
  char (far * pfun) ( );
  ```

  defines `pfun` as a far pointer (32 bits) to a function returning type **char**.

- Function declarations must match function definitions.

### ■ Examples

```
void char far fun(void);               /* small model */
void char far fun(void)
        {
        .
        .
        .
        }
```

In the example above, `fun` is declared as a function returning type **char**. The **far** keyword in the declaration means that `fun` must be called with a 32-bit call.

```
static char far * near fun( );          /* large model */
static char far * near fun( )
      {
       .
       .
       .
      }
```

In the large-model example above, fun is declared as a near function that returns a far pointer to type **char**. Such a function might be seen in a large-model program as a helper routine that is used frequently, but only by the routines in its own module. Since all routines in a given module share the same code segment, the function could always be accessed with a near call. However, you could not pass a pointer to fun as an argument to another function outside the module in which fun was declared.

```
void far *fun(void);                    /* small model */
void (far * pfun) ( ) = fun;
```

The small-model example above declares pfun as a far pointer to a function that has a **void** return type, and then assigns the address of fun to pfun. In fact, pfun could be used to point to any function accessed with a far call. Note that if the function pointed to by pfun has not been declared with the **far** keyword, or if it is not far by default, then calling that function through pfun would cause the program to fail.

```
double far * (far fun) ( );      /* compact model */
double far * (far *pfun) ( ) = fun;
```

The final example above declares pfun as a far pointer to a function that returns a far pointer to type **double**, and then assigns the address of fun to pfun. This might be used in a compact-model program for a function that is not used frequently and thus does not need to be in the default code segment. Both the function and the pointer to the function must be declared with the **far** keyword.

## B.3.4  Pointer Conversions

Passing pointers as arguments to functions may cause automatic conversions in the size of the pointer argument, since passing a pointer to a function forces the pointer size to the larger of the following two sizes:

- The default pointer size for that type, as defined by the memory model used during compilation.

  For example, in medium-model programs, data pointer arguments are near by default and code pointer arguments are far by default.

- The type of the argument.

If a function prototype with argument types is given, the compiler performs type checking and enforces the conversion of actual arguments to the declared type of the corresponding formal argument. However, if no declaration is present or the argument-type list is empty, the compiler will convert pointer arguments automatically to either the default type or the type of the argument, whichever is largest. To avoid mismatched arguments, you should always use a prototype with the argument types.

## ■ Examples

```
/* This program produces unexpected results in compact- or
** large-model programs.
*/

main( )

        {
        int near *x;
        char far *y;
        int z = 1;

        test_fun(x, y, z);    /* x is coerced to far pointer */

        }

int test_fun(ptr1, ptr2, a)
        int near *ptr1;
        char far *ptr2;
        int a;

        {
        printf("Value of a = %d\n", a);
        }
```

If the preceding example is compiled as a small-model program (with **/AS** option on the **QCL** command line) or medium-model program (with no memory-model options or the **/AM** option on the **QCL** command line), the size of pointer argument x is 16 bits, the size of pointer argument y is 32 bits, and the value printed for a is 1. However, if the preceding example is compiled with the **/AC** or **/AL** option, both x and y are automatically converted to far pointers when they are passed to test_fun. Since ptr1, the first parameter of test_fun, is defined as a near pointer argument, it takes only 16 bits of the 32 bits passed to it. The next parameter, ptr2, takes the remaining 16 bits passed to ptr1, plus 16 bits of the 32 bits passed to it. Finally, the third parameter, a, takes the leftover 16 bits from ptr2, instead of the value of z in the main function. This shifting process does not generate an error message, since both the function call and the function definition are legal, but in this case the program does not work as intended, since the value assigned to a is not the value intended.

To pass ptr1 as a near pointer, you should include a forward declaration that specifically declares this argument for test_fun as a near pointer, as shown below:

```
/* First, declare test_fun so the compiler knows in advance
** about the near pointer argument:
*/
int test_fun(int near*, char far *, int);

main( )

        {
        int near *x;
        char far *y;
        int z = 1;

        test_fun(x, y, z);      /* now, x will not be coerced
                                ** to a far pointer; it will be
                                ** passed as a near pointer,
                                ** no matter what memory
                                ** model is used
                                */

        }
int test_fun(ptr1, ptr2, a)
        int near *ptr1;
        char far *ptr2;
        int a;

        {
        printf("Value of a = %d\n", a);
        }
```

Note that it would not be sufficient to reverse the definition order for test_fun and main in the first example to avoid pointer coercions; the pointer arguments must be declared in a forward declaration, as in the second example.

## B.4   Setting the Data Threshold

■   **Option**

*/Gt⟦number⟧*

By default, the compiler allocates all static and global data items within the default data segment in the small and medium memory models. In compact- and large-model programs, only *initialized* static and global data items are assigned to the default data segment. The **/Gt** option causes all data items whose size is greater than or equal to *number* bytes to be allocated to a new data segment. When *number* is specified, it must follow the **/Gt** option immediately, with no intervening spaces. When *number* is omitted, the default threshold value is 256. When the **/Gt** option is omitted, the default threshold value is 32,767.

You can use the **/Gt** option only with compact- and large-model programs, since small- and medium-model programs have only one data segment. The option is particularly useful with programs that have more than 64K of initialized static and global data in small data items.

## B.5   Naming the Text Segment

■   **Option**

*/NT textsegment*

A "segment" is a contiguous block of binary information (code or data) produced by the Microsoft QuickC Compiler. Every module (that is, every object file produced by the compiler) has at least two segments: a text segment containing the program instructions, and a data segment containing the program data.

Each segment in every module has a name. The linker uses this name to define the order in which the segments of the program appear in memory when loaded for execution. (Note that the segments in the group named **DGROUP** are an exception.)

Text- and data-segment names are normally created by the QuickC compiler. In medium-model programs, the text from each module is placed in a separate segment with a distinct name, formed by using the module base name along with the suffix **_TEXT**. The data segment is named **_DATA**.

You can override the default text-segment name used by the QuickC compiler (thus overriding the default loading order) by using the **/NT** (for "name text") option. This option gives the text segment a new name in each module being compiled.

The *textsegment* argument used with the **/NT** option can be any combination of letters and digits. The space between **/NT** and *textsegment* is optional.

# APPENDIX C
# INTERFACING C
# WITH ASSEMBLY LANGUAGE

Mixed-language programming is the process of creating programs from two or more source languages. This capability allows you to combine the unique strengths of Microsoft® BASIC, C, FORTRAN, Pascal, and the Macro Assembler (**MASM**). Any one of these languages (in their recent versions) can call any of the others. Virtually all of the routines from each of these extensive language libraries are available to a mixed-language program.

For example, mixed-language programming helps you effectively use **MASM**. You can develop the majority of your program quickly with Microsoft C or FORTRAN, then call **MASM** for those few routines that are executed many times and must run with utmost speed.

Mixed-language programming also facilitates the transition from one language to another. For example, you may have a large FORTRAN program that you are converting to C. You can replace your FORTRAN subroutines, one by one, with corresponding C functions. C-generated code can come on line as soon as each function is written.

Finally, mixed-language programming is particularly valuable if you are marketing your own libraries. With the techniques presented here, you can produce libraries for any of the languages mentioned above, often with little change.

The details of mixed-language programming for the other high-level Microsoft languages are contained in the *Microsoft Mixed-Language Programming Guide.* This manual is included with Microsoft FORTRAN (Version 4.0 or later), Microsoft Macro Assembler (Version 5.0 or later), Microsoft Pascal (Version 3.3 or later), and Microsoft C (Version 5.0 or later).

This appendix focuses on the concepts, syntax, and programming methods necessary to write assembly-language routines usable with a C program. Refer to the *Microsoft Mixed-Language Programming Guide* for detailed information for the high-level language interfaces.

■   **Definitions**

The notational conventions used in this appendix are consistent with the conventions described in the user's guide for each Microsoft language. However, the following terms are used in specialized ways:

| Term | Definition |
| --- | --- |
| Routine | Any function, subprogram, subroutine, or procedure that can be called from another language. |
| | The concept is similar to that of a procedure in assembly language; however, the term "routine" is used in most contexts to avoid confusion with the Pascal keyword **procedure**. |
| Parameter | A piece of data passed directly between two routines. (External data are shared by all routines, but cannot be said to be passed.) |
| | Although elsewhere the term "argument" is sometimes used interchangeably with "parameter," in this appendix "argument" is used to refer to the particular values or expressions that are given for parameters. |
| Interface | A method for providing effective communication between different formats. With high-level languages, an interface is often established by some kind of formal declaration. |
| Formal parameter | A formal parameter is a dummy parameter declared in an interface statement or declaration. C uses parameter-type declarations rather than formal parameters. |

# C.1   Writing the Assembly Procedure

The Microsoft high-level languages all use roughly the same interface for procedure calls. This section describes the interface, which allows you to call assembly procedures by using the same methods as you do with Microsoft compiler-generated code. Procedures written with these methods can be called recursively and can be effectively used with the Stack Trace feature of the Microsoft® CodeView® window-oriented debugger.

The standard assembly-interface method consists of these steps:

1. Set up the procedure

2. Enter the procedure

3. Allocate local data (optional)

4. Preserve register values

5. Access parameters

6. Return a value (optional)

7. Exit the procedure

Sections C.1.1–C.1.7 describe each of these steps.

## C.1.1   Setting Up the Procedure

The linker cannot combine the assembly procedure with the calling program unless compatible segments are used and unless the procedure itself is declared properly. The following points may be helpful:

- Use the **.MODEL** directive at the beginning of the source file, if you have Version 5.0 of the Macro Assembler. This directive automatically causes the appropriate kind of returns to be generated (near for small or compact model, far otherwise). If you have a version of the assembler previous to 5.0, declare the procedure far (or near if the calling program is small- or compact-model QuickC).

- If you have Version 5.0 or later of the Microsoft Macro Assembler, use the simplified segment directives **.CODE** to declare the code segment and **.DATA** to declare the data segment. (Having a code segment is sufficient if you do not have data declarations.) If you are using an earlier version of the assembler, look up **SEGMENT**, **GROUP**, and **ASSUME** directives in Section C.4, "The Microsoft Segment Model."

- The procedure label must be declared public with the **PUBLIC** directive. This declaration makes the procedure available to be called by other modules. Also, any data you want to make public to other modules must be declared as **PUBLIC**.

- Global data or procedures accessed by the routine must be declared **EXTRN**. The safest way to use **EXTRN** is to place the directive outside of any segment definition (however, near data should generally go inside the data segment).

## C.1.2  Entering the Procedure

Two instructions begin the procedure:

```
push    bp
mov     bp,sp
```

This sequence establishes **BP** as the "framepointer." The framepointer is used to access parameters and local data, which are located on the stack. **SP** cannot be used for this purpose because it is not an index or base register. Also, the value of **SP** may change as more data are pushed onto the stack. The value of the base register **BP**, however, will remain constant throughout the procedure; consequently, each parameter can be addressed as a fixed displacement off of **BP**.

The instruction sequence above first saves the value of **BP**, since it will be needed by the calling procedure as soon as the current procedure terminates. Then **BP** is loaded with the value of **SP** in order to capture the value of the stack pointer at the time of entry to the procedure.

## C.1.3  Allocating Local Data (Optional)

An assembly procedure can use the same technique for allocating local data as that used by higher-level languages. To set up local data space, simply decrease the contents of **SP** in the third instruction of the procedure. (To ensure correct execution, you should always increase or decrease **SP** by an even amount.) Decreasing the contents of **SP** reserves space on the stack for the local data. The space must be restored at the end of the procedure.

In the following instructions, *space* is the total size in bytes of the local data. Local variables are then accessed as fixed, negative displacements off of **BP**.

```
push    bp
mov     bp,sp
        sub     sp,space
```

■  **Example**

```
push    bp
mov     bp,sp
sub     sp,4
.
.
.
mov     WORD PTR [bp-2],0
mov     WORD PTR [bp-4],0
```

The example above uses two local variables, each of which is two bytes in size. **SP** is decreased by four, since there are four bytes total of local data. Later, each of the variables is initialized to 0. These variables are never formally declared with any assembler directive; the programmer must keep track of them manually.

Local variables are also referred to as dynamic, stack, or automatic variables.

## C.1.4   Preserving Register Values

A procedure called from any of the Microsoft high-level languages should preserve the values of **SI**, **DI**, **SS**, and **DS** (in addition to **BP**, which is already saved). Therefore, push any of these register values that the procedure alters. If the procedure does not change the value of any of these registers, then the registers do not need to be pushed. Pop any registers you have previously pushed just before returning (as explained in Section C.1.7, "Exiting the Procedure").

The recommended method (used by the high-level languages) is to save registers after the framepointer is set and local data (if any) are allocated. In the following fragment, **DI** and **SI** (in that order) must be popped before the end of the procedure.

```
push    bp              ; Save old framepointer
mov     bp,sp           ; Establish current framepointer
sub     sp,4            ; Allocate local data space
push    si              ; Save SI and DI
push    di
  .
  .
  .
```

## C.1.5   Accessing Parameters

Once you have established the procedure's framepointer, allocated local data space (if desired), and pushed any registers that need to be preserved, you can write the main body of the procedure. In order to write instructions that can access parameters, consider the general picture of the stack frame after a procedure call, as shown in Figure C.1.

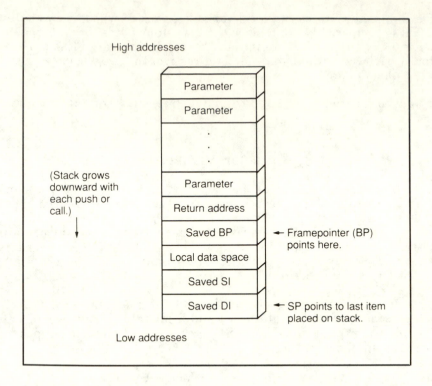

**Figure C.1  The Stack Frame**

The stack frame for the procedure is established by the following sequence of events:

1. The calling program pushes each of the parameters onto the stack, after which **SP** points to the last parameter pushed.

2. The calling program issues a **CALL** instruction, which causes the return address (the place in the calling program to which control will ultimately return) to be placed on the stack. This address may be either two bytes long (for near calls) or four bytes long (for far calls). **SP** now points to this address.

3. The first instruction of the called procedure saves the old value of **BP**, with the instruction `push bp`. **SP** now points to the saved copy of **BP**.

4. Use **BP** to capture the current value of **SP** with the instruction `mov bp,sp`. **BP** now points to the old value of **BP**.

5. Whereas **BP** remains constant throughout the procedure, **SP** may be decreased to provide room on the stack for local data or saved registers.

In general, the displacement (off of **BP**) for a parameter X is equal to

```
2 + size of return address
+ total size of parameters between X and BP
```

For example, consider a **FAR** procedure that has received one parameter, a two-byte address. The displacement of the parameter would be

```
Argument's displacement =   2 + size of return address
                        =   2 + 4
                        =   6
```

The argument can therefore be loaded into **BP** with the following instruction:

```
mov     bx,[bp+6]
```

Once you determine the displacement of each parameter, you may want to use string equates or structures so that the parameter can be referenced with a single identifier name in your assembly source code. For example, the parameter above at **BP+6** can be conveniently accessed if you put the following statement at the beginning of the assembly source file:

```
Arg1    EQU     [bp+6]
```

You could then refer to this parameter as `Arg1` in any instruction. Use of this feature is optional.

---

*Note*

> Microsoft high-level languages always push segment addresses before pushing offset addresses. Furthermore, when arguments larger than two bytes are pushed, high-order words are always pushed before low-order words.

---

## C.1.6   Returning a Value (Optional)

The Microsoft high-level languages share similar conventions for receiving return values. The conventions are the same when the data type to be returned is simple (that is, not an array or structured type) and is no more than four bytes long. This includes all near and far address types (in other words, all pointers and all parameters passed by reference).

| Data size | Returned in register |
|---|---|
| 1 byte | **AL** |
| 2 bytes | **AX** |
| 4 bytes | High-order portion (or segment address) in **DX**; low-order portion (or offset address) in **AX** |

When the return value is larger than four bytes, a procedure called by C must allocate space for the return value and then place its address in **DX:AX**. A convenient way to create space for the return value is to simply declare it in a data segment.

## C.1.7   Exiting the Procedure

Several steps may be involved in terminating the procedure:

1.  If any of the registers **SS**, **DS**, **SI**, or **DI** have been saved, these must be popped off the stack in the reverse order that they were saved.

2.  If local-data space was allocated at the beginning of the procedure, **SP** must be restored with the instruction `mov sp,bp`.

3.  Restore **BP** with `pop bp`. This step is always necessary.

4.  Finally, return to the calling program with `ret`. The C calling module will automatically adjust the stack with respect to the parameters that were pushed by the caller.

■   **Examples**

```
pop     bp
ret
```

The example above shows the simplest possible exit sequence. No registers were saved, no local data space was allocated, and the C calling convention is in use.

```
pop     di              ; Pop saved regs
pop     si
mov     sp,bp           ; Remove local-data space
pop     bp              ; Restore old framepointer
ret     6               ; Exit and restore 6 bytes of args
```

The example above shows an exit sequence for a procedure that has previously saved **SI** and **DI**, allocated local-data space, and uses a non-C calling convention. The procedure must therefore use `ret 6` to restore the six bytes of parameters on the stack.

## C.2   Calling Assembly-Language Routines from C

A C program can call an assembly procedure in another module, just as it would call a C function. In addition to the steps outlined in Section C.1, "Writing the Assembly Procedure," the following guidelines may be helpful:

1. Declare procedures called from C as far if the C module is compiled in large, huge, or medium model, and near if the C module is compiled in small or compact model.

   The **near** and **far** keywords can override these defaults. The correct declaration for the procedure is made implicitly when you use the .**MODEL** directive that is available in the Microsoft Macro Assembler, Version 5.0.

2. Observe the C calling convention.

   The C calling convention pushes parameters onto the stack in the reverse order in which they appear in the source code. For example, the C function call `calc(a,b);` pushes `b` onto the stack before it pushes `a`. In contrast with the other high-level languages, the C calling convention specifies that a calling routine always restores the stack immediately after the called routine returns control.

   The C convention makes calling with a variable number of parameters possible. (Because the first parameter is always the last one pushed, it is always on the top of the stack; therefore it has the same address relative to the framepointer, regardless of how many parameters were actually passed.) To call with a variable number of parameters, use the following steps:

   a. Return with a simple `ret` instruction. Do *not* restore the stack with `ret` *size*, since the calling C routine will restore the stack itself, as soon as it resumes control.

   b. Parameters are placed on the stack in the reverse order that they appear in the C source code. The first parameter will be lowest in memory (because it is the last parameter to be placed on the stack, and the stack grows downward).

  c. By default, C parameters are passed by value, except for arrays, which are passed by reference.

3. Observe the C naming convention.

  Include an underscore in front of any name which will be shared publicly with C. Only the first eight characters of any name are recognized by C, so do not make names shared with C longer than eight characters. Also, if you plan to link with the **/NOIGNORECASE** option, remember that C is case sensitive and does not convert names to uppercase.

In the following example program, C calls an assembly procedure that calculates $A * 2^B$, where A and B are the first and second parameters, respectively. The calculation is performed by shifting the bits in A to the left B times.

The C program uses an **extern** declaration to create an interface with the assembly procedure. No special keywords are required because the assembly procedure will use the C calling convention.

```
extern int power2(int, int);

main()
{
    printf("3 times 2 to the power of 5 is %d\n", power2(3,5));
}
```

To understand how to write the assembly procedure, consider how the parameters are placed on the stack, as illustrated in Figure C.2.

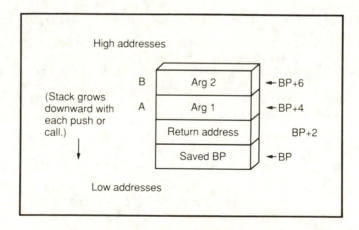

**Figure C.2  The C Stack Frame**

The return address is two bytes long, assuming that the C module is compiled in small or compact model. If the C module is compiled in large, huge, or medium model, then the addresses of Arg 1 and Arg 2 are each increased by two, to BP+6 and BP+8, respectively, because the return address will be four bytes long.

The first parameter, Arg 1, is lower in memory than Arg 2 because C pushes arguments in the reverse order that they appear. Each argument is passed by value.

The assembly procedure can be written as follows:

```
.MODEL SMALL
.CODE
        PUBLIC  _power2
_power2 PROC
        push    bp              ; Entry sequence - save old BP
        mov     bp,sp           ; Set stack framepointer

        mov     ax,[bp+4]       ; Load Arg1 into AX
        mov     cx,[bp+6]       ; Load Arg2 into CX
        shl     ax,cl           ; AX = AX * (2 to power of CX)
                                ; Leave return value in AX

        pop     bp              ; Exit sequence - restore old BP
        ret                     ; Return
_power2 ENDP
        END
```

The example above assumes that the C module is compiled in small model. The parameter offsets and the **.MODEL** directive will change for different models.

Note that ret without a size variable is used, since the caller will adjust the stack upon return from the call.

# C.3   Calling C from Assembly Language

High-level-language routines assume that certain initialization code has previously been executed; you can ensure that the proper initialization is performed by starting in a high-level language module, and then calling an assembly procedure. The assembly procedure can then call high-level-language routines as needed, as shown in Figure C.3.

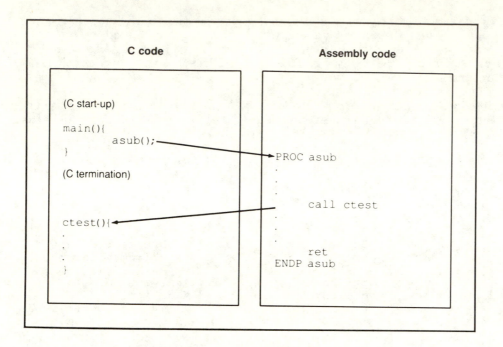

**Figure C.3  Assembly Call to C**

To execute an assembly call to a high-level language, you need to observe the following guidelines:

- Push each parameter onto the stack, observing the calling convention of the high-level language. Constants such as offset addresses must first be loaded into a register before being pushed.

- With long parameters, always push the segment or high-order portion of the parameter first, regardless of the calling convention.

- Execute a call. The call must be far unless the high-level-language routine is small model.

- If the routine used the C calling convention, then immediately after the call clear the stack of parameters with the instruction

  add sp, *size*

  where *size* is the total size in bytes of all parameters that were pushed.

# C.4   The Microsoft Segment Model

If you use the simplified segment directives by themselves, you do not need to know the names assigned for each segment. However, versions of the Macro Assembler prior to 5.0 do not support these directives. With older versions of the assembler, you should use the **SEGMENT**, **GROUP**, **ASSUME**, and **ENDS** directives equivalent to the simplified segment directives.

Table C.1 shows the default segment names created by each directive. Use of these segments ensures compatibility with Microsoft languages and will help you to access public symbols.

The table is followed by a list of three steps illustrating how to make the actual declarations, and an example program.

**Table C.1**

## Default Segments and Types for Standard Memory Models

| Model | Directive | Name | Align | Combine | Class | Group |
|-------|-----------|------|-------|---------|-------|-------|
| Small | .CODE | _TEXT | WORD | PUBLIC | 'CODE' | |
| | .DATA | _DATA | WORD | PUBLIC | 'DATA' | DGROUP |
| | .CONST | CONST | WORD | PUBLIC | 'CONST' | DGROUP |
| | .DATA? | _BSS | WORD | PUBLIC | 'BSS' | DGROUP |
| | .STACK | STACK | PARA | STACK | 'STACK' | DGROUP |
| Medium | .CODE | *name*_TEXT | WORD | PUBLIC | 'CODE' | |
| | .DATA | _DATA | WORD | PUBLIC | 'DATA' | DGROUP |
| | .CONST | CONST | WORD | PUBLIC | 'CONST' | DGROUP |
| | .DATA? | _BSS | WORD | PUBLIC | 'BSS' | DGROUP |
| | .STACK | STACK | PARA | STACK | 'STACK' | DGROUP |
| Compact | .CODE | _TEXT | WORD | PUBLIC | 'CODE' | |
| | .FARDATA | FAR_DATA | PARA | Private | 'FAR_DATA' | |
| | .FARDATA? | FAR_BSS | PARA | Private | 'FAR_BSS' | |
| | .DATA | _DATA | WORD | PUBLIC | 'DATA' | DGROUP |
| | .CONST | CONST | WORD | PUBLIC | 'CONST' | DGROUP |
| | .DATA? | _BSS | WORD | PUBLIC | 'BSS' | DGROUP |
| | .STACK | STACK | PARA | STACK | 'STACK' | DGROUP |

Table C.1 *(continued)*

| Model | Directive | Name | Align | Combine | Class | Group |
|-------|-----------|------|-------|---------|-------|-------|
| Large | .CODE | *name*_TEXT | WORD | PUBLIC | 'CODE' | |
| | .FARDATA | FAR_DATA | PARA | Private | 'FAR_DATA' | |
| | .FARDATA? | FAR_BSS | PARA | Private | 'FAR_BSS' | |
| | .DATA | _DATA | WORD | PUBLIC | 'DATA' | DGROUP |
| | .CONST | CONST | WORD | PUBLIC | 'CONST' | DGROUP |
| | .DATA? | _BSS | WORD | PUBLIC | 'BSS' | DGROUP |
| | .STACK | STACK | PARA | STACK | 'STACK' | DGROUP |

The directives in Table C.1 refer to the following kinds of segments:

| Directive | Description of Segment |
|-----------|------------------------|
| **.CODE** | Segment containing all the code for the module. |
| **.DATA** | Initialized data. |
| **.DATA?** | Uninitialized data. Microsoft compilers store uninitialized data separately because such data can be stored more efficiently than initialized data. |
| **.FARDATA** and **.FARDATA?** | Data that will not be combined with the corresponding segments in other modules. The segment of data placed here can always be determined, however, with the assembler **SEG** operator. |
| **.CONST** | Constant data. Microsoft compilers use this segment for items such as string and floating-point constants. |
| **.STACK** | Stack. Normally, this segment is declared in the main module for you and should not be redeclared. |

Use the following steps with Table C.1 to create actual directives:

1.  Use the indicated name, align type, combine type, and class in a segment definition. Thus, the code segment for small model would be declared as follows:

```
_TEXT    SEGMENT   WORD PUBLIC 'CODE'
```

If the combine type is private, simply do not use any combine type.

2. If you have segments in **DGROUP**, put them into **DGROUP** with the **GROUP** directive, as in

```
GROUP    DGROUP    _DATA _BSS
```

3. Use **ASSUME** and **ENDS** as you would normally. Bear in mind that, upon entry, **DS** and **SS** will both point to **DGROUP**.

The following example shows the C-assembly program from Section C.3, but without the simplified segment directives from Version 5.0 of the Microsoft Macro Assembler:

```
_TEXT    SEGMENT WORD PUBLIC 'CODE'
         ASSUME  cs:_TEXT
         PUBLIC  _Power2
_Power2 PROC
         push    bp              ; Entry sequence - save BP
         mov     bp,sp           ; Set stack frame

         mov     ax,[bp+4]       ; Load Arg1 into AX
         mov     cx,[bp+6]       ; Load Arg2 into CX
         shl     ax,cl           ; AX = AX * (2 to power of CX)
                                 ; Leave return value in AX

         pop     bp              ; Exit sequence - restore BP
         ret                     ; Return
_Power2 ENDP
_TEXT    ENDS
         END
```

# APPENDIX D
# ERROR-MESSAGE REFERENCE

This appendix lists error messages you may encounter as you develop a program and gives a brief description of actions you can take to correct the errors. The following list tells where to find error messages for the various components of the Microsoft QuickC Compiler:

| Component | Section |
|-----------|---------|
| The Microsoft QuickC Compiler | Section D.1, "Compiler Error Messages" |
| The command line used to invoke the Microsoft QuickC Compiler | Section D.2, "Command-Line Error Messages" |
| The Microsoft C run-time libraries and other run-time situations | Section D.3, "Run-Time Error Messages" |
| The Microsoft Overlay Linker, **LINK** | Section D.4, "LINK Error Messages" |
| The Microsoft Library Manager, **LIB** | Section D.5, "LIB Error Messages" |
| The Microsoft Program-Maintenance Utility, **MAKE** | Section D.6, "MAKE Error Messages" |

Note that compiler, command-line, and run-time error messages are listed alphabetically in this appendix.

See Section D.1.4 for information about compiler limits and Section D.3.3 for information about run-time limits.

# D.1   Compiler Error Messages

The error messages produced by the C compiler fall into three categories:

1. Fatal-error messages
2. Compilation error messages
3. Warning messages

The messages for each category are listed below in numerical order, with a brief explanation of each error. To look up an error message, first determine the message category, then find the error number. Each message that is generated within the QuickC environment appears in the error window;

the cursor is moved to the line that caused the error (see Section 7.3.4 for more information). Each message that is generated by compiling with the **QCL** command gives the file name and line number where the error occurs.

## Fatal-Error Messages

Fatal-error messages indicate a severe problem, one that prevents the compiler from processing your program any further. These messages have the following format:

*filename*(*line*)  :  `fatal error C1`*xxx*: *messagetext*

After the compiler displays a fatal-error message, it terminates without producing an object file or checking for further errors.

## Compilation-Error Messages

Compilation-error messages identify actual program errors. These messages appear in the following format:

*filename*(*line*)  :  `error C2`*xxx*: *messagetext*

The compiler does not produce an object file for a source file that has compilation errors in the program. When the compiler encounters such errors, it attempts to recover from the error. If possible, it continues to process the source file and produce error messages. If errors are too numerous or too severe, the compiler stops processing.

## Warning Messages

Warning messages are informational only; they do not prevent compilation and linking. These messages appear in the following format:

*filename*(*line*)  :  `warning C4`*xxx* : *messagetext*

You can use the **/W** option to control the level of warnings that the compiler generates. This option is described in Section 9.3.1.

# D.1.1  Fatal-Error Messages

The following messages identify fatal errors. The compiler cannot recover from a fatal error; it terminates after printing the error message.

| Number | Fatal-Error Message |
|--------|---------------------|

**C1000**      UNKNOWN FATAL ERROR
Contact Microsoft Technical Support

An unknown error condition was detected by the compiler.

Please report this condition to Microsoft Corporation, using the Product Assistance Request form at the back of this manual.

**C1001**      Internal Compiler Error
Contact Microsoft Technical Support

The compiler detected an internal inconsistency.

Please report this condition using the Product Assistance Request form at the back of this manual. Please include the file name and line number where the error occurred in this report; note that the file name refers to an internal compiler file, *not* your source file.

**C1002**      out of heap space

The compiler ran out of dynamic memory space. This usually means that your program has too many symbols and/or complex expressions.

To correct the problem, divide the file into several smaller source files, or break expressions into smaller subexpressions.

**C1003**      error count exceeds *n*; stopping compilation

Errors in the program were too numerous or too severe to allow recovery, and the compiler must terminate.

**C1004**      unexpected EOF

This message appears when you have insufficient space on the default disk drive for the compiler to create the temporary files it needs. The space required is approximately two times the size of the source file. This message can also occur when a comment does not have a closing delimiter (∗/), or when an #**if** directive occurs without a corresponding closing #**endif** directive.

**C1005**      string too big for buffer

A string in a compiler intermediate file overflowed a buffer.

| Number | Fatal-Error Message |
|--------|---------------------|

**C1006**    `write error on compiler intermediate file`

The compiler was unable to create the intermediate files used in the compilation process.

The following conditions commonly cause this error:

1.  Too few files in the

    `files=`*number*

    line of the **CONFIG.SYS** file (the compiler requires *number* to be at least 15)

2.  Not enough space on a device containing a compiler intermediate file

**C1007**    `unrecognized flag '`*string*`' in '`*option*`'`

The *string* in the command-line *option* was not a valid option.

**C1009**    `compiler limit`
`possibly a recursively defined macro`

The expansion of a macro exceeds the available space.

Check to see if the macro is recursively defined, or if the expanded text is too large.

**C1010**    `compiler limit : macro expansion too big`

The expansion of a macro exceeds the available space.

**C1012**    `bad parenthesis nesting - missing '`*character*`'`

The parentheses in a preprocessor directive were not matched; *character* is either a left or right parenthesis.

**C1013**    `cannot open source file '`*filename*`'`

The given file either did not exist, could not be opened, or was not found. Make sure your environment settings are valid and that you have given the correct path name for the file.

**C1014**    `too many include files`

Nesting of **#include** directives exceeds the 10-level limit.

| Number | Fatal-Error Message |
|--------|---------------------|

**C1015**  `cannot open include file 'filename'`

The given file either did not exist, could not be opened, or was not found. Make sure your environment settings are valid and that you have given the correct path name for the file.

**C1016**  `#if[n]def expected an identifier`

You must specify an identifier with the #**ifdef** and #**ifndef** directives.

**C1017**  `invalid integer constant expression`

The expression in an #**if** directive must evaluate to a constant.

**C1018**  `unexpected '#elif'`

The #**elif** directive is legal only when it appears within an #**if**, #**ifdef**, or #**ifndef** directive.

**C1019**  `unexpected '#else'`

The #**else** directive is legal only when it appears within an #**if**, #**ifdef**, or #**ifndef** directive.

**C1020**  `unexpected '#endif'`

An #**endif** directive appears without a matching #**if**, #**ifdef**, or #**ifndef** directive.

**C1021**  `bad preprocessor command 'string'`

The characters following the number sign (#) do not form a valid preprocessor directive.

**C1022**  `expected '#endif'`

An #**if**, #**ifdef**, or #**ifndef** directive was not terminated with an #**endif** directive.

**C1026**  `parser stack overflow, please simplify your program`

Your program cannot be processed because the space required to parse the program causes a stack overflow in the compiler.

To solve this problem, try to simplify your program.

| Number | Fatal-Error Message |
|--------|---------------------|

**C1027**    `compiler limit : struct/union nesting`

Structure and union definitions were nested to more than 10 levels.

**C1028**    *segment* `segment allocation exceeds 64K`

More than 64K of far data were allocated to the given segment. A single module can have only 64K of far data.

To solve this problem, either break declarations up into separate modules, reduce the amount of data your program uses, or compile your program with the Microsoft C Optimizing Compiler.

**C1032**    `cannot open object listing file '`*filename*`'`

One of the following statements about the file name or path name given (*filename*) is true:

1. The given name is not valid.
2. The file with the given name cannot be opened for lack of space.
3. A read-only file with the given name already exists.

**C1033**    `cannot open assembly-language output file '`*filename*`'`

One of the conditions listed under error message C1032 prevents the given file from being opened.

**C1034**    `cannot open source file '`*filename*`'`

One of the conditions listed under error message C1032 prevents the given file from being opened.

**C1035**    `expression too complex, please simplify`

The compiler was unable to generate code for a complex expression.

To solve this problem, break the expression into simpler subexpressions and recompile.

**C1036**    `cannot open source listing file '`*filename*`'`

One of the conditions listed under error message C1032 prevents the given file from being opened.

| Number | Fatal-Error Message |
|--------|--------------------|

**C1037**     `cannot open object file '`*filename*`'`

One of the conditions listed under error message C1032 prevents the given file from being opened.

**C1039**     `unrecoverable heap overflow in Pass 3`

The post-optimizer compiler pass overflowed the heap and could not continue.

Try recompiling with the Optimizations option turned on (within the QuickC programming environment) or with the **/Od** option (on the **QCL** command line), or try breaking up the function containing the line that caused the error.

**C1040**     `unexpected EOF in source file '`*filename*`'`

The compiler detected an unexpected end-of-file condition while creating a source listing or source/object listing.

This error probably occurred because the source file was edited during compilation.

**C1041**     `cannot open compiler intermediate file —`
`no more files`

The compiler could not create intermediate files used in the compilation process because no more file handles were available.

This error can usually be corrected by changing the `files=`*number* line in **CONFIG.SYS** to allow a larger number of open files (20 is the recommended setting).

**C1042**     `cannot open compiler intermediate file —`
`no such file or directory`

The compiler could not create intermediate files used in the compilation process because the **TMP** environment variable was set to an invalid directory or path.

**C1043**     `cannot open compiler intermediate file`

The compiler could not create intermediate files used in the compilation process. The exact reason is unknown.

| Number | Fatal-Error Message |
|---|---|

**C1044**      `out of disk space for compiler intermediate file`

The compiler could not create intermediate files used in the compilation process because no more space was available.

To correct the problem, make more space available on the disk and recompile.

**C1045**      `floating point overflow`

The compiler generated a floating-point exception while doing constant arithmetic on floating-point items at compile time, as in the following example:

```
float fp_val = 1.0e100;
```

In this example, the double-precision constant `1.0e100` exceeds the maximum allowable value for a floating-point data item.

**C1047**      `too many` *option* `flags,` '*string*'

The *option* appeared too many times. The *string* contains the occurrence of the option that caused the error.

**C1048**      `Unknown option` '*character*' `in` '*optionstring*'

The *character* was not a valid letter for *optionstring*.

**C1049**      `invalid numerical argument` '*string*'

A numerical argument was expected instead of *string*.

**C1050**      `code segment` '*segmentname*' `too large`

A code segment grew to within 36 bytes of 64K during compilation.

A 36-byte pad is used because of a bug in some 80286 chips that can cause programs to exhibit strange behavior when, among other conditions, the size of a code segment is within 36 bytes of 64K.

**C1052**      `too many #if/#ifdef's`

The program exceeded the maximum nesting level for #if/#ifdef directives.

| Number | Fatal-Error Message |
|--------|---------------------|

**C1053**     `DGROUP data allocation exceeds 64K`

More than 64K of variables were allocated to the default data segment.

For compact-, medium-, or large-model programs, compile with the **QCL** command and use the **/Gt** option to move items into separate segments.

**C1054**     `compiler limit : initializers too deeply nested`

The compiler limit on nesting of initializers was exceeded. The limit ranges from 10 to 15 levels, depending on the combination of types being initialized.

To correct this problem, simplify the data type being initialized to reduce the levels of nesting, or assign initial values in separate statements after the declaration.

**C1056**     `compiler limit : out of macro expansion space`

The compiler overflowed an internal buffer during the expansion of a macro.

**C1057**     `unexpected EOF in macro expansion; (missing ')'?)`

The compiler encountered the end of the source file while gathering the arguments of a macro invocation. Usually this is the result of a missing closing right parenthesis ( ) ) on the macro invocation, as in the following example:

```
#define print(a)      printf(string is (,#a))
main()
{
    print(the quick brown fox;
}
```

**C1059**     `out of near heap space`

The compiler ran out of storage for items that it stores in the "near" (default data segment) heap.

**C1060**     `out of far heap space`

The compiler ran out of storage for items that it stores in the far heap.

| Number | Fatal-Error Message |
|---|---|

Usually this error occurs in in-memory programs because the symbol table contains too many symbols. To fix this error, try compiling with the Debug option turned off, or try including fewer include files. If these solutions do not work, try compiling the program using the **QCL** command.

**C1061**      `compiler limit : blocks too deeply nested`

Nested blocks in the program exceeded the nesting limit allowed by the compiler.

To correct this problem, rewrite the program so that fewer blocks are nested within other blocks.

**C1063**      `compiler limit--compiler stack overflow`

Your program was too complex and caused the compiler stack to overflow. Simplify your program and recompile.

## D.1.2  Compilation-Error Messages

The messages listed below indicate that your program has errors. When the compiler encounters any of the errors listed in this section, it continues parsing the program (if possible) and outputs additional error messages. However, no object file is produced.

| Number | Compilation-Error Message |
|---|---|

**C2000**      `UNKNOWN ERROR`
`Contact Microsoft Technical Support`

The compiler detected an unknown error condition.

Please report this condition to the Microsoft Corporation, using the Product Assistance Request form at the back of this manual.

**C2001**      `newline in constant`

A new-line character in a character or string constant was not in the correct escape-sequence format ($\backslash$**n**).

**C2002**      `out of macro actual parameter space`

Arguments to preprocessor macros exceeded 256 bytes.

**C2003**      `expected 'defined id'`

The identifier to be checked in an #**if** directive was not found.

| Number | Compilation-Error Message |
|--------|---------------------------|

**C2004**      `expected 'defined(id)'`

An #**if** directive caused a syntax error.

**C2005**      `#line expected a line number`

A #**line** directive lacked the required line-number specification.

**C2006**      `#include expected a file name`

An #**include** directive lacked the required file-name specification.

**C2007**      `#define syntax`

A #**define** directive caused a syntax error.

**C2008**      `'`*character*`' : unexpected in macro definition`

The given character was used incorrectly in a macro definition.

**C2009**      `reuse of macro formal '`*identifier*`'`

The given identifier was used twice in the formal-parameter list of a macro definition.

**C2010**      `'`*character*`' : unexpected in formal list`

The given character was used incorrectly in the formal-parameter list of a macro definition.

**C2011**      `'`*identifier*`' : definition too big`

The given macro definitions exceeded 256 bytes.

**C2012**      `missing name following '<'`

An #**include** directive lacked the required file-name specification.

**C2013**      `missing '>'`

The closing angle bracket ($>$) was missing from an #**include** directive.

**C2014**      `preprocessor command must start as first non-whitespace`

Non-white-space characters appeared before the number sign (#) of a preprocessor directive on the same line.

| Number | Compilation-Error Message |
|--------|---------------------------|

**C2015**    too many chars in constant

A character constant containing more than one character or escape sequence was used.

**C2016**    no closing single quote

A character constant was not enclosed in single quotation marks.

**C2017**    illegal escape sequence

The character or characters after the escape character (\) did not form a valid escape sequence.

**C2018**    unknown character '0x*character*'

The given hexadecimal number did not correspond to a character.

**C2019**    expected preprocessor command, found '*character*'

The given character followed a number sign (#), but it was not the first letter of a preprocessor directive.

**C2020**    bad octal number '*character*'

The given character was not a valid octal digit.

**C2021**    expected exponent value, not '*character*'

The given character was used as the exponent of a floating-point constant but was not a valid number.

**C2022**    '*number*' : too big for char

The *number* was too large to be represented as a character.

**C2023**    divide by 0

The second operand in a division operation (/) evaluated to 0, giving undefined results.

**C2024**    mod by 0

The second operand in a remainder operation (%) evaluated to 0, giving undefined results.

| Number | Compilation-Error Message |
|--------|---------------------------|

**C2025**     '*identifier*' : enum/struct/union type redefinition

The given identifier had already been used for an enumeration, structure, or union tag.

**C2026**     '*identifier*' : member of enum redefinition

The given identifier had already been used for an enumeration constant, either within the same enumeration type or within another enumeration type with the same visibility.

**C2028**     struct/union member needs to be inside a struct/union

Structure and union members must be declared within the structure or union.

This error may be caused by an enumeration declaration that contains a declaration of a structure member, as in the following example:

```
enum a {
        january,
        february,
        int march;      /* structure declaration:
                        ** illegal
                        */
        };
```

**C2029**     '*identifier*' : bit-fields allowed only in structs

Only structure types may contain bit fields.

**C2030**     '*identifier*' : struct/union member redefinition

The *identifier* was used for more than one member of the same structure or union.

**C2031**     '*identifier*' : function cannot be struct/union member

The given function was declared to be a member of a structure or union.

To correct this error, use a pointer to the function instead.

| Number | Compilation-Error Message |
|--------|---------------------------|

**C2032**    '*identifier*' : base type with near/far/huge not allowed

The given structure or union member was declared with the **near** or **far** keyword.

**C2033**    '*identifier*' : bit-field cannot have indirection

The given bit field was declared as a pointer (*), which is not allowed.

**C2034**    '*identifier*' : bit-field type too small for number of bits

The number of bits specified in the bit-field declaration exceeded the number of bits in the given base type.

**C2035**    enum/struct/union '*identifier*' : unknown size

The given structure or union had an undefined size.

**C2036**    left of '*member*' must have struct/union type

The expression before the member-selection operator (—>) was not a pointer to a structure or union type, or the expression before the member-selection operator (.) did not evaluate to a structure or union. In this message, *member* is a member designator in one of the following forms:

—>*identifier*
.*identifier*

**C2037**    left of '—>' or '.' specifies undefined struct/union

The expression before the member-selection operator (—> or .) identified a structure or union type that was not defined.

**C2038**    '*identifier*' : not struct/union member

The given identifier was used in a context that required a structure or union member.

**C2039**    '—>' requires struct/union pointer

The expression before the member-selection operator (—> was a structure or union name, not a pointer to a structure or union as expected.

| Number | Compilation-Error Message |
|--------|---------------------------|

**C2040**     `'.' requires struct/union name`

The expression before the member-selection operator (.) was a pointer to a structure or union, not a structure or union name as expected.

**C2041**     `keyword 'enum' illegal`

The **enum** keyword appeared in a structure or union declaration, or an **enum** type definition was not formed correctly.

**C2042**     `signed/unsigned keywords mutually exclusive`

Both the **signed** and the **unsigned** keywords were used in a single declaration, as in the following example:

`unsigned signed int i;`

**C2043**     `illegal break`

A **break** statement is legal only when it appears within a **do**, **for**, **while**, or **switch** statement.

**C2044**     `illegal continue`

A **continue** statement is legal only when it appears within a **do**, **for**, or **while** statement.

**C2045**     `'identifier' : label redefined`

The given label appeared before more than one statement in the same function.

**C2046**     `illegal case`

The **case** keyword may appear only within a **switch** statement.

**C2047**     `illegal default`

The **default** keyword may appear only within a **switch** statement.

**C2048**     `more than one default`

A **switch** statement contained more than one **default** label.

| Number | Compilation-Error Message |
|--------|---------------------------|

**C2050**   `non-integral switch expression`

A switch expression was not integral.

**C2051**   `case expression not constant`

Case expressions must be integral constants.

**C2052**   `case expression not integral`

Case expressions must be integral constants.

**C2053**   `case value` *number* `already used`

The given case value was already used in this **switch** statement.

**C2054**   `expected '(' to follow '`*identifier*`'`

The context requires parentheses after the function *identifier*.

**C2055**   `expected formal parameter list, not a type list`

An argument-type list appeared in a function definition instead of a formal parameter list.

**C2056**   `illegal expression`

An expression was illegal because of a previous error. (The previous error may not have produced an error message.)

**C2057**   `expected constant expression`

The context requires a constant expression.

**C2058**   `constant expression is not integral`

The context requires an integral constant expression.

**C2059**   `syntax error : '`*token*`'`

The given token caused a syntax error.

**C2060**   `syntax error : EOF`

The end of the file was encountered unexpectedly, causing a syntax error. This error can be caused by a missing closing brace (}) at the end of your program.

| Number | Compilation-Error Message |
|--------|---------------------------|

**C2061**  `syntax error : identifier '`*identifier*`'`

The given identifier caused a syntax error.

**C2062**  `type '`*type*`' unexpected`

The given type was misused.

**C2063**  `'`*identifier*`' : not a function`

The given identifier was not declared as a function, but an attempt was made to use it as a function.

**C2064**  `term does not evaluate to a function`

An attempt was made to call a function through an expression that did not evaluate to a function pointer.

**C2065**  `'`*identifier*`' : undefined`

The given identifier was not defined.

**C2066**  `cast to function returning . . . is illegal`

An object was cast to a function type.

**C2067**  `cast to array type is illegal`

An object was cast to an array type.

**C2068**  `illegal cast`

A type used in a cast operation was not a legal type.

**C2069**  `cast of 'void' term to non-void`

The **void** type was cast to a different type.

**C2070**  `illegal sizeof operand`

The operand of a **sizeof** expression was not an identifier or a type name.

**C2071**  `'`*class*`' : bad storage class`

The given storage class cannot be used in this context.

**C2072**  `'`*identifier*`' : initialization of a function`

An attempt was made to initialize a function.

| Number | Compilation-Error Message |
|--------|---------------------------|

**C2073**  `'`*identifier*`'` `: cannot initialize array in`
`function`

An attempt was made to initialize the given array within a function.

Arrays can be initialized only at the external level.

**C2074**  `cannot initialize struct/union in function`

An attempt was made to initialize the given structure or union within a function. Structures and unions can be initialized only at the external level.

**C2075**  `'`*identifier*`'` `: array initialization needs curly`
`braces`

The braces ({ }) around the given array initializer were missing.

**C2076**  `'`*identifier*`'` `: struct/union initialization`
`needs curly braces`

The braces ({ }) around the given structure or union initializer were missing.

**C2077**  `non-integral field initializer '`*identifier*`'`

An attempt was made to initialize a bit-field member of a structure with a nonintegral value.

**C2078**  `too many initializers`

The number of initializers exceeded the number of objects to be initialized.

**C2079**  `'`*identifier*`'` `is an undefined struct/union`

The given identifier was declared as a structure or union type that had not been defined.

**C2082**  `redefinition of formal parameter '`*identifier*`'`

A formal parameter to a function was redeclared within the function body.

| Number | Compilation-Error Message |
|--------|---------------------------|

**C2083**   `array '`*identifier*`' already has a size`

The dimensions of the given array had already been declared.

**C2084**   `function '`*identifier*`' already has a body`

The given function had already been defined.

**C2085**   `'`*identifier*`' : not in formal parameter list`

The given parameter was declared in a function definition for a nonexistent formal parameter.

**C2086**   `'`*identifier*`' : redefinition`

The given identifier was defined more than once.

**C2087**   `'`*identifier*`' : missing subscript`

The definition of an array with multiple subscripts was missing a subscript value for a dimension other than the first dimension, as in the following example:

```
int func(a)
    char a[10][];          /* Illegal */
    {
    .
    .
    .
    }

int func(a)
    char a[][5];           /* Legal */
    {
    .
    .
    .
    }
```

**C2088**   `use of undefined enum/struct/union '`*identifier*`'`

The given identifier referred to a structure or union type that was not defined.

| Number | Compilation-Error Message |
|--------|---------------------------|

**C2089**    `typedef specifies a near/far function`

The use of the **near** or **far** keyword in a **typedef** declaration conflicted with the use of **near** or **far** for the declared item, as in the following example:

```
typedef int far FARFUNC( );
FARFUNC near *fp;
```

**C2090**    `function returns array`

A function cannot return an array. (It can return a pointer to an array.)

**C2091**    `function returns function`

A function cannot return a function. (It can return a pointer to a function.)

**C2092**    `array element type cannot be function`

Arrays of functions are not allowed; however, arrays of pointers to functions are allowed.

**C2093**    `cannot initialize a static or struct with address of automatic vars`

The program tried to use the address of an automatic variable in the initializer of a static item, as in the following example:

```
func ()
{
    int i;
    static int *ip=&i;
    .
    .
    .
}
```

**C2094**    `label 'identifier' was undefined`

The function did not contain a statement labeled with the given identifier.

| Number | Compilation-Error Message |
|--------|---------------------------|

**C2095**   *function* : actual has type void : parameter *number*

Formal parameters and arguments to functions cannot have type **void**; they can, however, have type **void** * (pointer to void).

**C2096**   struct/union comparison illegal

You cannot compare two structures or unions. (You can, however, compare individual members of structures and unions.)

**C2097**   illegal initialization

An attempt was made to initialize a variable using a non-constant value.

**C2098**   non-address expression

An attempt was made to initialize an item that was not an lvalue.

**C2099**   non-constant offset

An initializer used a nonconstant offset.

**C2100**   illegal indirection

The indirection operator (*) was applied to a nonpointer value.

**C2101**   '&' on constant

The address-of operator (&) did not have an lvalue as its operand.

**C2102**   '&' requires lvalue

The address-of operator must be applied to an lvalue expression.

**C2103**   '&' on register variable

An attempt was made to take the address of a register variable.

| Number | Compilation-Error Message |
|--------|---------------------------|
| C2104  | `'&' on bit-field` |
|        | An attempt was made to take the address of a bit field. |
| C2105  | `'operator' needs lvalue` |
|        | The given operator did not have an lvalue operand. |
| C2106  | `'operator' : left operand must be lvalue` |
|        | The left operand of the given operator was not an lvalue. |
| C2107  | `illegal index, indirection not allowed` |
|        | A subscript was applied to an expression that did not evaluate to a pointer. |
| C2108  | `non-integral index` |
|        | A nonintegral expression was used in an array subscript. |
| C2109  | `subscript on non-array` |
|        | A subscript was used on a variable that was not an array. |
| C2110  | `'+' : 2 pointers` |
|        | An attempt was made to add one pointer to another. |
| C2111  | `pointer + non-integral value` |
|        | An attempt was made to add a nonintegral value to a pointer. |
| C2112  | `illegal pointer subtraction` |
|        | An attempt was made to subtract pointers that did not point to the same type. |
| C2113  | `'-' : right operand pointer` |
|        | The right operand in a subtraction operation ($-$) was a pointer, but the left operand was not. |
| C2114  | `'operator' : pointer on left; needs integral right` |
|        | The left operand of the given operator was a pointer; the right operand must be an integral value. |

| Number | Compilation-Error Message |
|--------|---------------------------|

**C2115**   '*identifier*' : incompatible types

An expression contained incompatible types.

**C2116**   *operator* : bad *left* (or *right*) operand

The specified operand of the given operator was illegal for that operator.

**C2117**   '*operator*' : illegal for struct/union

Structure and union type values are not allowed with the given operator.

**C2118**   negative subscript

A value defining an array size was negative.

**C2119**   'typedefs' both define indirection

Two **typedef** types were used to declare an item and both **typedef** types had indirection. For example, the declaration of p in the following example is illegal:

```
typedef int *P_INT;
typedef short *P_SHORT;
/* this declaration is illegal */
P_SHORT P_INT p;
```

**C2120**   'void' illegal with all types

The **void** type was used in a declaration with another type.

**C2121**   typedef specifies different enum

An attempt was made to use a type declared in a **typedef** statement to specify both an enumeration type and another type.

**C2122**   typedef specifies different struct

An attempt was made to use a type declared in a **typedef** statement to specify both a structure type and another type.

**C2123**   typedef specifies different union

An attempt was made to use a type declared in a **typedef** statement to specify both a union type and another type.

| Number | Compilation-Error Message |
|--------|---------------------------|

**C2125**      '*identifier*': allocation exceeds 64K

The given item exceeds the size limit of 64K.

**C2126**      *identifier*: automatic allocation exceeds 32K

The space allocated for the local variables of a function exceeded the given limit.

**C2127**      parameter allocation exceeds 32K

The storage space required for the parameters to a function exceeded the limit of 32K.

**C2129**      static function '*identifier*' not found

A forward reference was made to a static function that was never defined.

**C2130**      #line expected a string containing the file name

A file name was missing from a **#line** directive.

**C2131**      attributes specify more than one near/far/huge

More than one of the keywords **near** and **far** were applied to an item, as in the following example:

```
typedef int near NINT;
NINT far a;          /* Illegal */
```

**C2132**      syntax error : unexpected identifier

An identifier appeared in a syntactically illegal context.

**C2133**      array '*identifier*' : unknown size

An attempt was made to declare an unsized array as a local variable, as in the following example:

```
int mat_add(array1)
    int array1[];       /* Legal */
    {
    int array2[];         /* Illegal */
    .
    .
    .
    }
```

| Number | Compilation-Error Message |
|--------|---------------------------|

**C2134**  *identifier* : `struct/union too large`

The size of a structure or union exceeded the compiler limit ($2^{32}$ bytes).

**C2135**  `missing ')' in macro expansion`

A macro reference with arguments was missing a closing parenthesis.

**C2137**  `empty character constant`

The illegal empty-character constant (`''`) was used.

**C2138**  `unmatched close comment '/*'`

The compiler detected an open-comment delimiter (`/*`) without a matching close-comment delimiter (`*/`).

This error usually indicates an attempt to use illegal nested comments.

**C2139**  `type following '`*type*`' is illegal`

An illegal type combination, such as the following, was used:

```
long char a;
```

**C2140**  `argument type cannot be function returning ...`

A function was declared as a formal parameter of another function, as in the following example:

```
int func1(a)
     int a( );      /* Illegal */
```

**C2141**  `value out of range for enum constant`

An enumeration constant had a value outside the range of values allowed for type **int**.

**C2142**  `ellipsis requires three periods`

The compiler detected a token consisting of two periods ( .. ) and assumed that an ellipsis ( ... ) was intended.

| Number | Compilation-Error Message |
|---|---|

C2143    `syntax error : missing 'token1' before 'token2'`

The compiler expected *token1* to appear before *token2*. This message may appear if a required closing brace (}), right parenthesis ()), or semicolon (;) is missing.

C2144    `syntax error : missing 'token' before type 'type'`

The compiler expected the given token to appear before the given type name.

This message may appear if a required closing brace (}), right parenthesis ()), or semicolon (;) is missing.

C2145    `syntax error : missing 'token' before identifier`

The compiler expected the given token to appear before an identifier.

This message may appear if a semicolon (;) does not appear after the last declaration of a block.

C2146    `syntax error : missing 'token' before identifier 'identifier'`

The compiler expected the given token to appear before the given identifier.

C2147    `array : unknown size`

An attempt was made to increment an index or pointer to an array whose base type has not yet been declared.

C2148    `array too large`

An array exceeded the maximum legal size ($2^{32}$ bytes).

C2149    *identifier*`: named bit-field cannot have 0 width`

The given named bit field had a zero width. Only unnamed bit fields are allowed to have zero width.

C2150    *identifier*`: bit-field must have type int, signed int, or unsigned int`

The ANSI C standard requires bit fields to have types of **int**, **signed int**, or **unsigned int**. This message appears only if you compiled your program with the **/Za** option.

| Number | Compilation-Error Message |
|--------|---------------------------|

**C2151**
`more than one cdecl/fortran/pascal`
`attribute specified`

More than one keyword specifying a function-calling convention was given.

**C2152**
*identifier* `: pointers to functions with`
`different attributes`

An attempt was made to assign a pointer to a function declared with one calling convention (**cdecl**, **fortran**, or **pascal**) to a pointer to a function declared with a different calling convention.

**C2153**
`hex constants must have at least 1 hex`
`digit`

**0x** and **0X** are illegal hexadecimal constants. At least one hexadecimal digit must follow the "x" or "X."

**C2154**
`'`*name*`' : does not refer to a segment`

The function *name* was the first identifier given in an **alloc_text** pragma argument list, and it is already defined as something other than a segment name.

**C2155**
`'`*name*`' : already in a segment`

The function *name* appeared in more than one **alloc_text** pragma.

**C2156**
`pragma must be at outer level`

Certain pragmas must be specified at a global level, outside a function body, and one of these pragmas occurred within a function.

**C2157**
`'`*name*`' : must be declared before use in`
`pragma list`

The function *name* in the list of functions for an **alloc_text** pragma was not declared prior to being referenced in the list.

**C2158**
`'`*name*`' : is a function`

The *name* was specified in the list of variables in a **same_seg** pragma, but was previously declared as a function.

| Number | Compilation-Error Message |
|--------|---------------------------|

C2159    `more than one storage class specified`

More than one storage class was given in a declaration, as in the following example:

```
extern static int i;
```

C2160    `## cannot occur at the beginning of a macro definition`

A macro definition began with a token-pasting operator ($\#\#$), as in the following example:

```
#define mac(a,b) ##a...
```

C2161    `## cannot occur at the end of a macro definition`

A macro definition ended with a token-pasting operator ($\#\#$).

C2162    `expected macro formal parameter`

The token following a stringizing operator ($\#$) was not a formal parameter name, as in the following example:

```
#define print(a) printf(#b)
```

C2163    `'string' : not available as an intrinsic`

A function specified in the list of functions for an **intrinsic** or **function** pragma is not one of the functions available in intrinsic form.

C2165    `'keyword' : cannot modify pointers to data`

The **fortran**, **pascal**, or **cdecl** keyword was used illegally to modify a pointer to data, as in the following example:

```
char pascal *p;
```

C2166    `lval specifies 'const' object`

An attempt was made to assign a value to an item declared with **const** storage class.

| Number | Compilation-Error Message |
|--------|---------------------------|

**C2167**   `'name' : too many actual parameters for intrinsic`

A reference to the intrinsic function *name* contains too many actual parameters.

**C2168**   `'name' : too few actual parameters for intrinsic`

A reference to the intrinsic function *name* contains too few actual parameters.

**C2169**   `'name' : is an intrinsic, it cannot be defined`

An attempt was made to provide a function definition for a function already declared as an intrinsic.

**C2171**   `'operator' : bad operand`

The given unary operator was used with an illegal operand type, as in the following example:

```
int (*fp)();
double d,d1;
.
.
.
fp++;
d = ~d1
```

**C2172**   *function* `: actual is not a pointer, parameter` *number*

An attempt was made to pass a non-pointer argument to a function that expected a pointer. The given number indicates which argument was in error.

**C2173**   *function* `: actual is not a pointer : parameter` *number* `: parameterlist` *number*

An attempt was made to pass a non-pointer argument to a function that expected a pointer. This error occurs in calls that return a pointer to a function. The first number indicates which argument was in error; the second number indicates which argument list contained the invalid argument.

| Number | Compilation-Error Message |
|--------|---------------------------|

**C2174**  *function* : actual has type void : parameter *number,* parameter list *number*

An attempt was made to pass a **void** argument to a function. Formal parameters and arguments to functions cannot have type **void**; they can, however, have type **void ∗** (pointer to **void**). This error occurs in calls that return a pointer to a function. The first number indicates which argument was in error; the second number indicates which argument list contained the invalid argument.

**C2175**  *function* : unresolved external

The given function is not defined in the source file, or built into the QuickC programming environment, or present in the Quick library (if any) that was loaded.

This error occurs only for single-module, in-memory programs. To solve this program, either define the function in the source file, load a Quick library containing the function, or (if the function is a standard C library function) create a program list for the program.

**C2177**  constant too big

Information was lost because a constant value was too large to be replaced in the type to which it was assigned. (1)

## D.1.3  Warning Messages

The messages listed in this section indicate potential problems but do not hinder compilation and linking. The number in parentheses at the end of an error-message description gives the minimum warning level that must be set for the message to appear.

| Number | Warning Message |
|--------|-----------------|

**C4000**  UNKNOWN WARNING
Contact Microsoft Technical Support.

The compiler detected an unknown error condition.

Please report this condition to Microsoft Corporation, using the Product Assistance Request form at the back of this manual.

| Number | Warning Message |
|--------|-----------------|
| C4001 | `macro 'identifier' requires parameters` |
| | The given identifier was defined as a macro taking one or more arguments, but it was used in the program without arguments. (1) |
| C4002 | `too many actual parameters for macro 'identifier'` |
| | The number of actual arguments specified with the given identifier was greater than the number of formal parameters given in the macro definition of the identifier. (1) |
| C4003 | `not enough actual parameters for macro 'identifier'` |
| | The number of actual arguments specified with the given identifier was less than the number of formal parameters given in the macro definition of the identifier. (1) |
| C4004 | `missing close parenthesis after 'defined'` |
| | The closing parenthesis was missing from an #if defined phrase. (1) |
| C4005 | `'identifier' : redefinition` |
| | The given identifier was redefined. (1) |
| C4006 | `#undef expected an identifier` |
| | The name of the identifier whose definition was to be removed was not given with the #undef directive. (1) |
| C4009 | `string too big, trailing chars truncated` |
| | A string exceeded the compiler limit on string size. |
| | To correct this problem, break the string into two or more strings. (1) |
| C4011 | `identifier truncated to 'identifier'` |
| | Only the first 31 characters of an identifier are significant. (1) |

| Number | Warning Message |
|---|---|

**C4014**    '*identifier*' : bit-field type must be unsigned

The given bit field was not declared as an **unsigned** type.

Bit fields must be declared as **unsigned** integral types. The compiler converted the given bit field accordingly. (1)

**C4015**    '*identifier*' : bit-field type must be integral

The given bit field was not declared as an integral type.

Bit fields must be declared as **unsigned** integral types. A conversion has been supplied. (1)

**C4016**    '*identifier*' : no function return type

The given function had not yet been declared or defined, so the return type was unknown.

The default return type (**int**) is assumed. (2)

**C4017**    cast of int expression to far pointer

A far pointer represents a full segmented address. On an 8086/8088 processor, casting an **int** value to a far pointer may produce an address with a meaningless segment value. (1)

**C4020**    too many actual parameters

The number of arguments specified in a function call was greater than the number of parameters specified in the argument-type list or function definition. (1)

**C4021**    too few actual parameters

The number of arguments specified in a function call was less than the number of parameters specified in the argument-type list or function definition. (1)

**C4022**    pointer mismatch: parameter *n*

The pointer type of the given parameter was different from the pointer type specified in the argument-type list or function definition. (1)

| Number | Warning Message |
|--------|-----------------|

**C4024**    `different types : parameter` *n*

The type of the given parameter in a function call did not agree with the type given in the argument-type list or function definition. (1)

**C4025**    `function declaration specified variable argument list`

The argument-type list in a function declaration ended with either a comma or a comma followed by ellipsis dots (,...), indicating that the function could take a variable number of arguments, but no formal parameters were declared for the function. (1)

**C4026**    `function was declared with formal argument list`

The function was declared to take arguments, but the function definition did not declare formal parameters. (1)

**C4027**    `function was declared without formal argument list`

The function was declared to take no arguments (the argument-type list consisted of the word **void**), but formal parameters were declared in the function definition, or arguments were given in a call to the function. (1)

**C4028**    `parameter` *n* `declaration different`

The type of the given parameter did not agree with the corresponding type in the argument-type list or with the corresponding formal parameter. (1)

**C4029**    `declared parameter list different from definition`

The argument-type list given in a function declaration did not agree with the types of the formal parameters given in the function definition. (1)

**C4030**    `first parameter list is longer than the second`

A function was declared more than once with different argument-type lists in the declarations. (1)

| Number | Warning Message |
|---|---|

**C4031**     `second parameter list is longer than the first`

A function was declared more than once with different argument-type lists. (1)

**C4032**     `unnamed struct/union as parameter`

The structure or union type being passed as an argument was not named, so the declaration of the formal parameter cannot use the name and must declare the type. (1)

**C4033**     `function must return a value`

A function is expected to return a value unless it is declared as **void**. (2)

**C4034**     `sizeof returns 0`

The **sizeof** operator was applied to an operand that yielded a size of zero. (1)

**C4035**     *identifier* `: no return value`

A function declared to return a value did not do so. (2)

**C4036**     `unexpected formal parameter list`

A formal-parameter list was given in a function declaration. The formal-parameter list is ignored. (1)

**C4037**     `'`*identifier*`' : formal parameters ignored`

No storage class or type name appeared before the declarators of formal parameters in a function declaration, as in the following example:

```
int *f(a,b,c);
```

The formal parameters are ignored. (1)

**C4038**     `'`*identifier*`' : formal parameter has bad storage class`

The given formal parameter was declared with a storage class other than **auto** or **register**. (1)

| Number | Warning Message |
|--------|-----------------|

**C4039**    `'`*identifier*`' : function used as an argument`

A formal parameter to a function was declared to be a function, which is illegal. The formal parameter is converted to a function pointer. (1)

**C4040**    `near/far/huge on '`*identifier*`' ignored`

The **near** or **far** keyword has no effect in the declaration of the given identifier and is ignored. (1)

**C4041**    `formal parameter '`*identifier*`' is redefined`

The given formal parameter was redefined in the function body, making the corresponding actual argument unavailable in the function. (1)

**C4042**    `'`*identifier*`' : has bad storage class`

The specified storage class cannot be used in this context (for example, function parameters cannot be given **extern** class). The default storage class for that context was used in place of the illegal class. (1)

**C4043**    `'`*identifier*`' : void type changed to int`

An item other than a function was declared to have **void** type. (1)

**C4045**    `'`*identifier*`' : array bounds overflow`

Too many initializers were present for the given array. The excess initializers are ignored. (1)

**C4046**    `'&' on function/array, ignored`

An attempt was made to apply the address-of operator (&) to a function or array identifier. (1)

**C4047**    `'`*operator*`': different levels of indirection`

An expression involving the specified operator had inconsistent levels of indirection. (1)

The following example illustrates this condition:

```
char **p;
char *q;
    .
    .
    .
p = q;
```

| Number | Warning Message |
|--------|-----------------|

C4048  `array's declared subscripts different`

An array was declared twice with different sizes. The larger size is used. (1)

C4049  `'operator' : indirection to different types`

The indirection operator (∗) was used in an expression to access values of different types. (1)

C4051  `data conversion`

Two data items in an expression had different types, causing the type of one item to be converted. (2)

C4052  `different enum types`

Two different **enum** types were used in an expression. (1)

C4053  `at least one void operand`

An expression with type **void** was used as an operand. (1)

C4056  `overflow in constant arithmetic`

The result of an operation exceeded 0x7FFFFFFF. (1)

C4057  `overflow in constant multiplication`

The result of an operation exceeded 0x7FFFFFFF. (1)

C4058  `address of frame variable taken, DS != SS`

The program was compiled with the default data segment (**DS**) not equal to the stack segment (**SS**), and the program tried to point to a frame variable with a near pointer. (1)

C4059  `segment lost in conversion`

The conversion of a far pointer (a full segmented address) to a near pointer (a segment offset) resulted in the loss of the segment address. (1)

C4060  `conversion of long address to short address`

The conversion of a long address (a 32-bit pointer) to a short address (a 16-bit pointer) resulted in the loss of the segment address. (1)

| Number | Warning Message |
|--------|-----------------|

**C4061** `long/short mismatch in argument: conversion supplied`

The base types of the actual and formal arguments of a function were different. The actual argument is converted to the type of the formal parameter. (1)

**C4062** `near/far mismatch in argument: conversion supplied`

The pointer sizes of the actual and formal arguments of a function were different. The actual argument is converted to the type of the formal parameter. (1)

**C4063** `'`*identifier*`' : function too large for post-optimizer`

The given function was not optimized because not enough space was available. To correct this problem, reduce the size of the function by dividing it into two or more smaller functions. (0)

**C4066** `local symbol table overflow - some local symbols may be missing in listings`

The listing generator ran out of heap space for local variables, so the source listing may not contain symbol-table information for all local variables.

**C4067** `unexpected characters following '`*directive*`' directive - newline expected`

Extra characters followed a preprocessor directive, as in the following example:

```
#endif   NO_EXT_KEYS
```

This is accepted in some versions of the Microsoft C Compiler, but not in Version 1.0 of the Microsoft QuickC Compiler. (1)

**C4068** `unknown pragma`

The compiler did not recognize a pragma and ignored it. (1)

| Number | Warning Message |
|--------|-----------------|

**C4069**  `conversion of near pointer to long integer`

A near pointer was converted to a long integer, which involves first extending the high-order word with the current data-segment value, *not* 0. (1)

**C4071**  `'`*identifier*`' : no function prototype given`

The given function was called before the compiler found the corresponding function prototype. (3)

**C4072**  `Insufficient memory to process debugging information`

You compiled the program with the **/Zi** option, but not enough memory was available to create the required debugging information. (1)

**C4073**  `scoping too deep, deepest scoping merged when debugging`

Declarations appeared at a static nesting level greater than 13. As a result, all declarations will seem to appear at the same level. (1)

**C4074**  `non standard extension used - '`*extension*`'`

The given nonstandard language extension was used when the Language Extensions option in the Compile dialog box was turned off, or when the **/Ze** option was in effect. These extensions are given in Section 8.1.4.6, "Using Microsoft Extensions to C: the Language Extensions Option." (If the **/Za** option is in effect, this condition generates an error.) (3)

**C4075**  `size of switch expression or case constant too large - converted to int`

A value appearing in a **switch** or **case** statement was larger than an **int** type. The compiler converts the illegal value to an **int** type. (1)

**C4076**  `'`*type*`' : may be used on integral types only`

The **signed** or **unsigned** type modifier was used with a non-integral type, as in the following example:

```
unsigned double x;
```

| Number | Warning Message |
|--------|-----------------|

**C4077**     `unknown check_stack option`

An unknown option was given with the old form of the **check_stack** pragma, as in the followling example:

```
#pragma check_stack yes
```

In the old form of the **check_stack** pragma, the argument to the pragma must be empty, +, or −.

**C4079**     `unexpected char 'character'`

An unexpected separator *character* was found in the argument list of a pragma.

**C4080**     `missing segment name`

The first argument in the argument list for the **alloc_text** pragma was missing a segment name. This happens if the first token in the argument list is not an identifier.

**C4082**     `expected an identifier`

There was a missing identifier in the list of arguments to a pragma.

**C4083**     `missing '('`

An opening left parenthesis was missing from the argument list for a pragma, as in the following example:

```
#pragma check_pointer on)
```

**C4084**     `expected a pragma keyword`

The token following the keyword **pragma** was not an identifier, as in the following example:

```
#pragma (on)
```

| Number | Warning Message |
|---|---|

**C4085**  `expected [on|off]`

An invalid argument was given for the new form of the **check_stack** pragma, as in the following example:

```
#pragma check_stack(yes)
```

**C4086**  `expected [1|2|4]`

An invalid argument was given for a **pack** pragma, as in the following example:

```
#pragma pack(yes)
```

**C4087**  `'name' : declared with void parameter list`

The given function was declared as taking no parameters, but a call to the function specified actual parameters, as in the following example:

```
int f1(void);
    .
    .
    .
f1(10);
```

**C4090**  `different 'const' attributes`

A pointer to an item declared as **const** was passed to a function where the corresponding formal parameter was a pointer to a non-**const** item. This means the item could be modified by the function undetected, as in the following example:

```
const char *p = "abcde";
int str(char *s);
.
.
.
str(p);
```

**C4091**  `no symbols were declared`

The compiler detected an empty declaration, as in the following example (2):

```
int ;
```

| Number | Warning Message |
|--------|-----------------|

**C4092**      `untagged enum/struct/union declared no symbols`

The compiler detected an empty declaration using an untagged structure, union, or enumerated variable, as in the following example:

```
struct {
    .
    .
    .
};
```

**C4093**      `unescaped newline in character constant in non-active code`

The constant expression of an #**if**, #**elif**, #**ifdef**, or #**ifndef** preprocessor directive evaluated to 0, making the following code inactive, and a new-line character appeared between a single or double quotation mark and the matching single or double quotation mark in that inactive code.

**C4095**      `too many arguments for pragma`

More than one argument appeared for a pragma that takes only one argument.

**C4096**      `huge item treated as far`

Since the Microsoft QuickC Compiler does not support the **huge** keyword, the item is treated as if it had been declared with the **far** keyword. If the item or function must be huge, recompile the program with the Microsoft C Optimizing Compiler.

**C4097**      `non-ascii character '`*hex-character*`' in string`

The given non-ASCII character was used in a string.

## D.1.4   Compiler Limits

To operate the Microsoft QuickC Compiler, you must have sufficient disk space available for the compiler to create temporary files that are used in processing. The space required is approximately two times the size of the source file.

Table D.1 summarizes the limits imposed by the C compiler. If your program exceeds one of these limits, an error message will inform you of the problem.

**Table D.1**

**Limits Imposed by the C Compiler**

| Program Item | Description | Limit |
|---|---|---|
| String literals | Maximum length of a string, including the terminating null character (\ **0**) | 512 bytes |
| Constants | Maximum size of a constant is determined by its type; see the *Microsoft C Language Reference* for a discussion of constants. | |
| Identifiers | Maximum length of an identifier | 31 bytes (additional characters are discarded) |
| Declarations | Maximum level of nesting for structure/union definitions | 10 levels |
| Preprocessor directives | Maximum size of a macro definition | 512 bytes |
| | Maximum number of actual arguments to a macro definition | 8 arguments |
| | Maximum length of an actual preprocessor argument | 256 bytes |
| | Maximum level of nesting for **# if**, **# ifdef**, and **# ifndef** directives | 32 levels |
| | Maximum level of nesting for include files | 10 levels |

The compiler does not set explicit limits on the number and complexity of declarations, definitions, and statements in an individual function or in a program. If the compiler encounters a function or program that is too large or too complex to be processed, it produces an error message to that effect.

# D.2   Command-Line Error Messages

Messages that indicate errors on the command line used to invoke the compiler have one of the following formats:

```
command line fatal error D1xxx: messagetext      Fatal error
command line error D2xxx: messagetext            Error
command line warning D4xxx: messagetext          Warning
```

If possible, the compiler continues operation, printing a warning message. In some cases, command-line errors are fatal and the compiler terminates processing. The messages in Sections D.2.1–D.2.3 indicate errors on the command line.

## D.2.1   Command-Line Fatal-Error Messages

The following messages identify fatal errors. The compiler driver cannot recover from a fatal error; it terminates after printing the error message.

| Number | Command-Line Fatal-Error Message |
|---|---|
| D1000 | UNKNOWN COMMAND LINE FATAL ERROR Contact Microsoft Technical Support |

The compiler detected an unknown fatal-error condition.

Please report this condition to Microsoft Corporation, using the Product Assistance Request form at the back of this manual.

D1001    could not execute '*filename*'

The compiler could not find the given file in the current working directory or in any of the other directories named in the **PATH** variable.

D1002          `too many open files, cannot redirect`
               `'`*filename*`'`

               No more file handles were available to redirect the output
               of the **/P** option to a file.

               Try editing your **CONFIG.SYS** file and increasing the
               value *num* on the line `files=`*num* (if *num* is less than 20).

## D.2.2   Command-Line Error Messages

When the compiler driver encounters any of the errors listed in this section, it continues compiling the program (if possible) and outputs additional error messages. However, no object file is produced.

| Number | Command-Line Error Message |
| --- | --- |

D2000          `UNKNOWN COMMAND LINE ERROR`
               `Contact Microsoft Technical Support`

               The compiler detected an unknown error condition.

               Please report this condition to Microsoft Corporation,
               using the Product Assistance Request form at the back of
               this manual.

D2001          `too many symbols predefined with -D`

               Too many symbolic constants were defined by using the **/D**
               option on the command line.

               The normal limit on command-line definitions is 16; you
               can use the **/U** or **/u** option to increase the limit to 20.

D2002          `a previously defined model specification`
               `has been overridden`

               Two different memory models were specified; the model
               specified later on the command line was used.

D2003          `missing source file name`

               You did not give the name of the source file to be compiled.

D2007          `bad `*option*` flag, would overwrite '`*string1*`' with`
               `'`*string2*`'`

               The specified option was given more than once, with
               conflicting arguments *string1* and *string2*.

| Number | Command-Line Error Message |
|--------|---------------------------|

**D2008**    `too many` *option* `flags,` `'`*string*`'`

Too many letters were given with the specified option (for example, with the **/O** option).

**D2009**    `unknown option` *character* `in` `'`*optionstring*`'`

One of the letters in the given option was not recognized.

**D2010**    `unknown floating point option`

The specified floating-point option (an **/FP** option) was not one of the valid options.

**D2011**    `only one floating point model allowed`

You specified more than one floating-point (**/FP**) option on the command line.

**D2012**    `too many linker flags on command line`

You tried to pass more than **128** separate options and object files to the linker.

**D2015**    `assembly files are not handled`

You gave a file name with an extension of **.ASM** on the command line.

Because the compiler cannot invoke the Microsoft Macro Assembler (**MASM**) automatically, it cannot assemble such files.

**D2018**    `cannot open linker cmd file`

The response file used to pass object-file names and options to the linker could not be opened.

This error may have occurred because another read-only file had the same name as the response file.

**D2019**    `cannot overwrite the source file,` `'`*name*`'`

You specified the source file as an output-file name.

The compiler does not allow the source file to be overwritten by one of the compiler output files.

| Number | Command-Line Error Message |
|--------|----------------------------|

D2020      `-Gc option requires extended keywords to be enabled (-Ze)`

The **/Gc** option and the **/Za** option were specified on the same command line.

The **/Gc** option requires the extended keyword **cdecl** to be enabled if library functions are to be accessible.

D2021      `invalid numerical argument 'string'`

A non-numerical string was specified following an option that required a numerical argument.

D2022      `cannot open help file, cl.hlp`

The **/HELP** option was given, but the file containing the help messages (**QCL.HLP**) was not in the current directory or in any of the directories specified by the **PATH** environment variable.

## D.2.3 Command-Line Warning Messages

The messages listed in this section indicate potential problems, but the errors do not hinder compilation and linking.

| Number | Command-Line Warning Message |
|--------|------------------------------|

D4000      `UNKNOWN COMMAND LINE WARNING`
                `Contact Microsoft Technical Support`

An unknown command-line error condition has been detected by the compiler.

Please report this condition to Microsoft Corporation, using the Product Assistance Request form at the back of this manual.

D4002      `ignoring unknown flag 'string'`

One of the options given on the command line was not recognized and is ignored.

D4003      `80186/286 selected over 8086 for code generation`

Both the **/G0** option and the **/G2** option were given; **/G2** takes precedence.

| Number | Command-Line Warning Message |
|---|---|

**D4004**    `optimizing for time over space`

This message confirms that the **/Ot** option is used for optimizing.

**D4005**    `could not execute '`*filename*`'; please insert diskette and press any key`

The **QCL** command could not find the specified executable file in the search path.

**D4006**    `only one of -P/-E/-EP allowed, -P selected`

More than one preprocessor output option was specified.

**D4007**    `-C ignored (must also specify -P or -E or -EP)`

The **/C** option must be used in conjunction with one of the preprocessor output flags, **/E**, **/EP**, or **/P**.

**D4009**    `threshold only for far/huge data, ignored`

The **/Gt** option was used in a memory model that has near data pointers. It can be used only in compact and large models.

**D4010**    `-Gp not implemented, ignored`

The DOS version of Microsoft C does not support profiling.

**D4013**    `combined listing has precedence over object listing`

When **/Fc** is specified along with either **/Fl** or **/Fa**, the combined listing (**/Fc**) is created.

**D4014**    `invalid value `*number*` for '`*string*`'. Default `*number*` is used`

An invalid value was given in a context where a particular numeric value was expected.

**D4017**    `conflicting stack checking options - stack checking disabled`

You gave both the **/Ge** and the **/Gs** options on the **CL** command line. The **/Gs** option takes precedence, so stack checking is disabled in the program.

# D.3   Run-Time Error Messages

Run-time error messages fall into four categories:

1. Floating-point exceptions generated by the 8087/80287 hardware or the emulator. These exceptions are listed and described in Section D.3.1.

2. Error messages generated by the run-time library to notify you of serious errors. These messages are listed and described in Section D.3.2.

3. Error messages generated by program calls to error-handling routines in the C run-time library—the **abort**, **assert**, and **perror** routines. These routines print an error message to standard error output whenever the program calls the given routine. For descriptions of these routines and the corresponding error messages, see the *Microsoft C Run-Time Library Reference*.

4. Error messages generated by calls to math routines in the C run-time library. On error, the math routines return an error value and some print a message to the standard error output. See the *Microsoft C Run-Time Library Reference* for descriptions of the math routines and corresponding error messages.

## D.3.1   Floating-Point Exceptions

The error messages listed below correspond to exceptions generated by the 8087/80287 hardware. Refer to the Intel documentation for your processor for a detailed discussion of hardware exceptions. These errors may also be detected by the floating-point emulator built into the standard QuickC library.

Using C's default 8087/80287 control-word settings, the following exceptions are masked and do not occur:

| Exception | Default Masked Action |
| --- | --- |
| Denormal | Exception masked |
| Underflow | Result goes to 0.0 |
| Inexact | Exception masked |

For information on how to change the floating-point control word, see the reference pages for **_control87** in the *Microsoft C Run-Time Library Reference*.

The following errors do not occur with code generated by the Microsoft QuickC Compiler or provided in the standard C library:

```
Square root
Stack underflow
Unemulated
```

The floating-point exceptions have the following format:

```
run-time error M61nn: MATH
- floating-point error: messagetext
```

The floating-point exceptions are listed and described below:

| Number | Floating-Point Exception |
|--------|--------------------------|
| M6101 | invalid |

An invalid operation occurred. These usually involve operating on NANs or infinities. This error terminates the program with exit code 129.

| M6102 | denormal |
|-------|----------|

A very small floating-point number was generated and may no longer be valid due to loss of significance. Denormals are normally masked, causing them to be trapped and operated on. This error terminates the program with exit code 130.

| M6103 | divide by 0 |
|-------|-------------|

An attempt was made to divide by 0. This error terminates the program with exit code 131.

| M6104 | overflow |
|-------|----------|

An overflow occurred in a floating-point operation. This error terminates the program with exit code 132.

| M6105 | underflow |
|-------|-----------|

An underflow occurred in a floating-point operation. (An underflow is normally masked so that the underflowing value is replaced with 0.0.) This error terminates the program with exit code 133.

| M6106 | inexact |
|-------|---------|

Loss of precision occurred in a floating-point operation. This exception is normally masked since almost any floating-point operation can cause loss of precision. This error terminates the program with exit code 134.

| Number | Floating-Point Exception |
|--------|--------------------------|

**M6107**    `unemulated`

An attempt was made to execute an 8087/80287 instruction that is invalid or not supported by the emulator. This error terminates the program with exit code 135.

**M6108**    `square root`

The operand in a square-root operation was negative. This error terminates the program with exit code 136. (Note: the **sqrt** function in the C run-time library checks the argument before performing the operation and returns an error value if the operand is negative; see the *Microsoft C Run-Time Library Reference* for details on **sqrt**.)

**M6110**    `stack overflow`

A floating-point expression caused a stack overflow on the 8087 or 80287 coprocessor or the emulator. (Stack-overflow exceptions are trapped up to a limit of seven levels in addition to the eight levels normally supported by the 8087 or 80287 coprocessor.) This error terminates the program with exit code 138.

**M6111**    `stack underflow`

A floating-point operation resulted in a stack underflow on the 8087 or 80287 coprocessor or the emulator. This error terminates the program with exit code 139.

**M6112**    `explicitly generated`

A signal indicating a floating-point error was sent using a `raise(SIGFPE)` call. This error terminates the program with exit code 140.

## D.3.2   Run-Time-Library Error Messages

The following messages may be generated at run time when your program has serious errors. Run-time error-message numbers range from R6000 to R6999.

A run-time error message takes the following general form:

```
run-time error R6nnn
- messagetext
```

| Number | Run-Time-Library Error Message |
|--------|-------------------------------|

**R6000**   `stack overflow`

Your program has run out of stack space. This can occur when a program uses a large amount of local data or is heavily recursive. The program was terminated with an exit code of 255.

To correct the problem, recompile using the **/F** option of the **QCL** command or relink using the linker **/STACK** option to allocate a large stack.

**R6001**   `null pointer assignment`

The contents of the **NULL** segment have changed in the course of program execution. The **NULL** segment is a special location in low memory that is not normally used. If the contents of the **NULL** segment change during a program's execution, it means that the program has written to this area, usually by an inadvertent assignment through a null pointer. Note that your program can contain null pointers without generating this message; the message appears only when you access a memory location through the null pointer.

This error does not cause your program to terminate; the error message is printed following the normal termination of the program. This error yields a nonzero exit code.

This message reflects a potentially serious error in your program. Although a program that produces this error may appear to operate correctly, it is likely to cause problems in the future and may fail to run in a different operating environment.

**R6002**   `floating point not loaded`

Your program needs the floating-point library, but the library was not loaded. The error causes the program to be terminated with an exit status of 255. This occurs in two situations:

1.  The program was compiled or linked with an option (such as **/FPi87**) that required an 8087 or 80287 coprocessor, but the program was run on a machine that did not have a coprocessor installed. To fix this problem, either recompile the program with the **/FPi** option or install a coprocessor. (See Section 9.3.5 of this manual for more information about these options and libraries.)

| Number | Run-Time-Library Error Message |
|---|---|

2. A format string for one of the routines in the **printf** or **scanf** families contains a floating-point format specification and there are no floating-point values or variables in the program. The QuickC compiler attempts to minimize the size of a program by loading floating-point support only when necessary. Floating-point format specifications within format strings are not detected, so the necessary floating-point routines are not loaded. To correct this error, use a floating-point argument to correspond to the floating-point format specification. This causes floating-point support to be loaded.

**R6003**    `integer divide by 0`

An attempt was made to divide an integer by 0, giving an undefined result. This error terminates the program with an exit code of 255.

**R6004**    `DOS 2.0 or later required`

The QuickC compiler cannot run on versions of DOS prior to 2.0.

**R6005**    `not enough memory on exec`

Errors R6005 through R6007 occur when a child process spawned by one of the **exec** library routines fails, and DOS could not return control to the parent process. This error indicates that not enough memory remained to load the program being spawned.

**R6006**    `bad format on exec`

The file to be executed by one of the **exec** functions was not in the correct format for an executable file.

**R6007**    `bad environment on exec`

During a call to one of the **exec** functions, DOS determined that the child process was being given a bad environment block.

| Number | Run-Time-Library Error Message |
|--------|-------------------------------|
| R6008 | not enough space for arguments |
| R6009 | not enough space for environment |

Errors R6008 and R6009 both occur at start-up if there is enough memory to load the program, but not enough room for the *argv* vector, the *envp* vector, or both. To avoid this problem, rewrite the **_setargv** or **_setenvp** routines.

R6012      Invalid near pointer reference

A null near pointer was used in the program.

This error occurs only if pointer checking is in effect (that is, if the program was compiled with the Pointer Check option in the Compile dialog box, the **/Zr** option on the **QCL** command line, or the **pointer_check** pragma in effect).

R6013      Invalid far pointer reference

An out-of-range far pointer was used in the program.

This error occurs only if pointer checking is in effect (that is, if the program was compiled with the Pointer Check option in the Compile dialog box, the **/Zr** option on the **QCL** command line, or the **pointer_check** pragma in effect).

R6015      unexpected interrupt

The program could not be run because it contained unexpected interrupts.

When it creates an in-memory program from a program list, QuickC automatically creates object files and passes them to the linker. The object files that QuickC passes to the linker contain interrupts that are required within the QuickC environment. However, you cannot run a program created from such object files outside of the QuickC programming environment.

## D.3.3    Run-Time Limits

Table D.2 summarizes the limits that apply to programs at run time. If your program exceeds one of these limits, an error message will inform you of the problem.

Table D.2

Program Limits at Run Time

| Item | Description | Limit |
|------|-------------|-------|
| Files | Maximum file size | $2^{32} - 1$ bytes (4 gigabytes) |
| | Maximum number of open files (streams) | 20[a] |
| Command line | Maximum number of characters (including program name) | 128 |
| Environment table | Maximum size | 32K |

[a] Five streams are opened automatically (**stdin**, **stdout**, **stderr**, **stdaux**, and **stdprn**), leaving 15 files available for the program to open.

# D.4   LINK Error Messages

This section lists and describes error messages generated by the Microsoft Overlay Linker, **LINK**.

Fatal errors cause the linker to stop execution. Fatal error messages have the following format:

*location* : `fatal error L1`*xxx*: *messagetext*

Nonfatal errors indicate problems in the executable file. **LINK** produces the executable file. Nonfatal error messages have the following format:

*location* : `error L2`*xxx*: *messagetext*

Warnings indicate possible problems in the executable file. **LINK** produces the executable file. Warnings have the following format:

*location* : `warning L4`*xxx*: *messagetext*

In these messages, *location* is the input file associated with the error, or LINK if there is no input file. If the input file is an **.OBJ** or **.LIB** file and has a module name, the module name is enclosed in parentheses, as shown in the following examples:

```
SLIBC.LIB(_file)
MAIN.OBJ(main.c)
TEXT.OBJ
```

Linker errors may occur when you invoke the linker implicitly with the
**QCL** command or explicitly with the **LINK** command. They may also
occur when you compile a program that has a program list, or when you
create an executable file on disk, within the QuickC environment. If linker
errors occur within the QuickC programming environment, QuickC
displays this message:

```
Errors during link phase
No .EXE file produced
```

To view the linker errors, press ENTER or click the OK command button.
The errors for the most recent linker pass are stored in a file named
**LINK.ERR**.

The error messages listed in this section may appear when you link object
files with the Microsoft Overlay Linker, **LINK**.

| Number | LINK Error Message |
|---|---|

**L1001**    *option* : option name ambiguous

A unique option name did not appear after the option indicator (/). For example, the command

```
LINK /N main;
```

generates this error, since **LINK** cannot tell which of the
three options beginning with the letter "N" was intended.

**L1002**    *option* : unrecognized option name

An unrecognized character followed the option indicator
(/), as in the following example:

```
LINK /ABCDEF main;
```

**L1004**    *option* : invalid numeric value

An incorrect value appeared for one of the linker options.
For example, a character string was given for an option
that requires a numeric value.

**L1006**    *option* : stack size exceeds 65535 bytes

The size specified for the stack was more than 65,535 bytes.

**L1007**    *option* : interrupt number exceeds 255

A number greater than 255 was given as a value for the
**/OVERLAYINTERRUPT** option.

| Number | LINK Error Message |
|--------|--------------------|

**L1008**   *option* : segment limit set too high

The limit on the number of segments allowed was set to greater than 3072 through use of the **/SEGMENTS** option.

**L1009**   *option* : CPARMAXALLOC : illegal value

The number specified in the **/CPARMAXALLOC** option was not in the range 1–65,535.

**L1020**   no object modules specified

No object-file names were specified to the linker.

**L1021**   cannot nest response files

A response file occurred within a response file.

**L1022**   response line too long

A line in a response file was longer than 127 characters.

**L1023**   terminated by user

You entered CONTROL+C.

**L1024**   nested right parentheses

The contents of an overlay were typed incorrectly on the command line.

**L1025**   nested left parentheses

The contents of an overlay were typed incorrectly on the command line.

**L1026**   unmatched right parenthesis

A right parenthesis was missing from the contents specification of an overlay on the command line.

**L1027**   unmatched left parenthesis

A left parenthesis was missing from the contents specification of an overlay on the command line.

| Number | LINK Error Message |
|--------|--------------------|

**L1043**    `relocation table overflow`

More than 32,768 long calls, long jumps, or other long pointers appeared in the program.

Try replacing long references with short references, where possible, and recreating the object module.

**L1045**    `too many TYPDEF records`

An object module contained more than 255 **TYPDEF** records. These records describe communal variables. This error can appear only with programs produced by the Microsoft QuickC Compiler or other compilers that support communal variables. (**TYPDEF** is a DOS term. It is explained in the *Microsoft MS-DOS Programmer's Reference* and in other reference books on DOS.)

**L1046**    `too many external symbols in one module`

An object module specified more than the limit of 1023 external symbols.

Break the module into smaller parts.

**L1047**    `too many group, segment, and class names in one module`

The program contained too many group, segment, and class names.

Reduce the number of groups, segments, or classes, and recreate the object file.

**L1048**    `too many segments in one module`

An object module had more than 255 segments.

Split the module or combine segments.

**L1049**    `too many segments`

The program had more than the maximum number of segments. (The **/SEGMENTS** option specifies the maximum legal number; the default is 128.)

Relink using the **/SEGMENTS** option with an appropriate number of segments.

| Number | LINK Error Message |
|--------|--------------------|

L1050        too many groups in one module

**LINK** encountered more than 21 group definitions (**GRPDEF**) in a single module.

Reduce the number of group definitions or split the module. (Group definitions are explained in the *Microsoft MS-DOS Programmer's Reference* and in other DOS reference books.)

L1051        too many groups

The program defined more than 20 groups, not counting **DGROUP**.

Reduce the number of groups.

L1052        too many libraries

An attempt was made to link with more than 32 libraries.

Combine libraries, or use modules that require fewer libraries.

L1053        symbol table overflow

The linker did not have enough memory to accommodate the symbolic information of the program (such as public, external, segment, group, class, and file names).

Combine modules or segments and recreate the object files. Eliminate as many public symbols as possible.

L1054        requested segment limit too high

The linker did not have enough memory to allocate tables describing the number of segments requested. (The default is 128 or the value specified with the **/SEGMENTS** option.)

Try linking again using the **/SEGMENTS** option to select a smaller number of segments (for example, use 64 if the default was used previously), or free some memory by eliminating resident programs or shells.

L1056        too many overlays

The program defined more than 63 overlays.

| Number | LINK Error Message |
|--------|--------------------|

**L1057**    `data record too large`

A **LIDATA** record (in an object module) contained more than 1024 bytes of data. This is a translator error. (**LIDATA** is a DOS term, explained in the *Microsoft MS-DOS Programmer's Reference* and in other DOS reference books.)

Note which translator (compiler or assembler) produced the incorrect object module and what the circumstances were. Please report this error using the Product Assistance Request form at the back of this manual.

**L1070**    *name*: `segment size exceeds 64K`

The specified segment contained more than 64K of code or data.

Try compiling and linking using the large model.

**L1071**    `segment _TEXT larger than 65520 bytes`

This error is likely to occur only in small-model C programs, but it can occur when any program with a segment named **_TEXT** is linked by using the **/DOSSEG** option of the **LINK** command. Small-model C programs must reserve code addresses 0 and 1; this range is increased to 16 for alignment purposes.

**L1072**    `common area longer than 65536 bytes`

The program had more than 64K of communal variables. This error cannot appear with object files generated by the Microsoft Macro Assembler, **MASM**. It occurs only with programs produced by the Microsoft QuickC Compiler or other compilers that support communal variables.

**L1080**    `cannot open list file`

The disk or the root directory was full.

Delete or move files to make space.

**L1081**    `out of space for run file`

The disk on which the **.EXE** file was being written was full.

Free more space on the disk and restart the linker.

| Number | LINK Error Message |
|--------|--------------------|

**L1083**   `cannot open run file`

The disk or the root directory was full.

Delete or move files to make space.

**L1084**   `cannot create temporary file`

The disk or root directory was full.

Free more space in the directory and restart the linker.

**L1085**   `cannot open temporary file`

The disk or the root directory was full.

Delete or move files to make space.

**L1086**   `scratch file missing`

An internal error occurred.

Note the circumstances of the problem and contact Microsoft Corporation, using the Product Assistance Request form at the back of this manual.

**L1087**   `unexpected end-of-file on scratch file`

The disk with the temporary linker-output file was removed.

**L1088**   `out of space for list file`

The disk on which the listing file was being written was full.

Free more space on the disk and restart the linker.

**L1089**   *filename* `: cannot open response file`

**LINK** could not find the specified response file. This usually indicates a typing error.

**L1090**   `cannot reopen list file`

The original disk was not replaced at the prompt.

Restart the linker.

**L1091**   `unexpected end-of-file on library`

The disk containing the library probably was removed.

Replace the disk containing the library and run the linker again.

| Number | LINK Error Message |
|--------|--------------------|

**L1093**      *filename*: `object not found`

The linker could not find the given object file.

Restart the linker and specify the correct object-file name.

**L1101**      `invalid object module`

One of the object modules was invalid.

If the error persists after recompiling, please contact Microsoft Corporation, using the Product Assistance Request form at the back of this manual.

**L1102**      `unexpected end-of-file`

An invalid format for a library was encountered.

**L1103**      `attempt to access data outside segment bounds`

A data record in an object module specified data extending beyond the end of a segment. This is a translator error.

Note which translator (compiler or assembler) produced the incorrect object module and the circumstances in which it was produced. Please report this error to Microsoft Corporation, using the Product Assistance Request form at the back of this manual.

**L1104**      *filename* : `not valid library`

The specified file was not a valid library file. This error causes **LINK** to abort.

**L1113**      `unresolved COMDEF; internal error`

Note the circumstances of the failure and contact Microsoft Corporation, using the Product Assistance Request form at the back of this manual.

**L1114**      `file not suitable for /EXEPACK; relink without`

For the linked program, the size of the packed load image plus packing overhead was larger than that of the unpacked load image.

Relink without the **/EXEPACK** option.

| Number | LINK Error Message |
|--------|--------------------|

**L2001**    `fixup(s) without data`

A **FIXUPP** record occurred without a data record immediately preceding it. This is probably a compiler error. (See the *Microsoft MS-DOS Programmer's Reference* for more information on **FIXUPP**.)

**L2002**    `fixup overflow at` *number* `in frame seg` *segname*
`target seg` *segname* `target offset` *number*

The following conditions can cause this error:

- A small-model program is compiled with the **/NT** option.

- A group is larger than 64K.

- The program contains an intersegment short jump or intersegment short call.

- The name of a data item in the program conflicts with that of a subroutine in a library included in the link.

- An **EXTRN** declaration in an assembly-language source file appeared inside the body of a segment, as in the following example:

```
code    SEGMENT public 'CODE'
        EXTRN   main:far
start   PROC    far
        call    main
        ret
start   ENDP
code    ENDS
```

  The following construction is preferred:

```
        EXTRN   main:far
code    SEGMENT public 'CODE'
start   PROC    far
        call    main
        ret
start   ENDP
code    ENDS
```

  Revise the source file and recreate the object file. (For information about frame and target segments, refer to the *Microsoft MS-DOS Programmer's Reference*.)

| Number | LINK Error Message |
|--------|--------------------|

**L2003**　　`intersegment self-relative fixup`

An intersegment self-relative fixup is not allowed.

**L2005**　　`fixup type unsupported`

A fixup type occurred that is not supported by the Microsoft linker. This is probably a compiler error.

Note the circumstances of the failure and contact Microsoft Corporation using the Product Assistance Request form at the back of this manual.

**L2012**　　`'name' : array-element size mismatch`

A far communal array was declared with two or more different array-element sizes (for example, an array was declared once as an array of characters and once as an array of real numbers).

**L2013**　　`LIDATA record too large`

A **LIDATA** record in an object module was larger than 512 bytes, the maximum legal size. This is a compiler error.

Please report this condition by using the Product Assistance Request form at the back of this manual.

**L2024**　　`name : symbol already defined`

One of the special overlay symbols required for overlay support was defined by an object.

**L2025**　　`'name' : symbol defined more than once`

Remove the extra symbol definition from the object file.

**L2029**　　`Unresolved externals`

One or more symbols were declared to be external in one or more modules, but they were not publicly defined in any of the modules or libraries. A list of the unresolved external references appears after the message, as shown in the following example:

```
EXIT in file(s):
 MAIN.OBJ (main.for)
OPEN in file(s):
 MAIN.OBJ (main.for)
```

| Number | LINK Error Message |
|---|---|

The name that comes before `in file(s)` is the unresolved external symbol. On the next line is a list of object modules that have made references to this symbol. This message and the list are also written to the map file, if one exists.

**L2041**      `stack plus data exceed 64K`

The combined size of the program stack segment plus **DGROUP** was greater than 64K; as a result, the program will not load correctly.

**L2043**      `starting address __aulstart not found`

When you build a Quick library using the **/Q** option, the linker expects to find the symbol **__aulstart** defined as a starting address.

**L4003**      `intersegment self-relative fixup at` *offset* `in segment` *name* `pos:` *offset* `Record type: 9C target external`

The linker found an intersegment self-relative fixup. This error may be caused by compiling a small-model program with the **/NT** option.

**L4012**      `load-high disables EXEPACK`

The **/HIGH** and **/EXEPACK** options cannot be used at the same time.

**L4015**      `/CODEVIEW disables /DSALLOCATE`

The **/CODEVIEW** and **/DSALLOCATE** options cannot be used at the same time.

**L4016**      `/CODEVIEW disables /EXEPACK`

The **/CODEVIEW** and **/EXEPACK** options cannot be used at the same time.

**L4020**      *name* `: code-segment size exceeds 65500`

Code segments of 65,501–65,536 bytes in length may be unreliable on the Intel 80286 processor.

| Number | LINK Error Message |
|--------|--------------------|

**L4021**    `no stack segment`

The program did not contain a stack segment defined with **STACK** combine type. This message should not appear for modules compiled with the Microsoft QuickC Compiler, but it could appear for an assembly-language module.

Normally, every program should have a stack segment with the combine type specified as **STACK**. You can ignore this message if you have a specific reason for not defining a stack or for defining one without the **STACK** combine type. Linking with versions of **LINK** earlier than 2.40 might cause this message, since these linkers search libraries only once.

**L4031**    *name* `: segment declared in more than one group`

A segment was declared to be a member of two different groups.

Correct the source file and recreate the object files.

**L4034**    `more than 239 overlay segments; extra put in root`

No more than 239 code segments can be defined in overlays. Any segments over this limit are assigned to the root.

**L4045**    `name of output file is` *name*

The linker displayed a default output-file name in the "Run file" prompt but changed the output-file name because the **/Q** option was used.

**L4050**    `too many public symbols`

The **/MAP** option was used to request a sorted listing of public symbols in the map file, but there were too many symbols to sort (more than 2048 symbols by default).

Relink using **/MAP:***number*. The linker produces an unsorted listing of the public symbols.

**L4051**    *filename* `: cannot find library`

The linker could not find the specified file.

Enter a new file name, a new path specification, or both.

| Number | LINK Error Message |
|--------|--------------------|

L4053       `VM.TMP : illegal file name; ignored`

**VM.TMP** appeared as an object-file name.

Rename the file and rerun the linker.

L4054       *filename* `: cannot find file`

The linker could not find the specified file.

Enter a new file name, a new path specification, or both.

# D.5   LIB Error Messages

Error messages generated by the Microsoft Library Manager, **LIB**, have one of the following formats:

{*filename* | LIB} : `fatal error U1`*xxx*: *messagetext*
{*filename* | LIB} : `error U2`*xxx*: *messagetext*
{*filename* | LIB} : `warning U4`*xxx*: *messagetext*

The message begins with the input-file name (*filename*), if one exists, or with the name of the utility. If possible, **LIB** prints a warning and continues operation. In some cases errors are fatal and **LIB** terminates processing. **LIB** may display the following error messages:

| Number | LIB Error Message |
|--------|-------------------|

U1150       `page size too small`

The page size of an input library was too small, which indicates an invalid input **.LIB** file.

U1151       `syntax error : illegal file specification`

A command operator such as a minus sign (−) was given without a following module name.

U1152       `syntax error : option name missing`

A forward slash (/) was given without a following option.

| Number | LIB Error Message |
|--------|-------------------|

**U1153**     `syntax error : option value missing`

The **/PAGESIZE** option was given without a value following it.

**U1154**     `option unknown`

An unknown option was given. Currently, **LIB** only recognizes the **/PAGESIZE** option.

**U1155**     `syntax error : illegal input`

The given command did not follow correct **LIB** syntax as specified in Chapter 10, "Creating Quick Libraries and Stand-Alone Libraries."

**U1156**     `syntax error`

The given command did not follow correct **LIB** syntax as specified in Chapter 10, "Creating Quick Libraries and Stand-Alone Libraries."

**U1157**     `comma or new line missing`

A comma or carriage return was expected in the command line but did not appear. This may indicate an inappropriately placed comma, as in the following line:

`LIB math.lib,-mod1+mod2;`

The line should have been entered as follows:

`LIB math.lib -mod1+mod2;`

**U1158**     `terminator missing`

Either the response to the "Output library" prompt or the last line of the response file used to start **LIB** did not end with a carriage return.

**U1161**     `cannot rename old library`

**LIB** could not rename the old library to have a **.BAK** extension because the **.BAK** version already existed with read-only protection.

Change the protection on the old **.BAK** version.

| Number | LIB Error Message |
|--------|-------------------|

**U1162**   `cannot reopen library`

The old library could not be reopened after it was renamed to have a **.BAK** extension.

**U1163**   `error writing to cross-reference file`

The disk or root directory was full.

Delete or move files to make space.

**U1170**   `too many symbols`

More than 4609 symbols appeared in the library file.

**U1171**   `insufficient memory`

**LIB** did not have enough memory to run.

Remove any shells or resident programs and try again, or add more memory.

**U1172**   `no more virtual memory`

Note the circumstances of the failure and notify Microsoft Corporation, using the Product Assistance Request form at the back of this manual.

**U1173**   `internal failure`

Note the circumstances of the failure and notify Microsoft Corporation, using the Product Assistance Request form at the back of this manual.

**U1174**   `mark: not allocated`

Note the circumstances of the failure and notify Microsoft Corporation, using the Product Assistance Request form at the back of this manual.

**U1175**   `free: not allocated`

Note the circumstances of the failure and notify Microsoft Corporation, using the Product Assistance Request form at the back of this manual.

**U1180**   `write to extract file failed`

The disk or root directory was full.

Delete or move files to make space.

| Number | LIB Error Message |
|--------|-------------------|

**U1181**   `write to library file failed`

The disk or root directory was full.

Delete or move files to make space.

**U1182**   *filename* `: cannot create extract file`

The disk or root directory was full, or the specified extract file already existed with read-only protection.

Make space on the disk or change the protection of the extract file.

**U1183**   `cannot open response file`

The response file was not found.

**U1184**   `unexpected end-of-file on command input`

An end-of-file character was received prematurely in response to a prompt.

**U1185**   `cannot create new library`

The disk or root directory was full, or the library file already existed with read-only protection.

Make space on the disk or change the protection of the library file.

**U1186**   `error writing to new library`

The disk or root directory was full.

Delete or move files to make space.

**U1187**   `cannot open VM.TMP`

The disk or root directory was full.

Delete or move files to make space.

**U1188**   `cannot write to VM`

Note the circumstances of the failure and notify Microsoft Corporation, using the Product Assistance Request form at the back of this manual.

| Number | LIB Error Message |
|--------|-------------------|

**U1189**   `cannot read from VM`

Note the circumstances of this error and notify Microsoft Corporation, using the Product Assistance Request form at the back of this manual.

**U1190**   `interrupted by user`

You terminated the **LIB** session before it had finished execution.

**U1200**   *name* `: invalid library header`

The input library file had an invalid format. It was either not a library file, or it had been corrupted.

**U1203**   *name* `: invalid object module near` *location*

The module specified by *name* was not a valid object module.

**U2152**   *filename* `: cannot create listing`

The directory or disk was full, or the cross-reference-listing file already existed with read-only protection.

Make space on the disk or change the protection of the cross-reference-listing file.

**U2155**   *modulename* `: module not in library; ignored`

The specified module was not found in the input library.

**U2157**   *filename* `: cannot access file`

**LIB** was unable to open the specified file.

**U2158**   *libraryname* `: invalid library header; file ignored`

The input library had an incorrect format.

**U2159**   *filename* `: invalid format` *hexnumber*`; file ignored`

The signature byte or word *hexnumber* of the given file was not one of the following recognized types: Microsoft library, Intel library, Microsoft object, or XENIX archive.

| Number | LIB Error Message |
|--------|-------------------|

**U4150**    *modulename* : module redefinition ignored

A module was specified to be added to a library but a module with the same name was already in the library. Or, a module with the same name was found more than once in the library.

**U4151**    *symbol*(*modulename*) : symbol redefinition ignored

The specified symbol was defined in more than one module.

**U4153**    *number* : page size too small; ignored

The value specified in the **/PAGESIZE** option was less than 16.

**U4156**    *libraryname* : output-library specification ignored

An output library was specified in addition to a new library name. For example, specifying

```
LIB new.lib+one.obj,new.lst,new.lib
```

where `new.lib` does not already exist causes this error.

# D.6   MAKE Error Messages

Error messages displayed by the Microsoft Program Maintenance Utility, **MAKE**, have one of the following formats:

{*filename* | MAKE} : fatal error U1*xxx*: *messagetext*
{*filename* | MAKE} : warning U4*xxx*: *messagetext*

The message begins with the input file name (*filename*), if one exists, or with the name of the utility. If possible, **MAKE** prints a warning and continues operation. In some cases, errors are fatal and **MAKE** terminates processing. **MAKE** generates the error messages listed in this section.

| Number | MAKE Error Message |
|---|---|

**U1001**  `macro definition larger than` *number*

A single macro was defined to have a value string longer than the number stated, which is the maximum length allowed.

Try rewriting the **MAKE** description file to split the macro into two or more smaller ones.

**U1002**  `infinitely recursive macro`

A circular chain of macros was defined, as in the following example:

```
A=$ (B)
B=$ (C)
C=$ (A)
```

**U1003**  `out of memory`

**MAKE** ran out of memory for processing the **MAKE** description file.

Try to reduce the size of the **MAKE** description file by reorganizing or splitting it.

**U1004**  `syntax error : macro name missing`

The **MAKE** description file contained a macro definition with no left side (that is, a line beginning with =).

**U1005**  `syntax error : colon missing`

A line that should be an outfile/infile line lacked a colon indicating the separation between outfile and infile. **MAKE** expects any line following a blank line to be an outfile/infile line.

**U1006**  *targetname* `: macro expansion larger than` *number*

A single macro expansion, plus the length of any string to which it may be concatenated, was longer than the number stated.

Try rewriting the **MAKE** description file to split the macro into two or more smaller ones.

| Number | MAKE Error Message |
|--------|--------------------|

**U1007**      `multiple sources`

An inference rule was defined more than once.

**U1008**      *name* `: cannot find file or directory`

The file or directory specified by *name* could not be found.

**U1009**      *command* `: argument list too long`

A command line in the **MAKE** description file was longer than 128 bytes, which is the maximum that DOS allows.

Rewrite the commands to use shorter argument lists.

**U1010**      *filename* `: permission denied`

The file specified by *filename* was a read-only file.

**U1011**      *filename* `: not enough memory`

Not enough memory was available for **MAKE** to execute a program.

**U1012**      *filename* `: unknown error`

Note the circumstances of the failure and notify Microsoft Corporation, using the Product Assistance Request form at the back of this manual.

**U1013**      *command* `: error` *errcode*

One of the programs or commands called in the **MAKE** description file returned with a nonzero error code.

**U1015**      *file* `: error redirection failed`

You entered the **MAKE** command with the **/x** *file* option, but **MAKE** could not redirect error output to the given file (for example, because the file was read only).

**U4000**      *filename* `: target does not exist`

This usually does not indicate an error. It warns the user that the target file does not exist. **MAKE** executes any commands given in the block description, since in many cases the outfile will be created by a later command in the **MAKE** description file.

| Number | MAKE Error Message |
|--------|--------------------|

**U4001**  dependent *filename* does not exist; target
*filename* not built

**MAKE** could not continue because a required infile did not exist.

Make sure that all named files are present and that they are spelled correctly in the **MAKE** description file.

**U4013**  *command* : error *errcode* (ignored)

One of the programs or commands called in the **MAKE** description file returned with a nonzero error code, and **MAKE** was run with the /I option. **MAKE** ignores the error and continues.

**U4014**  usage : make *options* [name-value ...] file
*options* = [/n] [/d] [/i] [/s] [/x file]

**MAKE** has not been invoked correctly.

Try entering the command line again with the syntax shown in the message.

# GLOSSARY

The definitions in this glossary are intended primarily for use with this manual, the *Microsoft C Language Reference,* and the *Microsoft C Run-Time Library Reference* . Neither individual definitions nor the list of terms is comprehensive.

**8087 or 80287 coprocessor**

Intel® hardware products that provide very fast and precise number processing.

**abstract declarator**

A declarator without an identifier, consisting of a type and, optionally, one or more pointer, array, or function modifiers.

**active page**

The area in memory where graphics output is written.

**aggregate types**

Arrays, structures, and unions.

**alias**

One of several alternative names for the same memory location.

**alternate math library**

A model-dependent floating-point library that uses a subset of the Institute of Electrical and Electronics Engineers, Inc. (IEEE) number format. Linking with this library results in the smallest, fastest programs available without a coprocessor, but sacrifices some accuracy in results.

**animation**

The process of creating graphics images that move on the screen.

**ANSI (American National Standards Institute)**

The national institute responsible for defining programming-language standards to promote portability of these languages between different computer systems.

**argument**

A value passed to a function.

**argument-type list**

In a function prototype, a list of abstract declarators, separated by commas, indicating the types of actual arguments in the function call. Used to make sure the actual arguments in the function call correspond to the formal parameters in the function definition.

**argc**

The traditional name for the first argument to the **main** function in a C source program. This argument is an integer specifying how many arguments are passed to the program from the command line.

**argv**

The traditional name for the second argument to the **main** function in a C source program. This argument is a pointer to an array of strings. Traditionally, the first string is the program name and each following string is an argument passed to the program from the command line.

**arithmetic conversion**

Conversion operations performed on items of integral and floating-point types used in expressions.

**arithmetic types**

Integral, enumeration, and floating-point data types.

**array**

A set of elements with the same type.

**ASCII (American Standard Code for Information Interchange)**

A set of 256 codes that many computers use to represent letters, digits, special characters, and other symbols. Only the first 128 of these codes are standardized; the remaining 128 are special characters that are defined by the computer manufacturer.

**associativity**

The precedence rules that apply when more than one operator is assigned to an operand. For example, in the expression *p++, the indirection operator (*) is applied before the unary increment operator (++).

**background color**

The color on which all drawing and color display takes place.

**base name**

The portion of the file name that precedes the file-name extension. For example, samp is the base name of the file samp.c.

**batch file**

A text file containing DOS commands that can be invoked from the DOS command line.

**binary expression**

An expression consisting of two operands joined by a binary operator.

**binary operator**

An operator used in binary expressions. Binary operators in the C language are the multiplicative operators (∗ /), additive operators (+ −), shift operators (<< >>), relational operators (< > <= >= == !=), bitwise operators (& ¦ ˆ), logical operators (&& ¦¦), and the sequential-evaluation operator (,).

**block**

A sequence of declarations, definitions, and statements enclosed within braces ({}).

**bounding rectangle**

The rectangular area used to define certain graphics operations.

**child process**

A new process started by a currently running process.

**clipping**

The limiting of graphics displays to a particular region of the screen, known as the clipping region.

**clipping region**

The rectangular portion of the screen where graphics output occurs.

**color value**

A unique ordinal value representing a displayable color.

**compact memory model**

A memory model that allows for more than one data segment and only one code segment.

**complex declarator**

A declaration containing more than one array, pointer, or function modifier.

**constant expression**

Any expression that evaluates to a constant and may involve integer constants, character constants, floating-point constants, enumeration constants, type casts to integral and floating-point types, and other constant expressions.

**coordinate system**

A system used to identify a screen location relative to the horizontal and vertical axes. Text is positioned in a character-based row and column coordinate system. Graphics figures are positioned in a pixel-based row and column coordinate system.

**core library**

The library of standard C routines that is built into the QuickC programming interface.

**current position**

The coordinate location given by an $(x, y)$ logical-coordinate pair that defines the pixel point where the next graphics operations will take place.

**current text position**

The coordinate location given by a ($row, column$) coordinate pair that defines the row and column point where graphics-based text operations will take place.

**declaration**

A construct that associates the name and the attributes of a variable, function, or type.

**declarator**

An identifier that can be modified with brackets ([ ]), asterisks (*), or parentheses (( )) to declare an array, pointer, or function type, respectively.

**definition**

A construct that initializes and allocates storage for a variable, or that specifies the name, formal parameters, body, and the return type of a function.

**directive**

An instruction to the C preprocessor to perform a specific action on source-program text before compilation.

**DOS interface functions**

Run-time library routines that provide access to DOS interrupts and system calls.

**emulator**

A floating-point-math package that provides software emulation of the operations of a math coprocessor.

**enumeration set**

The set of legal values defined for an enumeration type.

**enumeration type**

A user-defined data type that specifies a particular set of legal values.

**environment table**

The part of DOS that stores environment variables and their values.

**environment variable**

A variable stored in the environment table that provides DOS with information (where to find executable files and library files, where to create temporary files, etc.).

**errorlevel code**

See **exit code**.

**escape sequence**

A specific combination, comprising a backslash (\) followed by a letter or combination of digits, which represents white-space and nongraphic characters within strings and character constants.

**exit code**

A code returned by a program to DOS indicating whether or not the program ran successfully.

**expression**

A combination of operands and operators that yields a single value.

**external level**

The part of a C program outside of all function declarations.

**file handle**

A value returned by library functions that open or create files, used to refer to that file in later operations.

**file pointer**

A pointer that indicates the current position in an input or output stream. It is updated to reflect the new position each time a read or write operation takes place.

**fill mask**

An 8-by-8 array of bits, where each bit represents a pixel, that defines the mask to be used in filling figures. When a figure is filled, the fill mask is repeated over the entire area. If a bit in the array is a 1, the corresponding pixel in the figure is set to the current color. If a bit is 0, the corresponding pixel is unchanged. The default fill mask is **NULL**.

**filling**

The process of applying a fill mask to a specified area.

**foreground color**

A color used to display text and draw graphics images.

**formal parameters**

Variables that receive values passed to a function when the function is called.

**forward declaration**

A function declaration that establishes the attributes of a function so that it can be called before it is defined or called from a different source file.

**function**

A collection of declarations and statements returning a value that can be called by name.

**function body**

A compound statement containing the local variable declarations and statements of a function.

**function call**

An expression that passes control and actual arguments (if any) to a function.

**function declaration**

A declaration that establishes the name, return type, and storage class of a function that is defined explicitly elsewhere in the program.

**function definition**

A definition that specifies a function's name, its formal parameters, the declarations and statements that define what it does, and (optionally) its return type and storage class.

**function prototype**

A function declaration that includes a list of the names and types of formal parameters in the parentheses following the function name.

**fundamental data types**

A set of basic C data types, which includes all integer, character, floating-point, and enumeration types.

**global**

See **lifetime**; **visibility**.

**heap**

An area of memory set aside for dynamic allocation by a program.

**include file**

A text file that is merged into another text file through use of the #**include** preprocessor directive.

**internal level**

The parts of a C program within function declarations.

**keyword**

A word with a special, predefined meaning for the QuickC compiler.

### large memory model

A memory model that allows for more than one segment of code and more than one segment of data, but with no individual data items spanning a single segment.

### level

See **internal level**; **external level**.

### library

A file that stores related modules of compiled code. The linker extracts modules from the library and combines them with other program object modules to create executable program files.

### lifetime

The period during program execution in which a variable or function exists. An item with a "local" lifetime (a "local item") has storage and a defined value only within the block where the item is defined or declared.

### line style

A 16-bit array that defines the mask to be used in drawing lines. If a bit in the array is a 1, the corresponding pixel in the line is set to the current color. If a bit is 0, the corresponding pixel is unchanged. The default line style is 0xFFFF (a solid line).

### linked list

A data structure consisting of a list of entries, each of which includes a pointer to the next entry.

### local

See **lifetime**; **visibility**.

### logical coordinates

The coordinate system defined by the programmer. The logical-coordinate system origin can be positioned anywhere on the screen's physical-coordinate system. The default logical-coordinate system is identical to the physical-coordinate system which places the coordinates of the origin (0,0) at the top-left corner of the screen.

### logical origin

The origin given by the logical-coordinate pair (0,0). All subsequent graphics output is relative to the logical origin.

**loop optimization**

Optimizations that reduce the amount of code executed for each loop iteration in a program.

**low-level input and output routines**

Run-time library routines that perform unbuffered, unformatted I/O operations.

**lvalue**

An expression (such as a variable name) that refers to a memory location and is required as the left-hand operand of an assignment operation or the single operand of a unary operator.

**macro**

An identifier defined in a # **define** preprocessor directive to represent another series of tokens.

**manifest constant**

An identifier defined in a # **define** preprocessor directive to represent a constant value.

**medium memory model**

A memory model that allows for more than one code segment and only one data segment.

**member**

One of the elements of a structure or union.

**memory model**

One of the models that specifies how memory is set up for program code and data. (See **small memory model**, **medium memory model**, **compact memory model**, **large memory model**, and **huge memory model** for descriptions of standard memory models.)

**multidimensional array**

An array of arrays.

**naming classes**

Categories that the language sets up to distinguish between the identifiers used for different kinds of items.

## NAN

An abbreviation that stands for "not a number." The 8087 or 80287 coprocessor generates NANs when the result of an operation cannot be represented in the IEEE format. For example, if you try to add two positive numbers whose sum is larger than the maximum value permitted by the processor, the coprocessor returns a NAN instead of the sum.

## new-line character

The character used to mark the end of a line of a text file, or the escape sequence (\n) used to represent this character. In DOS "text mode," carriage-return–line-feed (CR-LF) combinations are translated into a single line-feed (LF) character on input, and line-feed characters are translated into carriage-return–line-feed combinations on output.

## null character

The ASCII character encoded as the value 0, represented as the escape sequence (\0) in a source file.

## null pointer

A pointer to nothing, expressed as the integer value 0.

## object

A region of memory that can be examined. A modifiable object can also have a value stored into it (that is, it can be altered as well as examined).

## object file

A file containing relocatable machine code, created as the result of compiling a source file.

## operand

A constant or variable value that is manipulated in an expression.

## operator

One or more symbols that specify how the operand or operands of an expression are manipulated.

## overlay

Part of a program that is read into memory from disk only if and when it is needed.

**palette**

A mapping of the color values (the actual displayable colors) to the legal pixel values for a given video mode. The CGA modes operate with a set of predetermined palettes. The EGA and VGA color modes operate with a redefinable palette of colors.

**parent process**

A process that generates a child process using one of the **spawn**, **exec**, or **system** families of run-time library functions.

**physical coordinates**

The coordinate system defined by the hardware. The physical-coordinate system has the origin (0,0) at the upper-left corner of the screen. The value of x increases from left to right the value of y increases from top to bottom. The default logical-coordinate system is identical to the physical-coordinate system.

**pixel**

A single dot on the screen. It is the smallest item that may be manipulated with the QuickC graphics library and it is the basic unit of the coordinate systems.

**pixel value**

The one-, two-, or four-bit representation of a screen pixel. It is the index into the palette of available colors.

**pointers**

A variable containing the address of another variable.

**pragma**

An instruction to the compiler to perform a particular action at compile time.

**precedence**

The relative position of an operator in the hierarchy that determines the order in which expressions are evaluated.

**preprocessor**

A text processor that manipulates the contents of a C source file during the first phase of compilation.

**preprocessor directive**

See **directive**.

**process**

A program being executed by DOS.

**prototype**

See **function prototype**.

**QCL**

The command used by the Microsoft C Optimizing Compiler to compile and link programs.

**RAM disk**

An area of memory that is used to load and save files in the same way as a disk drive but allows more rapid access to files than a disk drive. Unlike a disk drive, a RAM disk is not suitable for long-term storage because its contents are volatile—that is, they disappear if the machine is powered off.

**relocatable**

Not containing absolute addresses.

**remapping**

The process of altering the correspondence between color value and pixel value. Only EGA and VGA palettes may be remapped.

**run time**

The time during which a previously compiled and linked program is executing.

**run-time library**

A file containing the routines needed to implement certain functions of the Microsoft C language.

**scalar types**

In C, integral, enumerated, floating-point, and pointer types.

**scope**

The parts of a program in which an item can be referenced by name. The scope of an item may be limited to the file, function, block, or function prototype in which it appears.

**segment**

An area of memory, less than or equal to 64K long, that contains code or data.

**sequence point**

A point in a C program where all expressions lexically preceding the point are guaranteed to have been evaluated.

**side effects**

Changes in the state of objects that occur as a result of expression evaluation.

**sizeof operator**

A C operator that can be used to determine the amount of storage, in bytes, associated with an identifier or a type.

**small memory model**

A memory model that allows for only one code segment and only one data segment.

**source file**

A text file containing C-language code.

**stack**

A dynamically shrinking and expanding area of memory in which data items are stored in consecutive order and removed on a last in, first out basis.

**stack probe**

A short routine called on entry to a function to verify that there is enough room in the program stack to allocate local variables required by the function and, if so, to allocate those variables.

**static**

A storage class that allows variables to keep their values even after the program exits the block in which the variable is declared.

**stream functions**

Run-time library functions that treat data files and data items as "streams" of individual characters.

**string**

An array of characters, terminated by a null character (**\0**).

**string literal**

A string of characters and escape sequences delimited by double quotation marks (" "). Every string literal has a type of "array of **char**," an array of elements with **char** type.

**structure**

A set of elements, which may be of different types, grouped under a single name.

**structure member**

One of the elements of a structure.

**subscript expression**

An expression, usually used to reference array elements, representing an address that is offset from a specified base address by a given number of positions.

**symbolic constant**

See **manifest constant**.

**tag**

The name assigned to a structure, union, or enumeration type.

**ternary expression**

An expression consisting of three operands joined by the ternary operator (**? :**), used to evaluate either of two expressions depending on the value of a third expression.

**text color**

The color value to be used in all graphics-based text operations.

**text mode**

The file processing mode in which carriage-return–line-feed combinations are converted to a single line-feed character on input and reconverted to carriage-return–line-feed combinations on output.

**text window**

A window defined in row and column coordinates where text output to the screen will be displayed.

**tiling**

The process of applying a fill mask to an area of the screen.

**toggle**

The action of turning an option on or off.

**token**

The most fundamental unit of a C source program that is meaningful to the compiler.

**two's complement**

A type of base-2 notation used to represent positive and negative numbers in which negative values are formed by complementing all bits and adding 1 to the results.

**type**

A description of a set of values; for example, a variable of type **int** can have any of a set of integer values within the range specified for the type on a particular machine.

**type cast**

An operation in which an operand of one type is converted to an operand of a different type.

**type checking**

An operation in which the compiler verifies that the operands of an operator are valid or that the actual arguments in a function call are of the same types as the corresponding formal parameters in the function definition and function prototype.

**type declaration**

A declaration that defines the name and members of a structure or union type, or the name and enumeration set of an enumeration type.

**type name**

A specification of a particular data type that appears in variable declarations, in the formal-parameter lists of function prototypes, in type casts, and in **sizeof** operations.

### typedef declaration

A declaration that defines a shorter or more meaningful name for an existing C data type or for a user-defined data type. Names defined in a **typedef** declaration are often referred to as "typedefs."

### unary expression

An expression consisting of a single operand preceded or followed by a unary operator.

### unary operator

An operator that takes a single operand. Unary operators in the C language are the complement operators (– ~ !), indirection operator (*), increment (++) and decrement (– –) operators, address-of operator (&), and **sizeof** operator. The unary plus operator (+) is also implemented syntactically, but has no semantics associated with it.

### union

A set of values that have different types and occupy the same storage space.

### unresolved reference

A reference to a global or external variable or function that cannot be found, either in the modules being linked or in the libraries that are linked with those modules.

### usual arithmetic conversions

Type conversions performed by the Microsoft QuickC Compiler on operands of integral or floating-point types in an expression to bring the operands to a common type.

### video mode

The format used to display information on the screen. It defines the display characteristics.

### video page

A screen image stored in memory.

### viewport

A clipping region which sets the logical origin to the upper-left corner of the region.

**visibility**

The characteristic of a variable or function that describes the parts of the program in which it can be referenced by name. An item has global visibility if it is visible in all source files comprising the program; otherwise, it has local visibility in a single source file.

**visual page**

The area in memory that holds the current displayed graphics output.

**white-space character**

Characters that delimit items in a C source program, including space, tab, line-feed, carriage-return, form-feed, vertical-tab, and new-line characters.

**wild card**

One of the DOS characters (? and *) that can be expanded into one or more characters in file-name references.

# Microsoft® Product Assistance Request

Microsoft Product Support—Phone: (206) 882-8089

## Instructions

Use this form to request assistance or report problems with Microsoft software or hardware. You may also use this form to offer suggested product enhancements (use the space marked "Additional Information" at the end of the form). For comments on product documentation, use the documentation feedback form if one is included with your product.

We suggest you first make a copy of this form for future assistance requests. Then complete the form and mail it to Microsoft. All comments and suggestions become the property of Microsoft Corporation.

For a more rapid response, you may wish to call Microsoft Product Support at the number printed at the top of this form. Please have all the information requested on this form available when you call. For speed dialing, please read the README.DOC file included on one of your product disks. This file lists the three-digit phone code needed to reach the Microsoft support group for your product.

Name

Street

City            State            Zip

(    )                (    )

Phone: Daytime            Evening

## Diagnosing a Problem

To help us help you, please first answer the following questions if you are having a problem:

1. Can you reproduce the error or problem?
   ☐ Yes    ☐ No

2. Does the problem occur with another copy of the original disk of your Microsoft software?
   ☐ Yes    ☐ No

3. Does the problem occur with another system (if available)?
   ☐ Yes    ☐ No

4. If you were running other windowing or memory-resident software at the same time, does the problem also occur when you don't use the other software?
   ☐ Yes    ☐ No

If you still need help after answering these questions and consulting your documentation, use the rest of this form to request assistance with your Microsoft product. The more complete the information you provide, the more we will be able to help you.

## Product

Product name

Version number            Registration number

☐ Assistance request    ☐ Enhancement suggestion
☐ Other

## Software

### Operating System

Name/version number

### Windowing Environment

If you were running Microsoft® Windows or another windowing environment, give name and version number of windowing software:

### CD ROM Software

Name/version number

### Other Software

Name/version number of any other software you were running when problem occurred, including memory-resident software (such as keyboard enhancers or print spoolers):